T0035428

Mixed Signals

MIXED SIGNALS

HOW INCENTIVES
REALLY WORK

● ● ●

URI GNEEZY

Yale
UNIVERSITY PRESS
New Haven and London

Published with assistance from the Mary Cady Tew Memorial Fund.

Copyright © 2023 by Uri Gneezy.
All rights reserved.

This book may not be reproduced, in whole or in part, including
illustrations, in any form (beyond that copying permitted by Sections
107 and 108 of the U.S. Copyright Law and except by reviewers for the
public press), without written permission from the publishers.

Yale University Press books may be purchased in quantity for educational, business, or promotional use. For information, please e-mail
sales.press@yale.edu (U.S. office) or sales@yaleup.co.uk (U.K. office).

Set in Adobe Garamond type by Newgen North America.
Printed in U.S.A.

Library of Congress Control Number: 2022939728
ISBN 978-0-300-25553-9 (hardcover : alk. paper)
ISBN 978-0-300-27674-9 (paperback)

A catalogue record for this book is available from the British Library.

10 9 8 7 6 5 4 3 2 1

To my sisters Orit and Arza,
with love

Contents

CONTENTS

THREE

HOW INCENTIVES SHAPE THE STORY

FOUR

USE INCENTIVES TO IDENTIFY THE PROBLEM

FIVE

HOW INCENTIVES LEAD TO BEHAVIOR CHANGE

CONTENTS

Do as I Say, Not as I Do

I loved it when my son Ron reached the age when he started effectively communicating with us. Like other kids, he also started to experiment with lying. We told him he shouldn't lie—being honest is what separates the good guys from the bad guys. This moral lesson soon got me into trouble.

All was good until I took him to Disney World on a nice day in July. We waited in line to purchase tickets, and I saw the sign that said, "Under three years old: Free. Three and older: $117." When it was our time to pay, the smiling cashier asked me how old Ron was, and I replied, "Almost three." Technically I wasn't lying: he was almost three, but from the wrong side; his third birthday was a couple of months earlier. I paid for myself while the cashier kept smiling, and we went in to have fun.

What happened at the ticket booth and about half an hour later is shown on the next page.

When Ron said, "Daddy, I'm confused. You told me only bad guys lie, and you just did!" I tried the "do as I say, not as I do" approach, but I don't think it worked.

Before you judge my moral standards, it turns out that I'm not the only one who "rounds down" the age of their kids. An article on Vacationkids .com titled "Do You Lie about Your Kids to Get Family Vacation Deals?" reports that this question had been searched over two billion times (with a *b*) on Google![1] According to Google, I'm not alone.

Ron received two contradicting signals from me: what I said versus what I did in the face of a $117 incentive. In a nutshell, this book is about how to

"Do as I say, not as I do."

avoid such mixed signals: you say one thing, but when the incentives present themselves, you do something else.

What should Ron conclude regarding what I care about? What is the message that Ron heard? What happened when we approached the next ride is shown on the facing page.

The key is to understand that incentives send signals. Too often there's a conflict between what you say and what your incentives signal. You can tell everyone that you care about honesty; talk is cheap. For the claim to be credible, you need to back it up by taking actions that are costly to you, such as paying the full entrance fee. If you'll align what you say with the incentives you offer, the signal will be credible and easy to understand.

When you understand signals, you learn how to make incentives more effective. For example, what could Disney do to reduce the number of people lying about age? A simple option is to make people bring documentation, such as a birth certificate, to prove the age of their kids. That's probably a bad idea because you go to Disney World to be part of a big happy family, not to be policed. While requiring documentation would probably reduce the number of people lying, it would also create a lot of hassle and negative emotions.

Ron's takeaway was "do as I do, not as I say."

Take a minute to think about a solution.

Here's a solution that is based on signals: Disney could ask that the child be present when you buy the ticket. This would force you to face a mixed-signal dilemma like I did: Am I going to lie in front of my kid or pay $117? Disney can even take it a step further and ask the child to tell their own age, for example, by answering the question, "Did you already have your third birthday?" You can clearly coach your child to lie to the cashier, but boy, that is one strong and costly signal that lying is acceptable.

3

Mixed Signals at Work

There are many examples of incentives that send a confusing mixed signal, resulting in a different outcome than intended. As you will see in the pages ahead, even big companies often make such mistakes when designing their incentives.

Imagine a CEO who tells her employees how important it is to work as a team, but the incentives she designs for success are based on an individual's work. The result is simple: the employees would ignore what the CEO says and try to maximize their individual success and monetary gain, as they understand it from the incentives. You may conclude that to avoid such mixed signals, CEOs shouldn't use incentives at all. This book examines both perspectives and explores the middle ground that optimally shapes the incentives so that they are aligned with the intended messages and avoid mixed signals.

Examples of such mixed signals include the following:

- Encouraging teamwork but incentivizing individual success
- Encouraging long-term goals but incentivizing short-term success
- Inspiring innovation and risk-taking but punishing failure
- Emphasizing the importance of quality but paying for quantity

My goal is to show you how to be incentive smart—how to avoid these mixed signals and design incentives that are simple, effective, and ethical.

Controlling the Story

Look at the series of pictures in the figure from left to right. What do you see?[2]

When I ask a lecture audience this question, I hear some very creative and interesting answers. Some are literal, such as "A circle appears from the top left and moves toward the center, and the star moves out of the frame." Other replies are more creative: "How mediocrity wins over talent"; "It's

What's your story?

better to be a moon than a star"; "Only the strong survive"; or "The ball is being rejected."

The audience injects meaning into the abstract shapes to make sense of them. After having fun with the answers to the first question, I ask the audience to guess what happens next. Again, people have no problem filling in the gaps: "Don't worry, the star will come back to claim the center"; "We learn to live in an unfair world"; or "The circle is punished."

The psychology behind these reactions is interesting. Our brain tends to fill the gaps between pictures by creating a story out of what we see; instead of simple pictures of objects, our brain creates a narrative and even moral values such as fairness and punishment. Stories help us understand our experience by attaching meaning to complicated events that affect our lives. Stories have many uses: they help us memorize events, evaluate them, and make sense of the world.

Hence, mastering the ability to shape the story is important, and incentives done right can do just that. Take the example of Douglas Ivester, CEO of Coca-Cola, who in 1999 met with a Brazilian newspaper and discussed an incentive idea. The idea involved new technology in vending machines that automatically detected temperature; this information, Ivester mused, could be used for pricing at vending machines. Demand for Coca-Cola was higher on hotter days, so Ivester argued for increasing soda price when temperature rose.

Basic economics: when craving rises, so too should price. On a regular day, the price would be, say, $1.00. On a hot day, the vending machine would react and raise the price to $1.50, as shown on the next page. This type

Everyday price is $1.00; increases to $1.50 on hotter days.

of dynamic pricing isn't unusual—we see it in airlines, hotels, and many other industries.

When the word of temperature-controlled pricing got out, however, customers were not happy. The press picked it up and called Ivester's pricing plan a "cynical ploy to exploit the thirst of faithful customers."[3]

Coca-Cola had failed to shape the story. Ivester's mistake was to leave the story open for interpretation. Instead of just discussing the technical aspects of the idea, he should have framed the story. One idea is shown in the figure on the opposite page.

While describing the exact same reality, these options convey two very different stories. It's hard to imagine that giving incentives in the form of a discount on a cold day would meet a consumer pushback.

The Coca-Cola mistake shows how important it is to control the story and how incentives and their signals often do exactly that. We will discuss in detail how incentives can shape the story to your advantage.

Everyday price is $1.50; drops to $1.00 on colder days.

The Shape of Incentives

All animals, not just humans, react to incentives. Think about a lion in Tanzania hunting zebras. The lion needs to remain downwind in order to surprise the zebra. If it approaches from the wrong direction, all the zebras would escape, leaving the lions and their cubs hungry. The lion also needs to be careful when jumping on the zebra, as a zebra can kick back quite hard, thus injuring or even killing the lion. This calculated approach to hunting can easily be explained by incentives: the lion wants to eat and feed its cubs and doesn't want to get hurt in the process. It's not just food; a lion's social hierarchy and its dominance in the pack are also at stake. For example, it's more dangerous to be the first lion attacking, but being the brave one may pay off with some social status later on.

While both humans and lions react to incentives, there is a big difference between us when it comes to shaping incentives. Lions and other animals react to incentives like humans do, but they don't design incentives for others. It's hard to imagine lions in Tanzania designing rewards for lions far away, say in Kenya. Humans, on the other hand, are constantly busy constructing incentives, and our life is shaped by incentives that were designed by others.

If you think shaping incentives is inconsequential, think again. The twentieth century presented the largest ever economic experiment regarding shaping incentives: communism. Economics is at the core of communism because communism dictates how wealth is created and shared. Individuals create wealth, while the government owns and shares all the wealth created. The incentives to work and produce more in this economic structure are not to help yourself or your family but rather to help the community. It turned out that this type of incentives structure didn't do a good job at getting the world moving.

Here's a famous example that demonstrates this structural failing: in the late '80s, shortly before the collapse of the Soviet Union, an official from Moscow went to London to learn about bread distribution. When he asked the economist Paul Seabright, "Who's in charge of bread distribution in London?" Seabright's reply was, "Nobody."[4] There was a lot of effort going into distributing the bread, but it wasn't orchestrated by a central person or organization. Rather, the distribution was motivated by individual incentives. A British baker wakes up early in the morning and goes into the bakery to work hard, as they need money to pay rent and feed their family. The same is true for the farmers who grow wheat, the drivers who deliver bread to stores, and the storekeepers who sell it. This teamwork effectively functions because the market prices keep everyone in the supply chain motivated. The problematic supply of bread in Moscow wasn't due to the failure of the person in charge but rather to the failure of systemic incentives.

Cash Is Not the Only Game in Town

An important instrument in the functioning of markets was the creation of money. (Imagine that you had to pay for this book with a chicken!)

Money makes life much easier. But this book is not about money; it is about the interaction of important signals.

It helps to take a step back here and consider two different approaches to incentives. One simply focuses on the direct economic effect that makes the incentivized behavior more attractive: the more you would pay me to do something, the more likely I would be to do it. The other approach focuses on the indirect effect, which is more complex and can be split into two components: social signaling and self-signaling.

Social signaling captures the concern we have over what others might think of us. We want people to see us in a certain way, either to keep up a facade or because the image we project truly reflects our core values and beliefs.

Self-signaling is conceptually similar to social signaling with one fundamental difference: it represents the concern over what we can infer about ourselves from our behavior. We want to maintain a certain self-image—say, one that touts that we are good, smart, kind, and fair. Every time we behave in accordance with our identity, we view ourselves more positively.[5]

What happens once incentives are added to the mix? Let's put both approaches to work. Consider the following scenario: On a freezing December morning, you see your neighbor Sara carrying a large bag full of cans to the recycling center. You observe Sara's behavior and create a narrative: "Wow, Sara is awesome! She cares about the environment and is willing to sacrifice time and expend effort to help protect it." Sara socially signals to others that she is environmentally conscious. In all likelihood, her trip to the recycling center also serves as a positive self-signal; she could have placed the cans in the trash, but instead, she took the time and effort to recycle them in the bitter cold. She's probably quite happy with herself.

Now, consider the same scenario, only this time there's an incentive program aimed at encouraging people to recycle soda cans: for each soda can Sara recycles, she will receive five cents.

Does your original narrative that Sara is awesome still work? On day one of my economics training, I learned that more money is better than less, hence paying Sara should make her happy and incentivize her to recycle more. What could be wrong with that? Well, along with creating a financial gain (the economic effect), the incentive also changed the signals and the story. Sara is doing the exact thing you previously admired her for, only now she receives a couple of dollars in return. But instead of seeing her as a devoted environmentalist, you now see her as your cheap neighbor. In other words, the incentive changed the social signal that recycling sends.

The presence of incentives may change not only the social signaling but also how Sara feels about herself. Rather than feeling good each time she makes a trip to the recycling center, she may now wonder if it's worth going through all the trouble for a couple of bucks. In other words, the incentive also changed the self-signal that recycling sends.

These kinds of findings led Daniel Pink to declare in his book *Drive* that "most people believe that the best way to motivate is with rewards like money—the carrot-and-stick approach. That's a mistake."[6] I fully agree that the simplistic approach is wrong: cash is not always king. However, it doesn't mean that incentives don't work. The holy grail in designing incentives is to make the signals sent by incentives work and, at the same time, also to reinforce self- and social signaling in the desired direction.

Abracadabra?

Imagine waking up one morning to find an email from one of your heroes. It happened to me in 2012, and I couldn't have been happier. The email was from Thomas Schelling, a legendary economist who won the Nobel Prize in 2005. He wrote,

> I was reading your incentives paper and was reminded of an experience I had sixty years ago. I was in Washington from November '50 until September '53, first in the White House and then in the Office of the Director for Mutual Security. Morale was high; everyone felt engaged and worked hard.

Frequently on a Friday afternoon, a meeting would reach 7 P.M. or so and the chairman would ask whether we'd all rather hang around another hour or two or resume Saturday morning. There were lots of people with small children who would say, somewhat apologetically, that they shouldn't stay later, but Saturday A.M. at 9 or so was all right. Everybody always agreed. So, we spent dozens of Saturdays in interagency meetings.

One day in 1952, we were apprised of an executive order of the president that henceforth anybody who worked on Saturday was to receive overtime pay. I think there was some procedure to get certification of necessity, but I don't think I ever knew what the procedure was because I never again attended a Saturday meeting, nor did anyone else as far as I could tell.

I think two motives may have been involved. One was that we were all so highly motivated and enthusiastic about our work that the idea of getting paid took all the heroic excitement out of it. The other was that we wouldn't want someone to think we were eager for Saturday work because of the overtime pay.

Schelling's story is full of important behavioral insights on incentives waiting to be unpacked. Building on stories like this one, as well as years of rigorous research, this book will do just that. However, before we begin, what exactly is an incentive? Simply put, an incentive is a tool used to motivate people to do something they would not do otherwise.

The discussion around incentive schemes can often get quite heated. Should students be provided with incentives for school attendance, for reading, or for better grades? Should people receive incentives to recycle more, to donate blood, or to generally be better citizens? Should companies leverage incentives to reduce smoking, to encourage exercising, or to generally create better habits among their employees?

Some people believe that if you just give someone incentives, then—abracadabra!—success will magically follow. It's not that simple. While it's true that behavior is shaped by incentives, it's not magic. Sometimes incentives send mixed signals and achieve the opposite of what they were designed for. Other people deeply oppose incentive schemes, viewing them as immoral and even reprehensible. To them, incentives are instruments of manipulation used by malicious corporations aiming to trick hardworking folks into buying things they don't want or need.

My view is different. Incentives aren't inherently good or bad. It's the way we choose to use them that's either moral or not. Incentives can be used to get children addicted to cigarettes, sure, but they can also be used to save lives. Just like statistics and econometrics are not inherently moral or immoral but simply a useful tool, so too are incentives.

A disclaimer before we start: just because incentives can be powerful, it doesn't mean that we should accept them as our unquestioned masters. Think about a single parent who loses their job and with it their child's health insurance. This parent will be very motivated to find another job, more so than if the child's insurance had not been affected. But is this intensified job search really worth the cost? Is it okay to incentivize people by putting their child's health and well-being at risk? I very strongly believe that every child deserves to have full access to the health-care system, regardless of background and circumstances. While providing free health care for children might be a bad incentive for job-seeking parents, it is, in my view, the right thing to do. As powerful as incentives can be, they shouldn't be the only consideration in policy design.

My own work on incentives, which you'll read about throughout this book, covers a diverse range of topics, from increasing click-through rates on a website to improving employees' job retention, from eroding the practice of female genital mutilation in the Maasai tribe in Kenya to understanding why students in the US are perhaps not as bad at math as we might think. As you will see, incentives matter in various and sometimes unexpected ways.

Executives, parents, teachers, lovers—we're all pawns in the incentive game. Those who understand the rules of the game will gain the advantage.

Key principles from this book will seep not just into your work but also into your personal life. You may even find the secret to motivating yourself and finally achieve some of those personal goals you've had for just about forever, be it exercising more, taking more vacations, or being more productive.

This book is by no means an "abracadabra!" But I write in the hopes that after reading it, you will have the tools necessary to craft highly effective incentives while avoiding potentially detrimental mistakes.

PART ONE
How Signaling Wins Markets

● ● ●

The right signals could captivate consumers and win markets, while the wrong signals could backfire and lead to adverse outcomes. This lesson is well illustrated by an episode of *Seinfeld*.[1] In the episode, Jerry remembers that Elaine's birthday is coming up, and he needs to decide what to get her. Given Jerry and Elaine's past romantic relationship, he carefully considers the symbolism of each potential gift and struggles to choose. The birthday eventually arrives, and Jerry hands over a wrapped gift to Elaine, who is ecstatic about the surprise. While unwrapping the gift, Elaine's grin, however, quickly turns into a squint, then a grimace. "Cash? You got me cash?" Elaine questions rhetorically, "What are you, my uncle?" While Jerry is trying to justify his $182 gift, Kramer enters and gives Elaine his gift, which turns out to be a bench that Elaine has been looking for. Elaine hugs Kramer out of excitement and leaves Jerry baffled.

Why did a generous cash gift of $182 disappoint Elaine, while a bench that's worth much less monetarily make Elaine much happier? Jerry thought about the signal sent by his gift but made a poor choice. Elaine wanted a gift that signaled Jerry had put considerable thought into choosing the gift, but the cash signaled the exact opposite: it was lazy and thoughtless. On the other hand, Elaine loved Kramer's cost-effective gift, because it signaled care and consideration.

We all make mistakes like Jerry. Often we're too focused on the face value of our action or product and end up ignoring the consequential signals we're sending. What are the right signals, and how can we leverage them to achieve desirable results? The following chapters dive into the world of signaling: I'll discuss the types of signals, then showcase the power of effective signals and the dreadful outcomes of poor ones by examining a number of intriguing real-world examples. A win and a disaster are often separated merely by effective signals.

1

Credible Signals

My accountant, Jim, is full of energy. It's April 8, a week before Tax Day, and he has back-to-back meetings with procrastinating clients like me who blissfully ignore their taxes until the deadline. As he fills out my forms with impressive alacrity and a smile on his face, I check out the CPA diplomas on his wall. I notice that among them are pictures of him on this big motorcycle traversing through beautiful mountain roads. I look at these pictures and then back at Jim, a forty-three-year-old man with flecked black hair, sitting in his fourteenth-floor office with a view of downtown San Diego. Trying to reconcile the two images, I ask him what keeps him going so strong during this oh-so-stressful period in April, hoping he'll give me a bit of insight into his double life. I'm in luck: "In a couple of weeks, I'm taking off for my annual break," he replies, while his eyes glisten at the thought. He's got it all planned out: he's going to dust off his Harley, make sure his riding jacket still fits, get himself some new boots, shave his head . . . and get a neck tattoo.

If you ever happen to see Jim and his buddies entering a pub during their time off, you'd know immediately that although they ride nice bikes, they're not the real deal—they're not "bikers." Jim isn't really going to get a neck tattoo, and he isn't going to join Hells Angels. They wouldn't take him even if he wanted to. You can't be a Hells Angel for a month and then go back to the nice view from your downtown office like nothing had ever happened.

The Harley bike culture is hard to fake. Bikers love their Harleys as a lifestyle, not as a hobby—they are Harley to their core. They wear Harley shirts, Harley jackets, Harley boots, Harley rings . . . you get the picture. Jim has all of that, though. It's easy to notice how in love Jim and his buddies are with their Harley motorcycles, just like the "real" bikers. So, how can you distinguish between real Harley bikers and those like Jim, who take on the culture for a month every year?

You need what economists call a "costly signal": any piece of information that allows agents (such as employees or companies) to *credibly* inform others about their values, abilities, or preferences. In the case of bikers, this signal should be something that only real bikers would be willing to do. Material goods, such as jackets and boots, send weak signals, because many people can simply buy them. Jim is a case in point. Covering yourself in tattoos, on the other hand, sends a much stronger signal. If you were a "real" biker, you'd get tattoos to express your identity—not your temporary vacation identity but your everyday one. A tattoo is a good signal for the biker-culture club membership because getting one is too costly for the "fakers" who want to go back to their office life. You can imagine how Jim's boss would react if he came in one day with a winged skull etched onto his neck. A real Harley biker, the one getting the tattoo, gains direct utility from the fact that others see it and consider them to be part of the biker culture.

Jim's incentives decision is plotted in the game tree shown here. For context, game trees are a tool from game theory used to identify and explain how incentives can change a situation. These game trees may help you organize your thoughts about the decisions that people face. I'll use them all throughout this book. Let's start by really understanding Jim's decision.

Real Harley bikers go with Outcome #1—they get the neck tattoo, and it sends a strong signal that they're hard core. Reversible choices, such as haircuts, don't send such a credible signal. As Henry Farrell explains in the *Washington Post*, "This means that topknots and tattoos are different kinds of signals. Topknots, even extravagantly weird ones, verge perilously close

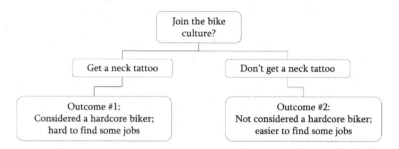

Getting a neck tattoo as a credible signal: utility of biker. If one cares enough about bike culture, Outcome #1 > Outcome #2 → get a neck tattoo. If not, Outcome #1 < Outcome #2 → don't get one.

to unconvincing 'cheap talk.' If a topknotted hipster changes his mind and decides to seek employment in a boring conventional job, all he needs to do is go for a haircut. Tattoos are much harder to get rid of, which means that they are much costlier signals."[1]

Ken, one of my MBA students, told me his workplace tattoo story. During his undergraduate studies at NYU, he worked as a valet in a fancy hotel in town. The valet guys had black uniforms that covered the tattoos on his right arm. All was fine in the winter, as he made good money (mostly tips) and did well in his job. Then it got hotter in New York, and the valet uniform was changed to short-sleeve shirts. With the new uniform, his tattoos were visible.

A couple of days into the new dress code, the hotel manager called Ken to his office. "I'm sorry, Ken," he said, "but you can't work as our hotel valet with such tattoos. It's against our policy." The manager had nothing against Ken's job performance; large tattoos were just not the message that the hotel wanted to send to its guests. The manager also assured Ken that he had nothing against him or against tattoos, only against displaying them at the front of the hotel. He even offered Ken a kitchen job, where guests wouldn't see him and his tattoos. Ken's story isn't unique, and that demonstrates tattoos' strong signaling power.

Note that signals may change their meaning over time. Forty years ago, many places wouldn't hire a man who didn't wear a necktie; I've been to offices in Silicon Valley where a necktie today would brand you as hopelessly out of touch. Likewise, a nose ring might have rendered you unemployable twenty years ago, but many places wouldn't bat an eye at a tasteful nose ring today. The same is true about tattoos. Not that long ago, tattoos were almost exclusively for sailors and prisoners. In contrast, many young "normal" people today have visible tattoos. Signals may change over time.

Whether you get a tattoo isn't the only decision that affects the signal. The location of the tattoo also alters the signal you send. If Ken had gotten his tattoo on his back, it would've had no effect on his valet job, as guests couldn't have seen it. What about tattoos on other parts of the body—what signals do they send? I'll leave the rest to the illustration shown here, with three different types of tattoos.

LOCAL SHOP IS HIRING FOR A NEW SHOP ASSISTANT

Different tattoos

Signals serve as a valuable tool for communicating private information that others possibly wouldn't believe if you simply told them. Talk is cheap—you could easily be pretending. Signals not only deliver messages but also make these messages credible. This value is not limited to preferences of the biker lifestyle. Say, for example, you want to hire someone to work for your company. Reading mountains of résumés and conducting interview after interview may reveal something about the applicants' true abilities or character, but they can fake it, much like Jim with his Harley merchandise. As a result, even after the most stellar interviews, employers still have good reason to remain skeptical, at least until the candidates signal something more credible.

Michael Spence created a seminal model about signaling in such job-market situations in 1973, and it landed him the Nobel Prize.[2] Spence's model showed that an applicant can resolve asymmetric information, in which they know how good they are, but the potential employer doesn't, by using costly signals that reveal important information about themselves in a credible way.

How can you tell if such a signal represents the applicant's true values, preferences, and abilities? Some information is fixed and can't be manipulated by the applicant and thus doesn't serve as a valuable message about the applicant's abilities. Age, race, or gender are examples. Signals, on the other hand, are information that can be shaped by the applicant's characteristics and controllable choices. Spence used education as an example of a signal you can find on an applicant's résumé that may tell you something deeper about them. His model includes two types of applicants: the "good" type and the "bad" type. The good type is the high-ability employee whom everyone is looking for. The employer can't tell what type the applicants are by simply reading a cover letter or even by means of an interview. But candidates can signal their true abilities through their level of education on their résumé. Investing in high-level and quality education credibly signals that the applicant is of the good type, and employers are willing to pay a higher salary for an applicant who has made this investment. As always with models, this is just a simplification. The signals are used as heuristics in making hiring decisions and may lead decision-makers to make mistakes.

Why is investing in education at a good academic institution a credible signal? Because it's difficult to achieve. One needs to invest time, effort, and passion into this long-term goal. This investment in education is less costly for the good type of applicant than for the bad type, because by definition, the good type is smarter and is more willing to work hard. Education is less taxing and more rewarding for them than for the bad type, who probably finds it extremely difficult or time-consuming. In this model, the expected future salary increase is worth the initial educational investment only for the good type of applicant, while being too costly for the bad type. As a result, the employer learns something important about the candidate who invested in education. Education has a credible signaling value because only good applicants have it.

Education isn't the only type of past behavior that can be a relevant signal. Imagine that one of the applicants you are interviewing is a former Navy SEAL. The initial training is hard, and it is even harder, both physically and mentally, to follow through, finish the regimen, and become a Navy SEAL. Among those who are able to do it, some find it much harder than others, depending on their type. So, even if the description of the position you are recruiting for doesn't include highly specialized tasks like landing in remote places and fighting enemies, being a former Navy SEAL reveals something fundamental about one's character that employers may find relevant and valuable.

Indicating education or special-ops training is clearly a very different way of signaling private information than getting a tattoo. Within a ten-minute drive from my home in San Diego are more than a dozen places that would be all too happy to give me a tattoo for the price of a dinner. Yet the cost of a tattoo goes far beyond its monetary value if it doesn't fit into your lifestyle. Hence, as we've discussed, getting one would credibly reveal your preferences. The credibility that comes with investing in something like education results from the fact that it is difficult and time-consuming; and the fact that you did so successfully signals something valuable about your abilities and character.

TAKEAWAY: Signals are a credible way to inform others about values, abilities, and preferences.

2

How Toyota Won the Hybrid Car Market

In chapter 1, we discussed how an individual can credibly signal information to others. How might a large organization or company use signaling insights to its advantage? If an organization knows that individuals use signals to reveal their preferences, abilities, and characteristics, could it turn that observation into a profitable strategy? Toyota did exactly that in the early 2000s.

In 1999, just a few months apart, Toyota and Honda introduced their hybrid cars to the US market. They were the first, and much anticipated, hybrid cars in mass production. Although there was a bit of competition in the beginning, Toyota won the market in just a few years and made its Prius one of the best-selling cars ever. Honda's hybrid lost. How did Toyota convince so many customers to purchase a hybrid car? And why did Honda fail?

The Advantage of Buying a Bad Car

The early hybrid cars were bad in nearly all dimensions, apart from fuel consumption. They were more expensive and offered less speed, acceleration, comfort, and safety than similarly priced nonhybrid cars on the market. You would imagine that offering such a bad car would not help Toyota win over customers. However, while these shortcomings certainly posed challenges, they also presented an opportunity, because getting an eco-friendly car, despite the car's being objectively "bad," sends a strong signal about the driver's environmental intentions. Consumers who chose to buy hybrid cars in the

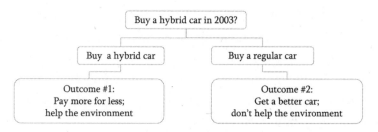

Buying a hybrid car as a credible signal: utility of buyer. If one cares enough about the environment, Outcome #1 > Outcome #2 → get a hybrid car. If not, Outcome #1 < Outcome #2 → get a regular car.

early days were making it abundantly clear that they were environmentally conscious and were willing to pay more for less to help the environment. If they weren't, why would they sacrifice their comfort and safety for it? Similar to investing in education, a hybrid car's cost with regard to its value for money was high, whereas the major benefit was helping the environment. By choosing to buy a Prius, consumers were announcing to themselves and to the world that they were the kind of person who's willing to sacrifice a lot for the environment. The original hybrid incentive game is plotted in the game tree shown here.

Today, buying a Prius no longer sends this kind of a signal—at least not as much as the early hybrid models did. The Prius is now a competitive car, even within the nonhybrid car market, offering an overall good deal that customers may find desirable regardless of their environmental leanings. For example, an Uber driver might find that a Prius saves a considerable amount of money on fuel, while also offering comfort and reliability. As such, many people today may choose to purchase a Prius even if they don't care that much about the environment. Because consumers no longer have to sacrifice much safety and comfort when purchasing a Prius today, the environmental signaling power is weakened by the car's other new advantages. If you are not convinced, think about the signal one sends by buying a Tesla—is it really all about the environment?

Prius Politics: Showing Off with the Bad Car

So, despite the inferior quality of these early hybrid cars, the ability to credibly signal one's environmental stance created a strong incentive to buy them. And because enough people were willing to buy these bad cars just to make this statement, an exploitable market was born. As we have already learned, Prius gave Toyota a real advantage over many years in the hybrid car market. What, then, did Toyota do that Honda missed?

Let's take a quick look at the companies' sales first. The graph below presents the US sales (global sales figures were similar) of Toyota and Honda hybrid cars between 2000 and 2010.[1] As you can see, it took some time for sales to pick up for both companies. Honda's first hybrid car was the Insight, a small, two-seater car that never really sold. Honda concluded that potential buyers didn't like the two-seater, and it introduced its new hybrid car,

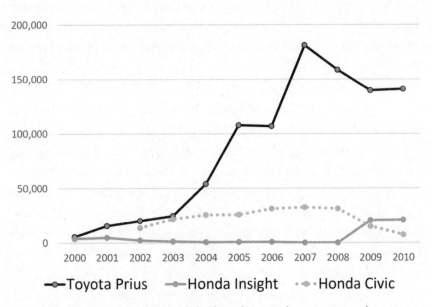

US sales of Honda and Toyota hybrid cars between the years 2000 and 2010. The vertical axis presents the number of cars sold per year.

based on the best-selling Honda Civic. The reasoning behind that choice is intuitive, and this design decision also surely made things easier for its engineers: starting with an existing model and simply modifying it makes life along the supply chain much easier.

Toyota, on the other hand, chose a different strategy that proved to make all the difference. The first generation of the Prius, produced between 1997 and 2003, was designed based on the Corolla, one of Toyota's best-selling cars. The second generation of the Prius was an improvement on many dimensions but had one crucial change that propelled it to success.

Instead of making the car look like any other sedan, with only a small plate on the back distinguishing it as a hybrid, the Prius was redesigned to have the distinct look that we are all familiar with now. When you drive into the parking lot at work with the newly designed Prius, everyone can see that you own a hybrid. This distinctiveness is extremely important for the people who buy the car to signal how much they care about the environment. After all, what's the value in signaling to others if they don't notice it? A small plate doesn't send much of a signal, because the receivers simply don't notice it—it's not that useful as a signal. A completely redesigned look, on the other hand, is nothing if not noticed everywhere and by everyone.

If you're not convinced that the Prius owners know exactly what they're doing, take a look at the vinyl sticker I saw on a Prius outside my house, shown on the following page.

Prius owners *like* the fact that their car is unique and doesn't look like what a typical person would consider "cool." When others see a Prius, they think that only someone who really cares about the environment would get such a car.

As the graph shows, the increase in sales came with this second-generation Prius, introduced in 2003. Sure, the car was better than the first-generation Prius, but so was the Honda Civic as compared to the Insight. However, only a small fraction of the buyers who chose a hybrid went for the Honda Civic. They wanted the distinct-looking Prius—they wanted to be noticed.

A proud Prius owner

This notion was confirmed in 2007 when the *New York Times* cited a study by CNW Marketing Research of Bandon, Oregon. The study found that 57 percent of the Toyota Prius buyers said they got it because "it makes a statement about me." Only 36 percent answered that they bought it because of its fuel economy, and even fewer (25 percent) mentioned low emissions. The article was titled "Say 'Hybrid' and Many People Will Hear 'Prius,'" and it hit the nail on the head. Its author, Micheline Maynard, started the article with a riddle: "Why has the Toyota Prius enjoyed such success, when most other hybrid models struggle to find buyers?" Her answer: buyers wanted everyone to know that they were driving a hybrid.[2]

Maynard interviewed people regarding their choice of the Prius to support her reasoning. She got similar messages across the board:

> I really want people to know that I care about the environment.
> —Joy Feasley, Philadelphia, PA

I felt like the Camry Hybrid was too subtle for the message I wanted to put out there. I wanted to have the biggest impact that I could, and the Prius puts out a clearer message.

—Mary Gatch, Charleston, SC

It wasn't just ordinary people who felt this way, either:

The Prius allowed you to make a green statement with a car for the first time ever.

—Dan Becker, head of the global warming program at the Sierra Club, San Diego, CA

In 2017, the *Washington Post*'s Robert Samuelson aptly called this phenomenon "Prius Politics," arguing that people bought Priuses to show off more than to reduce pollution.[3] In that same year, Honda's CEO admitted that "releasing a Civic Hybrid with little visual differentiation from more plebeian Civics was a mistake"—and with that, Toyota won the hybrid car competition.

TAKEAWAY: Accounting for signals can make all the difference in attracting customers and winning in a competitive marketplace.

3

It's Just Who I Am

The Value of Self-Signaling

The fact that the Prius signal was blatantly observable made it valuable—more valuable than the almost inconspicuous signal sent by purchasing a Honda hybrid. Recall the distinction between the two types of signaling discussed in the introduction: *self-signaling* and *social signaling*. Thus far, I've mostly discussed social signaling, which is a way to improve our social image—what other people think of us. Many of our choices, however, are driven by self-signaling considerations. People often get positive utility, or satisfaction, from signals they send to themselves, through actions indicating that they are good people.

Self-signaling and social signaling interact in quite interesting and inconspicuous ways. As always, the cleanest way to study such interactions is by experiments. Ayelet Gneezy, Gerhard Riener, Leif Nelson, and I ran a series of experiments to try to understand the way signals interact.[1] One was conducted in a Pakistani buffet restaurant, Der Wiener Deewan, located in a central Vienna district. The unique aspect of this restaurant is that it charges people using the "pay-what-you-want" (PWYW) pricing model. That is, when customers are done eating, they choose how much to pay for the meal; they can even pay nothing at all.

Before you begin to seriously question the business model, let me assure you, it works—at least to some degree. Many companies and organizations have utilized this business plan before. Radiohead, for example, released its album *In Rainbows* using a PWYW system on its website and achieved massive success—the album entered the *Billboard* chart at number one and sold millions worldwide, which generated more profit than the total sales of the band's previous album, even before the album's physical release.[2]

Inspired by the pricing scheme, the restaurant owners introduced PWYW to attract new customers when the restaurant first opened. Over the initial weeks, they found that payments approximately matched fixed-price expectations, and thus they decided to retain the PWYW pricing. The average payment ranged between €5.50 and €7.00 initially (similar to comparable restaurants in the area) and then decreased slightly. However, the drop in average payment was matched by an increase in the number of customers who seemed to like the PWYW pricing scheme and came in droves, yielding a slight increase in revenue.

Three months before we entered the picture, the median payment was €5.00, with a minimum of zero (which happened, at most, three or four times a day) and a maximum of €50.00 (which happened once, paid by a local communications company manager from a nearby building who added in writing, "That's what one does here, if I am not mistaken," on the bill). Generally, people paid to the waiter individually. In the rare cases in which one person paid for the entire table, the owner would divide the amount equally over the number of people to yield an individual payment estimate. This restaurant is just one demonstration of how PWYW can be sustained over a long period. Most customers simply didn't seem prepared to leave Der Wiener Deewan without paying. Why? The answer is probably that people care about the signals they are sending, both to themselves and to others, by paying.

To test for and disentangle social and self-signaling, we ran a field experiment. Field experiments are an important tool in behavioral research. While lab experiments are conducted in a "clean" environment that attempts to abstract from the naturalistic setting, field experiments test our theories "in the wild." When thinking about field experiments, we try to run our studies in naturalistic environments and use participants who are not aware that their decisions are being studied. As such, field experiments allow us to target the population of interest in its natural environment, resulting in findings that are more applicable to the relevant context.

Our field experiment consisted of two treatments, varying whether or not payment was made anonymously. In the "observed" treatment, customers filled out a questionnaire and returned it along with their payment to the waiter handling money and questionnaires at the counter. The waiter was instructed and trained to treat all customers the same and to record the amount paid on the questionnaire. The decision process is as follows:

> Eat lunch → Fill out a questionnaire → Give questionnaire and payment to *waiter*

In the "anonymous" treatment, customers also received the questionnaire and decided how much to pay. Before leaving, customers put their payment into an envelope and dropped it into a box near the entrance along with the questionnaire.

> Eat lunch → Fill out a questionnaire → Put questionnaire and payment in *sealed envelope*

In the observed treatment, customers paid €4.66 on average. A simple explanation of why they paid is that they cared about their social image— they didn't want to look cheap in front of the person collecting money from them. In other words, by paying a reasonable amount, they signaled to others that they are good people and thereby improved their social image.

How did customers in the anonymous treatment fare? In this treatment, signaling to others clearly cannot be at play. Think about it: if no one can see how much you pay, paying provides no social-image value. As a result,

PAY WHAT YOU WANT

Self-signaling: Am I a good person?

one might expect that if the customers only care about social signaling, they will pay nothing at all, as in the illustration.

What if they also care about their self-image? Eating a nice lunch and leaving without paying might make them feel bad, because they don't want to see themselves as the kind of people who take advantage of the restaurant's generosity. Engaging in self-signaling, they may still pay even though their payments go unobserved.

Our experimental design allowed us to tease apart the interactions between social and self-signaling and observe them in action. The observed treatment allowed us to analyze the combined effect of the two types of signals, whereas the anonymous treatment helped us isolate self-image considerations. Under this design, we can compare and contrast these two treatments and then uncover whether these signals reinforce each other. Take a second to think and make a guess. Did the "anonymous" customers pay less when they didn't have to worry about social pressure? If we simply assume that these two forces reinforce each other, we would expect that in the anonymous treatment, people would also pay, but less than the payments in the observed treatment.

As it turned out, customers in the anonymous treatment paid *more* than those in the observed treatment. That is, customers paid more when they were not observed, increasing payments by a statistically significant amount of €0.71 on average. We can clearly reject the notion that customers pay less when they are not observed.

Why did people pay more when their payments were anonymous, though? Our result not only supports the hypothesis that people often pay to enhance their self-image but also demonstrates that the two signals (self and social) don't just simply "add up." Because both signals push people to give more, it's easy to make the erroneous assumption that when both are present, the effect will always be stronger and people will give even more. We find that this assumption is not always consistent with behavior. When the two signals work in tandem, they can interact with each other and consequently change in value. If the employee observes your payment, you want to signal to them that you are a good person by paying a reasonable amount. However, being observed by others reduces the value of self-signaling. When you're observed, you feel like you are paying in part to impress the employee, and this signal to others therefore doesn't serve as a boost to your self-image. You don't feel like you are paying because you are a nice person—you feel like you are paying because you have to, or others will think negatively of you. On the other hand, when no one observes how much you pay, the self-signal is potentially stronger. You are paying even though no one is watching; thus, your self-image receives the full benefit of your generosity.

Self-Expression

Our finding demonstrated that signals don't necessarily add up. Sending a social signal may reduce the value of self-signaling, and the latter by itself may be more powerful, which is why adding the social signal in our experiment reduced overall payment. The Toyota Prius, however, did not suffer from this problem of social signals crowding out self-signals. In this case, the signals did add up. The branding expert Brad VanAuken discussed in his article "Toyota Prius—Vehicular Self-Expression" how the Prius's unique design was important to people who were using the brand as a self-expression statement. Marketers use the term *self-expression* to combine the two types of signaling we just discussed. VanAuken testified, "When driving my first Prius, I was always amused when I stopped next to a Hummer at a traffic light. I would look over at the Hummer driver smugly and think 'You gas hog, you selfish, wasteful person.' As a marketer who understands self-expressive brands, I was simultaneously imagining that he was looking over at me thinking, 'You enviro-wimp, I could crush your car as if it were a bug.' . . . Or maybe he was thinking that I was a 'self-righteous tree-hugger' or that I couldn't afford a car like his."[3]

The typical Prius owner enjoyed two aspects of the car. First, they were able to feel better about themselves (self-signaling). Second, they were happy members of the Prius club who could make fun of the Hummer club members (signaling to others). Combining the two signals is common in both sociology and marketing; put simply, we have a need for self-expression, and this need is fueled by our desire for the two signals. We use many of our choices, such as what we wear, eat, or drive, as opportunities for such self-expression.

However, when considering the use of incentives, disentangling self- and social signals is important. As our restaurant experiment demonstrated, the signals don't always add up and may detract from the goal itself if used without careful consideration. Pay attention to the incentive environment, as the interaction between the two signals, whether it's additive or conflicting, is context dependent. Understanding how incentives will be perceived in these terms can make a big difference when designing incentive schemes.

One important aspect to aid in this effort is to know the target audience. The Hummer driver wants to signal something very different than the

Prius driver. The Prius's revamped design was successful because it was properly aimed toward incentivizing the right group—we'll explore this more in depth shortly. For now, let's talk about how incentives and signals can really affect self-selection.

Case Study: Paying for Blood

Consider Jane, a lawyer who periodically takes the time to donate blood. The act is a bit unpleasant, which might actually be beneficial for her self-signaling: Jane can now not only feel good about her donation but also acknowledge that she's sacrificing her comfort for others. Jane may also enjoy some social-signaling when she mentions her donation while having dinner with friends. In her cost-benefit calculation, Jane gains more in good feelings than she loses in time and unpleasantness. Jane is not alone: about one hundred million donations are given annually worldwide.[4]

Of course, not everyone shares Jane's Samaritan drives. Take Joe, who works in the same law firm as Jane, but unlike Jane, he's a secretary. Joe's salary is predictably much lower than Jane's, and since he can use some extra cash, he drives for Uber after work to supplement his income. Joe doesn't donate blood. Why? First, he'd rather spend the time driving for Uber to earn more money. Second, he doesn't care that much about blood donation, and donating blood wouldn't make him feel that much better about himself.

The economics of blood donation are very interesting, because billions of dollars exchange hands in this market every year, but the donors are not paid. The US hospitals pay about $570 for a unit of blood and in turn charge their patients for it.[5] Blood banks always need more blood, and they in turn charge hospitals much more than the cost of collecting it. The demand is greater than the supply. The economic solution in such a case is simple: pay donors, and the supply will increase. If so, then why don't you get a wad of cash every time you donate blood?

Imagine that a blood bank approaches you and asks for help in designing such an incentive scheme for donors. Your intuition is simple: the

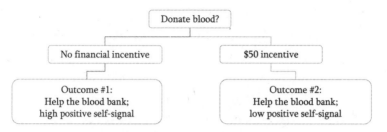

How money crowds out self-signaling

solution is to give each person who comes in to donate blood some compensation, say, $50, right? After all, the blood bank can charge more for it. Jane should be all the happier to visit, and Joe might even park his car for a couple of minutes to go donate and earn some cash. What could go wrong?

Your signals may clash. Monetary compensation affects one's bank account *and* alters the signal sent by donating blood. Jane enjoys the positive signal in the absence of any financial incentives, as shown in Outcome #1 of the game tree shown above, illustrating Jane's decision process. Offering her $50, though, results in Outcome #2 and changes everything. Over dinner with friends, she can no longer mention her nice behavior without her friends' judgmental assumptions, because they'd think she must be underpaid or, worse yet, cheap to do something like that for $50. Think back to the recycling example in the introduction: Sara went from the amazing environmentalist to your cheap neighbor with a simple incentive change. Like Sara, the $50 might even make Jane doubt her own motives for donating: Is she doing it because she's nice or because of the money she gets? Paradoxically, Jane may stop donating blood, because she prefers Outcome #1. Joe, on the other hand, may behave as you had hoped when designing your incentives (as long as they are large enough) and will become a frequent donor because he never cared as much about the positive signals that blood donation sent in the first place.

Richard Titmuss's 1970 book *The Gift Relationship: From Human Blood to Social Policy* pointed to this very effect.[6] He compared blood-donation systems in the US and the UK. At that time, the US blood banks paid donors for their blood, whereas the UK ones didn't. Titmuss argued that this difference in incentive design led to different types of people donating blood: there was a higher fraction of the "Jane type" in the UK and a higher fraction of the "Joe type" in the US. The result was that the blood donated in the US, where many donors were drug addicts who needed money, was of a lower quality, with a higher chance of being infected with hepatitis B. This difference in the composition of donor types, Titmuss continued, was the result of a change in the relevant norm associated with blood donation. Norms, established by the incentive scheme, complete the story and affect both signals—what you think about your actions and what others think about them.

The current incentive involved in the market for blood is explained further by the fact that when donors in wealthy countries are asked why they donate blood, the majority say they do so for purely altruistic reasons: they want to help their community, friends, and relatives.[7] And, indeed, most of the blood (over 75 percent) collected in such countries comes from volunteers.[8] In fact, high-income countries are unwilling to even consider paying money to donors, to a great extent because of Titmuss-like arguments: they don't want the norm associated with blood donation to be monetary.

The overall impact of incentives in the case of blood donation depends largely on the size and type of incentives. If incentives come in the form of petty cash, the norm may shift, and the backfire effect on the Jane-type donors might be larger than the appeal to the Joe-type donors. In this case, one is better off not offering incentives at all to avoid changes in motivation.

However, countries that don't allow cash incentives for blood donations have shown that small noncash incentives may work, as, when done correctly, noncash incentives don't provoke donors to doubt their motives. Switching up both the type (financial to nonfinancial) and size ($50 cash to $1 pen) still may not affect the Joe-type donors, but field experiments have revealed that they can be used to convince people like Jane to donate more often or to move people who are "almost there" to join the donors. One study used medals and social rewards (in the form of recognition in the local newspaper in an Italian town).[9] Another gave Australian Jane-type blood donors "Blood Service pens."[10] Such studies show that incentives in the form of small gifts can have a positive effect on donation in the short run, without downsides in the long run.[11]

Why do these small tokens of recognition motivate donors? Clearly, Jane doesn't need another pen. However, with this one, she can casually bring it out in a meeting and more easily signal to people that she's a blood donor. The pen also enhances self-signal. After all, it is nice to be reminded every time she picks up her pen just how good of a person she is.

TAKEAWAY: Signals change how people feel about themselves (self-signaling) and how others perceive them (social signaling). To enhance signaling, consider both signal size and type.

PART TWO
Avoid Mixed Signals

• • •

Our choices and actions send messages to others about our values. Consider a manager who communicates to her employees in a call center that "customer care is the most important thing for our company." That's a signal to others regarding values. Now, imagine that the manager sets the incentives such that employees are paid by the number of calls they answer. This incentive sends a very different signal about what the manager is looking for: it's about being fast, which comes at the expense of quality of care. Such mixed signals leave the employees confused about the manager's values and expectations.

This mixed signals problem is channeled into a simple question: What should be rewarded? In many cases, performance is multifaceted, but compensation is only given to one aspect of performance, typically the one that is easiest to measure. Simple "one-aspect" compensation sends a clear message to the workers: concentrate on what we're paying you for and ignore everything else. For example, it might be easy to measure how many shirts factory workers produce, but if we reward them only for the number of shirts produced, what will happen to the quality of the shirts? Would workers be just as careful making sure the stitches are straight and symmetric? If we pay our salesperson just based on the dollar amount of their sales, they might sell more, but customers might be less satisfied with the service they receive and will be less likely to come back and buy from our company in the future.

Economists struggle with the best way to incentivize behavior under such "multitasking" conditions.[1] In some cases, if you can only incentivize one dimension (such as quantity) because it is too complicated to measure the other dimensions (such as quality), it may be better to avoid "contingent incentives"—incentives that depend on performance—altogether. There are clever ways to avoid the problem by making other dimensions of performance count. We'll discuss these problems and their solutions in this part.

The important lesson is that when you use incentives to reward an action or outcome, you need to understand and control how the incentives affect the tension between different goals. Otherwise, you're sending conflicting messages. Companies often have "talking points" that mean next to nothing, instead of having a strong and clear message that is supported by their incentives. Look at some of the common conflicting messages that companies send in the figure below.

The mixed signals arising from the conflict between what companies say they want and how they set their incentives is present in all these messages.

Encouraging…	But incentivizing…
o *Quality*	o *Quantity*
o *Innovation*	o *Safe bets and punishing failure*
o *Long-term goals*	o *Short-term success*
o *Teamwork and cooperation*	o *Individual success*

How incentives can send mixed signals

Each case of mixed signals in the figure will be discussed in turn in the following chapters, and I'll speak to how companies can avoid these mixed signal problems. Note that in the examples in the figure, signals are the interpretation of what the executive expects the worker to do. That is, they help workers interpret the expectations of the people who set the incentives.

4

When More Is Less

Incentivizing Quantity at the Expense of Quality

> Well, then, says I, what's the use you learning to do right when it's trouble-some to do right and ain't no trouble to do wrong, and the wages is just the same?
>
> —*Mark Twain,* The Adventures of Huckleberry Finn

Suzan, at age forty-five, was promoted to be the manager of a call center that employs about a hundred people. She joined the company a couple of years earlier and is now tasked with setting the compensation for her team. Jack is one of the team members: he is twenty-nine years old, lives with his girlfriend, and attends a part-time local law school. His dream is to become a successful lawyer; the call center job is his bread, not his dream.

Suzan is frustrated today, because she can't simply set compensation based on effort, since there's no good measure of it at the call center. While Suzan can't fully monitor Jack's effort, she can alter his incentive structure to try to motivate him to work harder. Initially, Suzan considers trying the one extreme method that many employers turn to: a fixed wage. With this option, Jack gets paid as long as he shows up to work and answers calls. Is time a good enough proxy for Jack's effort, though? The eight hours Jack logs every day could be spent leisurely answering calls in a careless fashion, with many coffee and Facebook breaks in between. If time is not a good metric for effort, what should Suzan use instead? The number of calls Jack makes? The number of clients he helps? The volume of coffee he drinks?

Let's say Suzan uses the number of calls instead of time, as many employers in her position opt to do. If the number of calls simply depends on Jack's effort and is easy to measure, then Suzan need not worry about Facebook breaks: the more calls he makes, the more money he earns.

It seems straightforward, doesn't it? It is, if the number of calls is the only metric Suzan cares about. Is the signal she wants to send Jack, "make as many calls as you can"? If she cares about the quality of calls as well, she might be disappointed. Consider the type of calls Jack may face. Some are easy and fast, while others are longer and harder to deal with. If paid by the number of calls, Jack receives a signal that, for example, it is fine to "accidentally" drop calls that he considers as getting too complicated. This would not be beneficial to the customer or for the center. Jack would also be less polite and patient with the callers, as he would rather simply try to end the calls as fast as possible. This chapter is about how simply incentivizing quantity could create problems if you care about other dimensions, such as quality.

As in the case of Suzan and Jack, it's often easier to measure the number of assignments completed or products assembled than to evaluate the quality of work. In such cases, it is tempting to incentivize quantity—indeed, that is the route many companies take. This metric, however, creates a problem for companies that truly care about quality (e.g., ones for which positive customer reviewers are integral to their success): it sends the wrong signal. Companies can emphasize the importance of quality as often as they want, but they end up sending the opposite signal when they set incentives that solely reward quantity.

Who Sends Mixed Signals?

Governments join private companies in making this mixed signal mistake. In the mid-nineteenth century, the US government set out to build its first transcontinental railroad. The department in charge hired the Union Pacific Railroad Company to do the job, instructing it to build the most efficient track possible. The department also created an incentive based on quantity: it decided to pay per mile of track built.

In the 1860s, the colorful Thomas C. Durant entered the story. A medical doctor by training, Durant switched to business and bought over $2 million in shares of the Union Pacific Railroad Company, thus gaining control of it by selecting its president. He "hired" Crédit Mobilier of America as an independent contractor for the construction of the railroad. But Crédit Mobilier was only a business front and was in fact owned by Union Pacific investors. Durant used this business front to cheat the government out of tens of millions of dollars by inflating the actual cost of construction. One way to inflate the cost was by unnecessarily adding miles to the tracks: after all, the more miles of track built, the more money the company earned.[1]

This outcome was clearly not what the government wanted when it created the per-mile incentive. While there's nothing wrong with incentivizing quantity, miles built is just a proxy for quality and not the actual measure of efficient track. A better incentive could have included a temporal component (e.g., a fixed payment for finishing the track on time, without pay based on miles, which is an easily inflatable number), combined with quality controls, since a mandated time frame could also lead to a neglect of quality.

The consequences of mistakenly increasing quantity at the expense of quality could be irreversible. Take fossil recovery as an example. Back in the nineteenth century, paleontologists in China recruited local peasants to help find fossils at a dig site. They motivated the peasants by paying a reward per fossil *fragment* submitted. They incentivized quantity, and that's exactly what they got: the wily peasants smashed the bones they found, which significantly increased their earnings but of course decreased the scientific value of the artifacts. Simple incentives are great, but the incentive that the paleontologists created was too simple. They would have benefited from adding another dimension in their incentives—say, the size of the fossil.

Why add a dimension, rather than switching one simple incentive out for another? The Soviets learned the answer to this question the hard way. In the Soviet Union, state glass-production factories once paid managers and employees on the basis of the weight of the glass they produced. This incentive spurred workers to produce glass that was exceedingly heavy, to the point of being almost opaque. The factory heads recognized this, but instead of adding a dimension to the incentive, they simply traded the incentive based on weight out for an incentive based on size: they switched to paying based on the square meters of glass produced. This new incentive solved the heavy glass problem but created an altogether different problem: the glass produced became so thin that windows often shattered while being transported or installed.[2]

Why Tel Aviv Minibuses Drive before They Close Their Doors

All these stories convey that when you push people to increase one dimension of their output, you can create unintended effects on the other dimensions. You need to make sure what you incentivize is indeed what you want to encourage. Understanding this effect is key. The economist Austan Goolsbee of the University of Chicago made this point in an article he wrote for *Slate* magazine.[3] Goolsbee tries to avoid bad highway traffic during his daily commute. He's learned to save time by mastering all the different routes and taking another route if the highway is jammed. Fellow drivers around the world commiserate . . . except for bus drivers. Buses wait in traffic jams and don't seek faster routes, even when doing so wouldn't affect the stops they have to make—after all, they have no stops to make on the highway. The delays caused by highway traffic make buses a far less attractive option than alternative transportation.

Why don't bus drivers use shortcuts? Is it because it's hard to find a faster route? Not so much—even if you don't know the roads, it's easy to find a faster route using GPS-based apps that tell you the fastest route given current traffic. Maybe a better question is, Why would bus drivers make an effort to find the fastest route possible *when they're not incentivized to*? Bus drivers are paid by the hour. Once they finish their routes, they simply turn back and continue driving until the end of their shift. They are not motivated to take shortcuts and serve more passengers because of the way their incentives are structured.

In a 2015 study, Ryan Johnson, David Reiley, and Juan Carlos Muñoz showed that Chilean bus drivers are acutely aware of incentives and react quickly to changes in incentive structure.[4] When they're paid an hourly wage like the US bus drivers, they have no incentives to look for the fastest route and increase the number of passengers they serve. In our terminology, they receive a signal that it is fine to "take their time." But by changing the incentive structure such that the drivers' pay is based on the number of passengers carried during their shift instead, they receive a signal that this is what management cares about, and their behavior changes dramatically. This alternative incentive structure motivates drivers to reduce delays. They find ways, just as you and I do, to be faster when they drive. They also spend more time on the road and take shorter breaks.

In Tel Aviv, you can observe a similar phenomenon as in Chile, but the problem with a simple pay-per-passenger incentive becomes more apparent. On some of the busier routes, minibuses, which are operated by private drivers who pocket the passenger fees, compete with regular buses operated by drivers who are paid by the hour. I love riding these minibuses when I'm in Tel Aviv because I get to observe strategic behavior in the wild. The minibus drivers are always strategizing with their friends over the radio, planning where to go based on which locations have a larger number of potential passengers. They keep track of the bus schedule as well and try to always be seconds ahead of the bus, so they can pick up the passengers who are waiting at the bus stops.

The figure on the next page tells the story. All in all, this strategic behavior translates to faster service from these minibus drivers. However, in

GUESS: WHO'S PAID PER HOUR, AND WHO'S PAID PER PASSENGER?

Fast and furious or take your time? It's all in the driver's incentives

addition to being faster, they are also much more aggressive, which makes the ride less pleasant for many passengers. They often leave the station as soon as the passenger steps on board, before passengers have a chance to sit and even before they have fully shut the doors. You need to be quick on your feet, literally. In line with this anecdote, the Chilean study found that when bus drivers are incentivized to be fast and increase the number of passengers they pick up, they are also involved in a greater number of accidents, and passengers report a less pleasant riding experience.

When choosing how to pay the drivers, the company needs to consider what's more important: efficiency or safety and comfort? After deciding the relative importance, the company can choose the incentives that align its goals with that of the driver and avoid sending mixed signals. Alternatively, you can find some creative solutions to tackle the quality dimension at the same time. A large natural experiment on rideshare shows us how.

The Rideshare Case

Let's first look at your friendly neighborhood yellow cab company. Sam drives for this cab company and receives an hourly wage. You can imagine why Sam, under this fixed wage, doesn't have a particularly strong motivation to think strategically about the best places to look for rides. He also enjoys long lunch breaks instead of spending that time driving around. After all, as long as he isn't spotted slacking off, he'll get paid the same amount no matter how long or how hard he works.

Compare Sam to Kate, who drives for Uber. She and her fellow Uber drivers are at the other extreme: they are paid per ride, and they keep their earnings minus the percentage they pay to the Uber platform. Hence, Kate's earnings depend on how much she drives: drive more, earn more. She and her fellow rideshare drivers have more motivation to optimize rides with regard to speed and distance, much like the minibus drivers in Tel Aviv, and might work harder than Sam and his fellow cabbies at the taxi company.

Kate may choose to put all her energy into getting more rides, neglecting the service aspect of her job. Ride-sharing companies understood the risk but found a solution: add another incentive dimension, namely, *allow passengers to rate drivers*. At the end of your Uber ride, you can rate the driver on a scale of one to five stars. When you order a ride, the accumulated rating of the driver over many passengers is displayed on your screen. If the rating is low, you may choose to book a different driver. Moreover, if you choose to give your driver a low rating, you are prompted to indicate why: safety, cleanliness, politeness, and the like. The stakes are high: Uber's algorithm monitors these ratings, and drivers who don't meet a certain threshold can no longer drive for the company.

This rating system was a simple solution that motivated drivers to provide good service, because it put the user experience and customer service back in focus. Note that the rating system is cheap and effective, but it didn't replace the original pay-per-ride incentive. Ride-sharing companies *added* it to the original incentive structure and thereby found a way to simultaneously incentivize drivers to be efficient and provide good service.

No such mechanism is in place for traditional taxi drivers. Fixed pay aside, even those who are independent or receive a share of their revenue only have the incentive to maximize the number of rides, increasing speed at the expense of comfort and safety. If the passenger doesn't file an official complaint against them, they have no extrinsic motivation to provide good service. You'd think that if they worked for a company, like Sam does, they'd be rewarded somewhat for service and not tarnishing the company's good name—not even close. Nicole Tam spoke for many of us when she wrote in the *Hawaii Business Magazine* about her riding experience:

> [My friends and I] caught a taxi that was waiting at the parking lot. The ride was short, but hot and unpleasant. The driver was hostile and the seven-seat van looked old, smelled moldy, and was dirty and strewn with tissues and plastic bags. I wanted to pull out my phone and use an app to vent by giving him a lousy rating that everyone could see, but the only way to complain was to take down his taxi license number and call the cab company to complain verbally.
>
> When I ride with Uber and Lyft, the drivers are almost always civil, the vehicles are rarely messy and I can rate my experience in their apps right after my trip is done.[5]

Now, things have changed. The competition that rideshare apps brought to taxi companies forced customer service into the spotlight. Analyzing data from more than a billion cab rides, a report in the *Atlantic* revealed that customer complaints to the Taxi and Limousine Commission in New York and Chicago steadily declined after rideshare companies entered the game.[6] Why? The data suggest that at least some of the decrease in complaints is related to the fact that due to the new competitive pressure, taxi drivers are now trying to improve the ride quality. In some cities, the cab companies have launched their own apps to try to combat rideshare apps, and these apps also include ratings.

Case Study: Fee for Service

One of my research assistants for this book, Will, recently bought an electric skateboard and had been cruising all around town with it. He enjoys the speed and adrenaline, as often the board would go up to a thrilling twenty miles per hour. After weeks of limit testing, Will was eventually punished for his recklessness, crashing and injuring his knees. He went to the emergency room to seek medical help. At the hospital, a doctor immediately ordered an array of different scans. After the doctor examined the physical scans, he suggested that Will come back for a second checkup two weeks later and even mentioned the potential need to undergo a minor surgery. The doctor also prescribed Will plenty of pain-killing medications as well as sleeping-aid drugs. The dosage prescribed was enough for Will to be knocked out for weeks. Will's knees ended up healing completely after a week and a half of resting, and he only finished about a quarter of the prescribed medication.

Will's experience isn't uncommon. In a 2015 survey, out of the 435 ER physicians asked about the tests they order, more than 85 percent admitted that they call for too many tests despite knowing that the results won't aid their decision in choosing treatments.[7] Why do doctors often order a surplus of unnecessary tests and treatments? It's because they are incentivized to do so by the fee-for-service (FFS) system, under which health-care providers are paid according to the service they provide, not based on outcomes. The more tests, surgeries, and scanning a patient undergoes, the more providers are paid. Under such a system, doctors are incentivized to overprescribe treatments and services even if they are not helpful.

The FFS, which started in the mid-1960s when Medicare was introduced, is still the dominant mode of health-care payment in the US, representing over 90 percent of revenue in primary care practices.[8] It's easy for a doctor to tell patients like Will, "Why not do an electrocardiogram to see if there are any problems?" Under the FFS, both the health-care provider and the hospital earn money for each such test—a lot of money, actually. The National Academy of Medicine estimates that the US health-care industry wastes $765 billion a year on unnecessary procedures, which is about a quarter of the annual health-care spending.[9] While the FFS is not the only reason for overtreatment, it sure contributes to the waste. The FFS often incentivizes physicians to neglect simple solutions when more complex and expensive plans are available, for which the doctors are directly compensated. This incentive structure is one of the reasons that US per capita health-care spending is almost twice the average of other wealthy countries, yet this astronomical spending comes with poorer outcomes.[10] The quantity is there, but the quality isn't.

One of the reasons the FFS and the incentives to overtreat can survive is that typically the insurance company covers most of the cost. My daughter had a procedure recently; the bill was $64,000. Fortunately, my university health-care insurance paid for most of it; my copay was only $250. The rest of the cost is spread among all the members of my health insurance company. For example, while it was very nice that my daughter had her own private room in the hospital, we might have opted to share her room if that could have saved us thousands of dollars. We're fortunate to have such insurance; two-thirds of Americans who file for bankruptcy cite medical issues as a key contributor to their financial downfall.[11] Patients who pay the full cost might have tried to shop around, as we do when we make large purchase decisions; but often the system doesn't allow for such freedom. If we wanted to remodel our house, for example, we'd probably get estimates from a few contractors and choose the one that offers us the most cost-effective outcome. However, if someone else would pay for the remodeling, say, the insurance company, we would probably shop around less. Similarly, when the insurance pays for our treatment, we want to have the best treatment possible, regardless of the price. And often we might feel that more treatments equal a better treatment, but that's not necessarily the case.

Let's consider Jane and Ashley, both healthy women who are pregnant and due for delivery. Jane goes to her local hospital and chats with her physician about the optimal delivery method. The physician tells Jane that they have to perform a risk analysis, specifically conducting a fetal heart tracing examination to see if the baby is safe for natural labor. After the analysis, the physician concludes that the fetal heart tracing shows possible abnormality, thus strongly recommending that Jane undergo a C-section.

When Ashley consults her physician at another hospital, her physician also recommends conducting a fetal heart tracing examination to see if the baby is safe for natural labor. After the analysis, the result is the same as in Jane's case: the fetal heart tracing shows possible abnormality. However, the physician's conclusion is drastically different. She explains the situation to Ashley and recommends the natural delivery mode, with some extra monitoring for the fetal heart rate.

While C-section can lower the risk of birth injuries and is sometimes desirable when the woman has life-threatening labor conditions like placenta previa and cord prolapse, vaginal birth is usually the preferred delivery mode.[12] C-sections on average have a higher chance of maternal death, cause more blood loss, have a higher chance of infection, cause more problems for future deliveries, and come with longer recovery periods.[13]

Then why did Jane's physician recommend that she have a C-section? It turns out that Jane's physician is handsomely compensated for every C-section procedure she performs, whereas Ashley's physician receives no extra financial compensation for her C-section procedures when compared to vaginal birth. This behavior doesn't necessarily mean that the doctor doesn't care about the patient's health. As we will discuss later in the book, doctors may deceive themselves to believe that they are acting in the patient's best interest. According to some calculations, incentivized doctors make a few hundred dollars more for every C-section. This makes economic

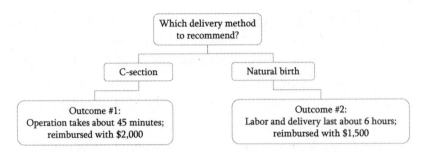

Incentivized physician's delivery recommendation: physician's utility.
Outcome #1 takes less time and has higher monetary gain → chooses Outcome #1.

sense to the hospital that could also earn a few thousand dollars more for each C-section procedure.[14] Given this pay structure, on top of the doctors' individual incentives, there is the additional top-down pressure exerted by hospitals that pushes doctors to recommend C-sections.

Although C-sections have similar underlying costs of procedure as vaginal birth, C-section deliveries tend to receive a much higher reimbursement. Research has shown that there is a strong positive effect of reimbursement fee differentials on the use of C-section delivery.[15] In other words, the larger the difference between reimbursement fees of C-section and vaginal birth, the more likely it is that a physician is going to perform a C-section. To illustrate this incentivized perspective, a simplified physician decision process is plotted in the game tree shown above. Note that the illustration takes an extreme position by ignoring the costs and benefits to the patient.

This is why Jane's and Ashley's physicians made completely different decisions when facing the same abnormality. Jane's physician could easily justify performing a more profitable C-section when there is any deviation from labor normality, whereas it takes more evidence to persuade Ashley's physician to shift away from natural labor, given the lack of additional financial benefits for either option.

The Jane and Ashley scenario is based on real data. About one in three babies are delivered by C-section today, significantly increasing from about one in five babies being delivered by C-section in the 1990s.[16] While a woman's having a C-section itself isn't a problem if the doctors make an objective and informed decision, many doctors' decisions are clouded by financial incentives and institutional pressure.

In addition to financial incentives, physicians' decisions are also affected by their patients' knowledge. Let's say that Jane, though educated, has little to no knowledge about labor treatments, whereas Ashley is a physician who has the necessary medical knowledge to make independent judgments. Would the physicians treat physician mothers differently than other mothers? This is exactly the comparison done by recent research, and the answer is yes: physician mothers are less likely to have an unnecessary C-section and are overall 7.5 percent less likely to receive a C-section than nonphysician mothers.[17]

Patients' knowledge has an interesting interaction with financial incentives. Normal (nonphysician) mothers like Jane have a higher C-section rate in hospitals with financially compensated C-sections, but what about physician mothers? While physicians can normally benefit financially by recommending C-sections, they could endure a loss of patients' satisfaction if they make unnecessary recommendations to a knowledgeable patient. In line with this reasoning, physician mothers like Ashley actually don't seem to have their delivery method affected by the physician's financial compensations. This indicates that while incentivized physicians are comfortable recommending intensive treatments to mothers who lack the relevant knowledge, they refrain from doing so with physician mothers, as patients' knowledge serves as an effective neutralizer.

This treatment difference based on patients' knowledge leads to other significant consequences as well. A physician mother like Ashley and her infant would have lower morbidity rates than a nonphysician mother like Jane and her infant, all while using less of the hospital's resources. Ashley also would have lower hospital charges, have a shorter recovery time, and be less likely to have a vacuum extraction. If all patients were treated as the most informed physicians, C-section rates would be reduced, and hospital charges would be cut by $2 billion. At the end of the day, however, most mothers aren't as knowledgeable as informed physicians and are still under the pressure of potential overtreatment.

Another important problem posed by the FFS is that health-care providers have no incentives to invest in the prevention of illness or injury. We know that investing in prevention has a much higher return-on-investment rate. As Ben Franklin once said, "An ounce of prevention is worth a pound of cure." More recently, Barack Obama has argued that "too little is spent on prevention and public health."[18] Preventable causes of death have been estimated to be responsible for nine hundred thousand deaths annually—nearly 40 percent of total yearly mortality in the United States.[19] But there's no money for the physician or the hospital in keeping us healthy; there is a lot of money in treating us when we're sick!

A recent book called *The Long Fix: Solving America's Health Care Crisis with Strategies That Work for Everyone*, by Vivian Lee, gives some great examples of this dynamic. The book was covered in an episode of Shankar Vedantam's *Hidden Brain* podcast.[20] The podcast emphasizes how the FFS is a major reason for medical mistakes that are consequences of actions such as overdiagnosis and overtreatment. It is a clear case in which the quality of the treatment suffers because of a focus on increasing quantity. Lee gives the example of a patient who has a headache. The physician believes with 99.9 percent confidence that the patient has a regular headache that will pass by itself. The chance of a brain tumor is very low, but it's there. In Europe, such a patient would probably be given some simple medication and kept under observation. But in the US, because the physician might be afraid of a lawsuit and the family might be anxious, the patient will be sent for a brain MRI. The hospital and the physician will earn a couple of thousand dollars, and everyone will be satisfied. But such tests come with a cost. For example, there might be an ambiguous finding that will send the patient to have an unnecessary procedure.

How can we reduce the conflict of interest and disproportionate financial compensations in the medical field overall? There are a few alternative payment models that carry different incentive schemes. For example, "capitation models" pay physicians on the basis of the total number of patients under their care. This system gives health-care providers incentives to keep these patients healthy.[21] Some insurance companies understood this. When I worked with Humana, one of the largest health insurance companies in the world, the company was paid a fixed fee per Medicare member. As long as the member was healthy, Humana earned money from insuring them. Hence, we worked on trying to create incentives for members to get preventive medical care, such as receiving an annual flu shot. Another preventive-care example applies to readmission to hospitals. A large fraction of patients who are released from hospitalization have to be readmitted within a month, at a very high cost. Our study showed that many of these rehospitalizations could be prevented by simple, cost-effective treatments, such as sending a nurse to the patient's home and making sure they are doing well and taking their medication as prescribed. However, while this payment model conserves resources, it creates a different trade-off between quality and quantity. For physicians to maximize their total number of patients, they are incentivized to see each patient as little as possible, instead of treating them to the best of their ability.

One alternative is to give physicians a monthly salary, without additional incentives. While this model mitigates physicians' biased preference for overtreatment or undertreatment, it lacks the financial motivation for physicians to work hard. This is similar to the cab drivers who work hourly wages: physicians under this scheme are simply working to fill time.

Another incentive model is the pay-for-performance (P4P), in which physicians' pay is based on metric-driven outcomes, best practices, and patients' satisfaction. While it is more complex than the other models, data show that P4P helps prevent the quantity-quality trade-off and improves overall patient satisfaction by incentivizing physicians' payment with important value-based criteria.[22] In the example of giving birth, physicians now have an incentive to tailor delivery methods to individual pregnant mothers to maximize metric-driven outcomes and patients' satisfaction, instead of choosing a delivery method that is the most convenient and profitable.

The US medical-care industry is currently undergoing a gradual shift to value-based medicine by nudging health-care providers to transition toward P4P programs. While most hospitals are still utilizing the FFS models, P4P programs are causing many hospitals to pay attention to a range of previously unincentivized factors.

The lesson is clear: incentives could affect life-and-death decisions. Always control for potential quality loss by adding another dimension to your incentive, like how rideshare apps added rating systems or how hospitals added outcome metrics. By doing so, you signal that while you care about quantity, quality is also important to you, thus fixing the inherent mixed signal problem.

An economics professor shared a story that sums it up nicely: he once used incentives to try to shape the behavior of his children. When his daughter was being potty-trained, he implemented the following incentive scheme: she would receive a jellybean every time she used the toilet. A few years later, when her younger brother needed to be potty-trained, the professor built on his incentive scheme: his daughter would receive a treat every time she helped her brother use the toilet. His toddler gamed the system. How? In her words, "I realized that the more that goes in, the more that comes out, so I was just feeding my brother buckets and buckets of water."[23]

TAKEAWAY: If you incentivize quantity, make sure that quality is not compromised.

Encouraging Innovation but Punishing Failure

A person who never made a mistake never tried anything new.

—*Albert Einstein*

Thomas Edison's search for a filament for the lightbulb is quite inspiring. After trying two thousand different materials, his assistant complained, "All our work is in vain. We have learned nothing. Not sure if we can use an electricity properly."[1] Edison's reply suggests that their failures had not gone to waste: "Oh, we have come a long way and we have learned a lot. We know that there are two thousand elements which we cannot use to make a good light bulb." We know the ending of this story. According to Edison's account, "Before I got through I tested no fewer than 6,000 vegetable growths, and ransacked the world for the most suitable filament material. . . . The electric light has caused me the greatest amount of study and has required the most elaborate experiments. I was never myself discouraged, or inclined to be hopeless of success. I cannot say the same for all my associates."[2]

For many companies, success depends on innovation, and innovation requires a degree of risk-taking that comes with inevitable failures. Companies that succeed do so by introducing a new product or service that's well received by the marketplace. They take risks that end up being worth it. The success of just one attempt can more than compensate for the failure of others. What separates successful companies from unsuccessful ones is often how they deal with failures and how they manage when promising ideas fall flat.

When a company encourages its employees to innovate but then punishes them when their new approach fails (e.g., through delaying promotions), it sends a mixed signal. Punishing failure deters people from taking risks and trying new ideas. Even worse, it can reduce the ability to learn from failures, as people would try to hide them. A culture that accepts mistakes and encourages discussing and learning from them results in more risk-taking and more failures but ultimately more successes. Cultivate a culture that allows for exploration and encourages even the wildest of ideas, and it just might pay off.

Admittedly, it's easier said than done. It can be challenging to create an environment in which high-performing, achievement-driven, competitive individuals can thrive but also feel comfortable sharing and publicly analyzing their mistakes. But remember, a culture in which everyone feels like they can readily admit failures naturally extends to a reduced fear of making them in the first place. In such an environment, daring innovation would flourish. At worst, people would admit their ideas did not work, and someone else could suggest an alternative new approach, potentially turning past failures into the cornerstones of future breakthroughs.

The Israeli Air Force (IAF) is an example of an organization that has successfully created this unique type of culture through practice and effort. It encourages innovation and does not punish failures, ensuring that it is not sending a mixed signal. IAF pilots are taught from an early stage that learning from mistakes is crucial to preventing similar ones in the future. Consider the case of a "near accident"—a case in which an accident almost happens, such as when two fighter jets pass within a short distance of each other during flight. The IAF treats such a case as it would treat an actual accident. That way, pilots learn that the difference between an accident and a "near accident" is often simply luck. By treating mistakes seriously and openly, IAF pilots improve and learn how to avoid such incidents in the future. To make learning efficient, the pilots need to be open and share their mistakes, even ones that could've passed unnoticed by their commanders.

To be more specific, let's take a high-stakes example from the IAF during the Yom Kippur War in 1973. Two formations of F-4 fighters set out to strike the Syrian headquarters in Damascus, a mission that was critical in stopping the Syrian army. Each jet quartet was led by a veteran qualified pilot. As fortune (or lack thereof) would have it, the weather that day was terrible for airstrikes. A layer of clouds covered the whole area of operation, such that planes could only fly below or above it. If they flew below, they would be able to see the target, but everyone on the ground would easily see them, making them easy targets. If they flew above, they would be safer but unable to see where the target was. One leader saw the weather, realized that both options were bad, turned around, and aborted the mission. The other decided to fly above and by sheer chance discovered a hole in the clouds just above the target. His formation was able to attack and destroy the target. During the debrief, the commander commended *both* leaders, asserting that both decisions were sound. His message was clear: every leader was free to make decisions without being afraid of punishment for failure.

Of course, not all failures or mistakes are encouraged, nor should they be—mistakes that result from bad intentions, inattention, or lack of experience or ability are not constructive for any organization. The risks that are encouraged are the ones that test new ideas and directions. Even if the new direction seems wrong to some, exploring it might prove profitable in the end.

A high failure rate is associated with innovation, and aiming to reduce failure rates is not always a useful strategy. In the book *Origins of Genius*, Dean Keith Simonton claims that the most creative people have the greatest number of failures because they try the most ideas.[3] Creative geniuses don't have a higher success rate than their more ordinary counterparts do; they just try more. This led the organizational psychologist Bob Sutton to suggest that companies should not punish failure but rather inaction.

The most creative people—and companies—don't have lower failure rates; they fail faster and cheaper, and perhaps learn more from their setbacks, than their competitors. One of the biggest impediments to faster and cheaper failures is that once people have made a public commitment to some course of action and have devoted a lot of time and energy to it, they become convinced that what they are doing is valuable independently of the facts. . . . One antidote to such misguided commitment is to provide people with incentives for pulling the plug as early as possible on failing projects.[4]

Peter Kim took this idea to heart when he was appointed the head of research and development (R&D) at Merck, where he introduced a "kill fee" to the pharmaceuticals company.[5] He noticed upon arrival that many scientists at the company kept chasing dead ends in order to avoid admitting to failure and suffering potential consequences. To reduce this costly behavior, Kim introduced a bonus to scientists who pulled the plug on failed projects early and moved on to new creative ideas. Kim turned the incentive on its head to fix the mixed signal problem: he rewarded failure instead of punishing it. Menlo Innovations had the same reasoning in mind when it made the slogan "make mistakes faster" part of its culture. The company understood that mistakes are a part of innovation and encouraged its employees to experiment with new ideas by rewarding them for failing quickly.

In a TED Talk, Astro Teller, director of Alphabet's R&D "X" division, discussed many of the failed ideas that his team came up with. He's proud of the bad ideas that his team worked on and that they killed the ideas when they failed:

You cannot yell at people and force them to fail fast. People resist—they worry, "What will happen to me if I fail? Will people laugh at me? Will I be fired?" . . . The only way to get people to work on big risky things [is to] make that the path of least resistance for them. [Here at X], we work hard . . . to make it safe to fail. Teams kill their ideas as soon as the evidence is on the table because they're rewarded for it. They get applause from their peers, hugs and high-fives from their managers, too, and me in particular. They get promoted for killing fast. We have bonused every single person on teams that ended their projects, from teams as small as two to teams as big as thirty.[6]

Most of the projects his team worked on had failed, true, but this culture of rewarding fast failures led to wild successes, such as an early start on self-driving cars. Other companies have learned from this example and followed suit. For example, the huge Indian company Tata Group looks for innovations, knowing that they help expand the business. Before retiring, chairman Ratan Tata started a prize, called the "Dare to Try" award, for the best failed innovation, proclaiming, "Failure is a gold mine!" Just like that, he sent the signal that both failures and successes should be rewarded in the pursuit of innovation.[7]

The Cost of Not Innovating

There are examples of giants tumbling down from the top due to being overly conservative in their thinking. Blockbuster's fall from industry domination to bankruptcy is a great such example of how avoiding change and fearing failure can lead to stagnation and eventually elimination. Blockbuster, founded by David Cook in 1985, quickly became America's number-one video chain and dominated the video-rental market.[8] By the late '90s, the company had a market value of $3 billion and owned over nine thousand rental stores in the US. Apart from rental fees, the DVD giant's main revenue model relied on penalizing its customers by collecting late fees. At its prime, Blockbuster was collecting $800 million in late fees annually from its massive sixty-five million registered customers.[9] Inevitably, there were many frustrated customers who despised the punishment, which at times was significant. Reed Hastings, the founder of Netflix, was one of these frustrated customers.

After being charged a $40 late fee from Blockbuster, an annoyed Hastings decided to start his own movie-rental company in 1997. Netflix quickly grew with its new digital platform and the subscription-based business model: for $20 a month, the subscribers could rent as many movies as they wanted with no return deadline or late fees; whenever the subscribers sent back the DVDs they watched, the new ones were sent to them. In 2000, with leverage obtained from the initial success of Netflix's online platform, Hastings flew to Dallas to negotiate a partnership with Blockbuster. He proposed that Netflix run Blockbuster's online sector, and in exchange, Blockbuster would promote Netflix services in its stores. John Antioco, the Blockbuster CEO at the time, laughed at the idea and rejected Hastings. As you know, he didn't have the last laugh.[10]

The rest was known history. With millions of subscribers and massive savings accumulated from not needing to establish retail locations, Netflix was able to innovate its online platform to incorporate revolutionary streaming services in 2007 and eventually expanded its massive success across the globe in the early 2010s.[11] Netflix was earning $116 million in 2009, while Blockbuster was losing $516 million. Slowly and painfully, Blockbuster closed all but one of its retail stores.

Why did Blockbuster fail to transition? Sometimes the biggest enemy can be one's current success. While Netflix was shifting away from DVD rental and developing its innovative domain, Blockbuster was stuck to its profitable yet slowly dying status quo. Blockbuster attempted various strategies to rescue the failing business, but most of them were tangential and risk averse. Blockbuster had a chance to transition and streamline itself, but the company's board was too scared of failure. The signal board members received was that they should find a way to keep the traditional model; they were not incentivized to look for a change. CEO Antioco, a few years after rejecting the Netflix acquisition offer, realized that Netflix posed an immense threat. He attempted to convince his board to discontinue the late-fee business model and heavily invest in an online platform to answer the newer generation's need of digital service. However, the company's board was blinded by the still significant profits at the time, thus shying away from the costly transition process.

Jim Keyes, a chairman at Blockbuster and the major voice of transition opposition, highlighted that the transition plan would cost the company $200 million and that discontinuing the late-fee model would cut revenue by an additional $200 million. Convinced by Keyes's scary estimation, the board rejected Antioco's advancing vision and eventually fired him in 2005. To a great extent, Antioco was fired because he offered a creative change that would deviate significantly from the way Blockbuster operated. Keyes took over as the new CEO and reversed Antioco's last-ditch effort to save the company, in order to increase short-term profit. Stagnating with the safety plan, Blockbuster went bankrupt a few years later.

Don't Look Back

While some companies are terrified of potential failure, some exhibit extraordinary entrepreneurial spirit and flexibility. Sir Richard Branson, an English business magnate, founded the Virgin brand in the '70s and has since then launched more than four hundred companies under the Virgin Group. The Virgin brand quickly grew in the '80s, and Branson never stopped venturing. He dipped his toes into all kinds of water: from Virgin Media to Virgin Mobile, Virgin Cosmetics to Virgin Clothing, Virgin Airlines to Virgin Cars.[12]

Some failed. For example, in 1994, a soda producer approached Branson with his own homemade soda. Amazed by the taste, Branson administered a blind test between the original soda, Coke, and Pepsi at his child's school. After seeing the overwhelmingly positive result of the homemade soda, Branson decided to invade the soda industry by launching Virgin Cola. As a David taking on the Goliaths—Coca-Cola and Pepsi—Virgin Cola was surprisingly popular in the UK right away. Riding high on the momentum, Branson launched Virgin Cola in the US in the same year, attracting much media attention with the stunt of Branson riding a tank in Times Square crushing a wall of Coca-Cola cans. The momentum didn't last long, however, as the industry titans started their counterattack. Virgin Cola started to disappear from retailer store shelves around the world. It turns out that Coca-Cola gave retailers "offers they couldn't refuse" to cut off Virgin Cola's rollout. With such a "systematic kneecapping job," Branson soon declared the end of Virgin Cola. While he lost a lot of money in the process, and we as consumers may have lost a great soda, Branson wasn't upset at Coke's sabotage and Virgin Cola's failure and optimistically derived a valuable lesson from the venture. He said that the experience taught him to "only go into businesses where [they] were palpably better than all the competition." He claimed to be someone who will "fight tooth and nail to make something succeed," but the moment he realizes that "it's not going to succeed, the next day [he] would have forgotten about it" and moved on to the next venture.[13]

Branson never stopped innovating, and failures only pushed him forward with new opportunities. When asked about his everlasting entrepreneurship, Branson credited his mother for ingraining the idea of not spending too much time regretting the past. He stated that he and his team are never let down by mistakes and failures. "Instead, even when a venture has failed, [they] try to look for opportunities, to see whether [they] can capitalize on another gap in the market."[14] This risk-seeking spirit has seeped top-down into the layers of his companies and the hearts of his employees, thus establishing a healthy and innovative company culture.

If you want to encourage innovation, you need to motivate your team to take risks. This means that your team might fail, and fail again, but that's okay. Don't tell your team to take risks and then punish them for failure—

it'll lead to less innovation and more wasted resources, as people will try to make their ideas work even when evidence is stacked against them. The message is loud and clear: encourage risk-taking and reward failures.

TAKEAWAY: If you want innovation and risk-taking, don't send a mixed signal by punishing failures—reward them!

6

Encouraging Long-Term Goals but
Rewarding Short-Term Results

Eliminating your competition and increasing prices is an Econ 101 tactic. As consumers, we don't appreciate such behavior, and it may also be illegal, as is the case in the following example. In June 2012, Bazaarvoice bought PowerReviews. As a result of this acquisition, Bazaarvoice stock price soared above $20, and its executives realized $90 million of stock.[1] Why did Bazaarvoice purchase PowerReviews? To kill the competition. "Bazaarvoice is the dominant commercial supplier of product ratings and reviews platforms in the United States, and PowerReviews was its closest rival. Before the transaction, PowerReviews was an aggressive price competitor, and Bazaarvoice routinely responded to competitive pressure from PowerReviews. As a result of the competition between Bazaarvoice and PowerReviews, many retailers and manufacturers received substantial price discounts. . . . Bazaarvoice sought to stem competition through the acquisition of PowerReviews." Bazaarvoice's glory days didn't last long. In January 2013, the US Department of Justice launched an antitrust complaint that forced Bazaarvoice to divest PowerReviews and caused its stock price to drop below $7, which was a large loss to shareholders.[2]

Were Bazaarvoice executives so badly misinformed that the complaint came as a surprise? Apparently not. They expected it and chose to take the risk. The complaint quotes internal company documents in which senior

70

Bazaarvoice executives describe PowerReviews' role in the market, clearly showing that they knew the risk.

If it wasn't ignorance, then why did Bazaarvoice executives make the move? The executives saw dollar signs, $90 million to be exact, and took the short-term gain despite knowing the possible long-term consequences for the company.

Imagine that shareholders are hiring a new CEO for their firm. When hiring her, they communicate their goals to her, emphasizing the importance of the company's long-term success. While confident in the new CEO's ability, shareholders also want to incentivize her to perform well. To that end, they make a large part of her compensation based on equity in the company, overlooking the fact that equity may be based on short-term performance.

Given the new CEO's incentives, you shouldn't be surprised that she will concentrate on delivering short-term results, a behavior termed "short-termism." She might divert resources away from anything that doesn't pay in the short term. For example, imagine that the company outsources the delivery of its products. It might be profitable for the company to invest in its own fleet of trucks to streamline operations, but such an investment would cause short-run losses and only yield profit in the long run. Why would the CEO risk losing her job and bonus to invest in a new fleet? To inflate short-term profits, she would not invest in new technology that incurs costs now but improves performance in the long run. She would make decisions that aid her in meeting short-term profit targets at the expense of long-term success of the company.

Evidence supports short-termism: executives who receive this mixed signal say they would delay or sacrifice projects that create long-term value if they come at the expense of short-term gains.[3] As the Bazaarvoice example shows, short-termism could also affect the risks a company takes. A recent paper further illustrates the problem with using short-term incentives to motivate CEOs. In the paper, the CEOs are considered to have short-term incentives if their equity is scheduled to vest in an upcoming quarter (e.g., if they are set to fully own shares of the company in, say, the next year). The authors show that short-term incentives are significantly correlated with re-ductions in investment growth. Stock returns are more positive in the two quarters surrounding the equity vest but more negative in the following years. In other words, the CEOs act on the short-term incentives, making short-sighted decisions that sacrifice the company's lasting success.[4]

In some cases, a CEO is replaced after the company's stock underper-forms for just a few quarters. CEOs are incentivized to say that they'll invest for the future, as that's what shareholders want to hear, but instead fixate on the present, since they want to be employed for the long run. As an incen-tive designer, you must structure CEO incentives to highlight that while you want good short-term results, you also care about long-term success. One way to make a CEO care more about the long run is by escrowing the CEO's equity for a longer period.[5] Escrow is a process whereby an asset is held by a third party on behalf of two other parties until the fulfillment of predetermined obligations. In the case of company management, an escrow ensures that the executives who receive equity as a bonus to their compensa-tion would wait for the obligated period to pass before they could sell the stock.[6] The US Council of Institutional Investors (CII) recommends,

> Executive compensation should be designed to attract, retain, and incentivize executive talent for the purpose of building long-term shareholder value and promoting long-term strategic thinking. CII considers "the long-term" to be at least five years. Executive rewards should be generally commensurate with long-term return to the company's owners. Rewarding executives based on broad measures of performance may be appropriate in cases where doing so logically contributes to the company's long-term shareholder return.
>
> For some companies, emphasis on restricted stock with ex-tended, time-based vesting requirements—for example, those that might begin to vest after five years and fully vest over 10 (includ-

ing beyond employment termination)—may provide an appropriate balance of risk and reward, while providing particularly strong alignment between shareholders and executives.[7]

The goal of this suggestion is to reduce the weight that short-term outcomes receive relative to long-term ones. The restricted stock ensures that executives don't have tunnel vision on short-term results and that they evaluate positive and negative long-term performance, just as shareholders do.

Extending Tenure

Another way to align the goals of shareholders and a CEO is to extend the guaranteed tenure—this alleviates the CEO's concern of being replaced if the company underperforms in the short term. The problem with short-term tenure is well illustrated in politics. The length of tenure affects long-term considerations. Consider a governor who is deciding whether to invest in infrastructure, say, new bridges or trains. In the long run, it would prevent accidents and might even be very profitable, as a new train could bring tourists and their wallets to town. But the governor has short-term incentives: the governor wants to win the next election in a couple of years. The governor recognizes that losing a reelection will probably be the end of their political career, so they have strong incentives to gear actions toward reelection. Given this strong short-term incentive, why would a governor invest in a new train that would take at least a decade to see its benefits? To build such a train, the governor would have to divert resources from projects with a shorter timeline and possibly even increase taxes. These policies would not make them popular among the people and would hurt their reelection chances. To add insult to injury, the new train would probably only be ready after they've been booted from office, and the successor would be the one who reaps the fruits of the project.

How can we fix the mixed signals that we're giving to our politicians? The solution seems simple: get rid of the limits on the duration of tenure. Without having to worry about reelection every four years, the governor can focus on investing in the future, knowing that they will be there to enjoy the fruits. However, politics is an area in which extended tenure may not be such a great idea, as it may end up being costlier than the original problem. Even though a four-year tenure incentivizes short-term considerations, I personally prefer this system over the unconstrained alternative, for it means we live in a democracy in which the leader has to answer to voters.

Politics aside, incentivizing long-term success by extending tenure is typically not so costly. Consider how basketball coaches choose who'll play in certain games. Do they send out their MVPs or give some game time to promising but inexperienced younger players? Giving playing time to such players would probably reduce the immediate success of the team but would allow the players to gain necessary experience. If the coach is facing the risk of a midseason firing, conditional on the first few games of the season, they would probably choose to play it safe and rely on the experienced players. If the coach knows that their position is guaranteed for the first season, they will invest more in improving the entire team and would probably see the efforts pay off in the long run.

Teaching to the Test

Short-term incentives are prevalent beyond business and politics—they're affecting every classroom in our public-school system. Traditionally, public-school teachers are paid based on their experience, education level, and seniority. In recent years, however, there has been much discussion and implementation of an alternative incentive structure: performance pay, where teachers' salary and bonuses are tied to students' performance.[8]

At least twenty states in the past decade have implemented some form of pay for performance for teachers, and this number is growing, thanks to the Teacher Incentive Funds, a federal grant program that sponsors performance-based plans.[9] The program had a five-fold increase in funds in just one year, from $97 million in 2009 to $487 million in 2010.[10] In the following decade, the annual funding continued to stay in the hundreds of millions, with 2016 having $225 million.[11]

The pay for performance approach was further propelled by the No Child Left Behind Act. In 2002, the act introduced standards-based education reform and required states to develop and report student assessments, such as annual nationwide standardized tests, in order to receive federal education funding. If the schools don't live up to the required standard of improvements mandated by the federal government, they could face punishments like decreased funding and a pay cut for teachers.[12] This could disproportionally affect poor public schools, as they're already low on funding; thus, a funding reduction can snowball into worse performance and more funding cuts in subsequent years. With so much at stake, does the performance-pay incentive structure work? Intuitively, to encourage teachers to put more effort into their jobs and to filter those who don't fit the job, good teachers should be rewarded. This way, schools could attract more motivated teachers and obtain better student achievement in the long run.

The problem is in the details. In order to tie pay to students' performance, schools need an objective measure of performance. To that end, performance is measured using standardized testing, giving teachers the short-term goal of "teaching to the test." Do we really want teachers to put all their effort in teaching their students how to ace the standardized test? The heavy emphasis on testing has several negative consequences on long-term student learning. A curriculum that heavily focuses on preparing students to do well on mandated exams narrows the range of knowledge and skills, thus sacrificing a holistic understanding of the material, let alone teaching students to enjoy learning.

Rachel Tustin, a US public-school teacher, says she spends weeks of a school year on standardized testing, during which she must give up valuable days of learning for testing instructions, preparations, and reviews. As a teacher who doesn't teach the subjects of mathematics, reading, or writing, Tustin finds it "a bitter pill to swallow" that she must sacrifice her teaching to make time for these objectively quantifiable subjects.[13] Tustin isn't alone. According to a report from the Center on Education Policy in 2016, 81 percent of teachers think their students spend too much time on standardized testing. Many teachers have to "strip topics down to the bare bones just to get them covered in time," giving up the interactive activities that help students learn the material.[14] Due to the time crunch, teachers lose room for creativity and student engagement. The curriculum becomes streamlined, compressed, and dry, thus significantly diminishing students' interest in learning.

Contrast this cookie-cutter teaching style to Finland's liberal educational approach: Finnish teachers can customize their lesson plans and select their own textbooks. They have plenty of creative freedom because they aren't required to administer standardized tests. Without the enforcement of standardized tests and tying teachers' paychecks to students' performance, Finland consistently places at the top of the Programme for International Student Assessment (PISA), an international test administered to high school students in fifty-seven developed countries, while American students constantly struggle to achieve high placements on this assessment (we will discuss the problems with PISA in chapter 13). The success of the Finnish system suggests that the constant pressure and focus of mandated exams isn't helping American students' performance relative to other international students. In addition to Finland's exceptional test performance, it also has an impressively low high-school dropout rate (less than 1 percent, compared to around 25 percent in the US).[15]

The debate about using teacher and school incentives is going on along these two dimensions: the supporters say that it's important to motivate educators and that such incentives work; the opposition argues that this short-term incentive cost is detrimental to the long-term goals of education, as the pay for performance incentive sends mixed signals to teachers. It adds a dollar sign to students' learning process. Many teachers are heavily motivated by intrinsic values, such as the value of facilitating student growth, but this incentive structure signals a potentially damaging message: you should substitute this long-term goal with short-term success in tests.

This debate is a good example of a situation in which the decision is broader than simply examining the incentive effect. Different people may have different values. The goal of the economists here is to use economic reasoning and collect data regarding how well each system works. In the book *The Why Axis*, John List and I discussed some of these experiments that are designed to inform decision-makers.[16] In particular, experiments can determine what type of incentives and signals work in different communities, recognizing that one size doesn't fit all. Economists can explain the trade-offs between short- and long-term goals. Policy makers should then base their decisions on these trade-offs and experimental data, understanding the advantages and disadvantages of each system.

If you want to encourage long-term considerations, you need to make sure that your short-term incentives do not have too much weight. You will probably observe less success in the short run, but that's fine if it serves your long-run goals. Don't tell your team to work for the long run and then punish them when the short-run outcomes are not great. Make sure that the timeline of your incentives coincides with that of your ultimate goals.

TAKEAWAY: If you want to motivate long-term success, don't incentivize (only) short-term success.

7

Encouraging Teamwork but
Incentivizing Individual Success

A Star Is Born

In a 2010 interview, Facebook founder Mark Zuckerberg discussed paying $47 million to acquire FriendFeed, a company that used social networks as a tool for discovering information relevant to the users. Friend-Feed's product seemed secondary to the price; it was really the people at FriendFeed whom Zuckerberg was after. When asked why he paid so much, Zuckerberg said, "Someone who is exceptional in their role is not just a little better than someone who is pretty good. . . . They are 100 times better." Zuckerberg's point of view is echoed by Marc Andreessen, the cofounder of Netscape—among other companies—and a high-profile Silicon Valley venture capitalist: "The gap between what a highly productive person can do and what an average person can do is getting bigger and bigger. Five great programmers can completely outperform 1,000 mediocre programmers."[1]

An example of the importance of "exceptional" talent is the American football quarterback Tom Brady. Brady played for the New England Patriots for twenty seasons, contributing to his team winning, among many other achievements, six Super Bowl titles. It is no wonder he is widely regarded as the greatest player to ever play the sport.[2] When the 2019 season reached its end, Brady wanted to negotiate a longer-term contract with the Patriots, allowing him to retire with the New England team. Owner Robert Kraft and coach Bill Belichick were reluctant, however, both preferring to offer the aging player a short-term deal.[3] So, after twenty seasons, Brady left the most successful team in the world and moved to the Tampa Bay Buccaneers, who have never been considered a powerhouse NFL team. The team has won the Super Bowl only once, in 2002, long before Brady joined it. The rest is history: in Brady's first season with Tampa Bay, he led the team to win Super Bowl LV over the Kansas City Chiefs. If you're wondering, the New England Patriots didn't do well after Brady left.

But sometimes it's not enough to have the star. Take Lionel (Leo) Messi, one of the best soccer players in the history of the game, as an example. According to the official website of FC Barcelona, where he played at the time, "Leo Messi is the best player in the world. Technically perfect, he brings together unselfishness, pace, composure and goals to make him number one." Under his leadership in the sixteen seasons he played in the club, FC Barcelona won more than two dozen league titles and tournaments and became one of the best clubs in the world. Messi also has unprecedented individual achievements: he's won more awards than any other player in history.[4]

Like most great soccer players, Messi also plays with his national team (Argentina in his case) in international events such as the World Cup and Copa America. While doing so well with his club, Messi hasn't won a major tournament with his national team. Why? After all, he's *the* star player. A 2018 *Guardian* article, titled "Messi's in a Mess and Doesn't Seem to Fit into the Argentina Collective," reflects on this: "We know Messi is great, but we're confused and sad for him. He is such a pure Barcelona product, but with Argentina right now, Messi's in a mess. Something is missing—is it unity, faith? Messi doesn't seem to fit into the collective. They have so many talented strikers, so many skillful attacking players and yet they don't seem to know how to get the best out of them. They are really struggling. Is it the system? Is there a certain spirit missing?"[5]

As it turns out, sometimes even the biggest star can't win without his team. It could simply be a lack of chemistry between Messi and the Argentinian players. It could be that FC Barcelona was tailored to support his amazing talent and hence is a better fit for his style of play. It could also be that both teams are equally good and supportive but Messi himself doesn't play the same with his home-nation team. As Daniel Passarella, captain of the Argentina team that won the 1978 World Cup, said, "He's a great player who can give a lot to any team. But when he plays for Barcelona, he has a different attitude. He's better there. Sometimes these things happen. You play well for a team and they love you, but you don't feel at ease and something doesn't fit. I don't know what it is, but it should be something you feel inside."[6]

Team versus Individuals

Messi's example demonstrates that we shouldn't just care about the individual talent. What happens when organizations emphasize the importance of teamwork but use individual incentives? Individual incentives have many advantages: they motivate people to work harder because the payoff is directly associated with their own performance, and they attract better people to the job while maintaining the high-performing individuals. It is also often more straightforward to measure the performance of an individual than that of a group.

It's fine to set individual incentives if you want to increase individual effort. The mixed signal happens when you set individual incentives but emphasize the importance of team effort. Which would your employee take to heart: Do they follow the talking points or the money? They follow the money. When one should care about team effort and performance, the drawbacks of individual incentive schemes may be larger than the benefits we just considered. Individual incentives encourage people to focus on their own performance and not on that of the team. It can lead to competitiveness and even sabotage in order to boost relative performance, which is detrimental to collaboration.

When you want to encourage teamwork, you need to use team incentives—incentives that are offered to the entire team for meeting a goal. If they're designed with care, team incentives can encourage individuals to collaborate, communicate effectively with each other, and foster a stronger sense of community. Consider the practice of mentoring within companies. The success of new employees often depends on the quality of the mentoring they receive from more experienced colleagues. If the organization focuses on individual incentives, the experienced employees would be less enthusiastic to spend their valuable time showing new employees the ropes. Even if they liked mentoring and wanted to do it, the individual incentives would send the signal that the organization wanted them to focus only on their own performance. Moreover, the quality of mentoring might be affected, as the new employee they're training could be a future competitor. This mixed signal would be costly to the organization because the return on mentoring is often very high. If the organization instead incentivizes based on team performance, the experienced employees would be motivated to spend time helping new employees, with the understanding that it truly is what the organization wants.

Yet team incentives could backfire by encouraging "free riding." Some members of the team may reduce their effort with the expectation that someone else on the team will pick up the slack. If enough members of the team behave in this way, the overall performance of the team will suffer. Differential contribution to the goal could increase resentment and tension in a team, and if the team fails to reach the goal, the blame game starts.

The right balance between individual and team incentives depends on the situation. Consider an obstacle race between teams. The winning team is the one with the runner crossing the finish line first. Individual incentives make sense here: you want to be able to attract and keep the best talent, and you want to reward them. You also want the entire team to work together to support the fastest member; hence, you might want to add some team incentives—but they aren't the driving force.

Now, consider instead an obstacle race in which in order to win, the entire team must cross the line first. In this case, it all depends on the slowest person on the team. The whole team competes, but the team's success depends on whether its slowest runner finishes faster than the slowest runner on the other team. This kind of competition calls for very different incentives, ones that drive the entire team toward helping the slowest rather than the fastest member.

This example is commonly seen in research and development races. Some R&D situations require one brilliant person to come up with a brilliant idea that will win the competition. Other R&D situations require the team to work together to advance several dimensions of the research in order to win the distance race.

Want Drama?

When we think about price competition, we have in mind large companies cutting prices to win market share. The cola price war between Coke and Pepsi keeps the price of soft drinks down. Headlines such as "A War Is Breaking Out between McDonald's, Burger King, and Wendy's—and That's Great News for Consumers" always make us happy, as they should.[7]

When we think about such big companies, should we think about them as one "unitary player" or as a team? Sometimes the company itself is not one big happy family. There can be tension, competition, and conflict within a company regarding how to set prices. While often ignored, the internal organization of these companies and the possibility of conflicting interests within them are central to behavior. Gary Bornstein and I wanted to look deeper into this drama and see how the structure of an organization affects the way it competes with other companies and the resulting market prices.[8]

Consider, for example, an airline that is interested in buying new aircrafts for its fleet. The two main competitors in this market are the Boeing 737 and the Airbus A320. To simplify, assume that the airline's purchase decision is based solely on price. This market has two players competing by cutting each other's prices. The CEO of Boeing is trying to undercut the CEO of Airbus, and vice versa.

Alternatively, one can consider a market with more complex (and probably more realistic) organizations, each consisting of alliances of firms that are responsible for a different part of the airplane (engine, avionics, etc.). Each firm in the alliance sets its price independently, and the price of the airplane is the sum of the prices demanded by the individual firms. While all the members in the Boeing alliance have a common interest in setting a competitive price and winning the competition against Airbus, each individual member also has an interest in maximizing its own share in the group's profit. Say that Boeing is buying its engines from General Electric. Boeing can't just switch the engine on its 737—moving its business to another engine manufacturer would be costly and time-consuming. Hence, General Electric's goal is to charge as much as possible for the engine while keeping its price low enough for Boeing to win the contract.

Since we can't run experiments with Boeing and Airbus, Gary and I created a laboratory game to mimic such competition. We created a market with competition between two teams (think Boeing and Airbus) called Team A and Team B. Each team consisted of three players (think engine, avionics, and components and parts). These "players" were students taking part in our experiment and making money on the basis of their decisions.

We asked players to set a price between $2 and $25. The team's price was simply the total price of its three players. Say that in Team A, player 1 sets the price at $10, player 2 at $15 and player 3 at $5. In this case, Team A's price is $10 + $15 + $5 = $30. Then, Team A's price was submitted to the competition between the two teams. The team whose total price was lower won the competition and was paid its price (ties were split). In our example, if the total price of Team B was below $30, then it won; if it was above $30, then Team A won. In this simple game, each team wants to have the highest price possible to maximize payoffs, as long as it's lower than that of the competition.

An interesting comparison emerges from the two ways team profits were distributed among the three team members. In the team incentives case, profits for winning were divided equally among its members, each earning exactly one-third of the total profit. In the preceding example, if Team A won, every player would be paid $10.

In the individual incentives case, each individual player was paid the price they asked for if the team won. In the preceding example, player 1 would win $10; player 2, $15; and player 3, $5. As you can imagine, giving individual incentives to players changes the dynamic completely. Price competition is expected to drive prices down. However, in the case of individual incentives, each player has an opportunity, indeed a temptation, to free ride. If the other players on the team settle for a low price, each player can demand a higher price and still, possibly, win. In Team A's example, player 2 was able to pocket $15 because player 3 was "nice" and had only a modest demand. With team incentives, where profits are split equally, the opportunity of free riding is eliminated.

In our experiment, we let participants play this game one hundred times, each time with a different team, and observed the dynamic. Our prediction was that the drama in the individual incentive case would prevent prices from falling too sharply. Indeed, that's what we found. After one hundred rounds, the mean price in the team incentives case was under $12, while the mean price in the individual incentives case was two and a half times higher, at $30.

This experiment is a simple demonstration of how the choice of team versus individual incentive schemes within an organization changes the internal dynamic. Want drama? Give your people individual incentives and let them go after each other. Want a more peaceful and possibly less ambitious organization? Use team incentives. Whatever you do, make sure the incentive structure within the team serves your goal.

Case Study: Team versus Individual Incentives in Sport

Imagine that you are Alexis Sánchez, a professional soccer player and the forward of Manchester United in 2019. It's the third game of the season in the Premier League, the top-level competition of the English football league system. With the opposing team failing a coordinated attack, you get possession of the ball and run a swift counterattack. You quickly progress through the field toward the opposing goal. Right outside the penalty area, you are facing an important decision. You can maneuver your way around the remaining two defenders and try to score yourself—say that you'll have a 40 percent probability of success. Or you can pass the ball to your teammate Paul Pogba, who has an open position fifteen yards out—say that you believe he'll have a 60 percent probability of success.

What would you do? From the team's perspective, the latter option is clearly preferable, as it's more likely to score a goal. Why would Sánchez hesitate to pass the ball to Pogba, though? If all incentives were based on the team's success, it would be an easy choice. However, this is not the case. Sánchez, the highest earner at Manchester United at the time, had a bonus clause in his contract that would earn him an additional £75,000 for every goal and £20,000 for every assist.[9] This type of individual incentive creates a trade-off between a team's overall success and a player's own compensation. In the player's case, even though passing the ball is more beneficial for the team, a shooting attempt could be much more lucrative given the disparity between goal and assist bonuses. To illustrate Sánchez's perspective more clearly, his decision process is plotted in the game tree and shown in the illustration on the next page.

On top of conflicting motivations, this type of individual incentive could also cause division within a team. In October 2019, Sánchez and Pogba had a dispute on the field over who should take a penalty kick. Pogba, the other big scorer of the team, received £50,000 for every goal and £20,000 for every assist. Knowing their incentives, it is no surprise that they both wanted the scoring bonus.[10] The division also extends beyond individual disagreements. An English national newspaper reported that the disparity between Pogba's and Sánchez's bonuses and those of the rest of the squad at the club had caused anger and dissatisfaction among teammates.[11] The individual contract bonuses backfired, as the team's atmosphere suffered, leading to animosity among teammates.

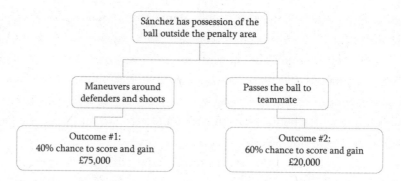

Sánchez's utility. *Outcome #1 has an expected value of £30,000 (£75,000*40%). Outcome #2 has an expected value of £12,000 (£20,000*60%). Expected value Outcome #1 > Outcome #2 → Sánchez chooses to shoot.*

TEAM VS. INDIVIDUAL INCENTIVES

Let's go for it!

Despite the potential downsides of big individual compensation, Manchester United has a track record of giving out astronomical goal bonuses. To give you some more figures, Romelu Lukaku was promised £10 million for scoring twenty-three goals per season during his first four years at the club.[12] And Zlatan Ibrahimović had earned over £3.69 million in goal bonuses in the 2017 season alone, with up to £184,900 per goal.[13] Manchester United is not alone in having individual compensation—they are very common in most big clubs.

For instance, in Liverpool forward Roberto Firmino's contract in 2016, his scoring bonuses incrementally increased as he scored more in the season, with up to £85,000 per goal after scoring sixteen goals.[14] While Firmino also made £31,000 for every assist he contributed, it was far less than the amount he earned for scoring once he had five goals under his belt in the season.[15]

In contrast, some teams emphasize winning over individual performance. For example, contracts from Major League Soccer (MLS) offer players the same amount of bonus compensation for a goal or an assist, thus minimizing the conflict between individual gain and the team's success. Such contracts align the signals: the real goal of the team and that of the players are now the same. A downside is that stars who score many goals may prefer to choose a team that disproportionally compensates individual success.

This incentive problem in sports isn't unique to soccer. NFL players also get a combination of individual and team incentives. Just like soccer, the teams' goal is clear: to win, make the playoffs, and place as high as possible in the league. But management often believes that simply giving team incentives is not enough to motivate individual players, so many players also have contract-based individual performance incentives that are dependent on their game statistics, such as yardage, yards per attempt, and touchdowns.[17] In 2007, Baltimore Ravens defensive end Terrell Suggs had a contract clause incentivizing him with a whopping $5.5 million bonus for reaching a target number of sacks.[18] For those who are unfamiliar, a sack happens when a quarterback is tackled behind the line of scrimmage before he can throw a forward pass. How could this incentive change the way Suggs approaches the game? He would probably be more risk-seeking and take more chances when attempting to sack the opposing quarterback. While it can be rewarding to be aggressive on the field, it's not always optimal for the team to look for sacks and risk giving up crucial running plays. Suggs did end up successfully reaching the required number of sacks and earning the multimillion-dollar bonus, but the Ravens finished the season with a poor record.[19]

In addition to the contract-based bonuses, NFL players are also eligible to receive another form of individual incentive: a performance-based fund from the league. In the 2019 season, NFL players received a substantial total of $147.95 million performance-based pay. The fund compensates players on the basis of a player index, calculated by computing the ratio of a player's playing time to salary. In other words, the pay increases as the player's playing time increases and salary decreases.[20] Under this performance pay structure, players are incentivized often to choose field time over their health. As playing time is equivalent to money for many players, they choose to play with injuries or pain, since spending time recovering could mean losing some of the performance pay. This individual incentive could end up causing more harm than good for a team's long-term success if its key players continuously sacrifice their health and recovery for bonus pay.

In this chapter, we have discussed some aspects of individual incentives in teams. The individual incentives of team members are introduced to motivate players. Are these incentives really needed? In the long run, players are compensated for their success, both intrinsically with regard to their pride as players and in future contracts that include team-based incentives. Isn't that enough? The cost of individual incentives in this case is not trivial. Management sends players a strong signal: you should do your best for the team to win. It's all about teamwork, team success, and so on. However, the individual incentives send a very different signal: we expect *you* to score the goal. This mixed signal could be costly.

The examples we've discussed show that the choice between individual and team incentives depends on the nature of the work and the desired outcome. In some cases, when you care about the single "best" athlete, go ahead and use individual incentives. But if you decide to do so, don't send mixed signals by also promoting team collaboration while incentivizing individual contributions. In the case where you care about team effort, align your incentives with this goal.

Of course, there are also creative ways to combine the two incentives. For example, in chapter 12, on awards, we'll talk about offering special awards that will encourage team investment without overshadowing individual effort (e.g., the "best mentor award"). Alternatively, consider using both individual and team incentives—pay a bonus to the entire team for winning a game and a bonus to everyone who scores a goal.

TAKEAWAY: Make sure the balance between team and individual incentives is in line with your goals.

PART THREE
How Incentives Shape the Story

•   •   •

I hope that by now you're convinced that incentives send signals that shape the story. Behavioral economists and psychologists have found systematic ways in which different framings of incentives affect the meaning we assign to the story and behavior. In this part, we'll discuss some of these psychological regularities and how they can be used to achieve our goals.

8

Stakes and Mistakes

I have a strange hobby: collecting stories on incentives gone wrong. These funny anecdotes show that people are much more creative than we usually give them credit for. In this chapter, I'll share some of these stories with you. You'll discover, as I did, that quite unfortunately, those who design incentives repeat the same mistakes time and time again—a pity, given the powerful potential that smart incentives hold.

Why Does Wells Fargo Need to Reestablish Itself?

Recently, Wells Fargo introduced a curious twist to its brand marketing, dubbed the "Reestablished" campaign. The reason the bank felt the need to reestablish itself is rather prosaic. In September 2016, the bank's reputation went up in flames because of a scandal involving widespread fraud—the result of bad incentives aimed at generating higher sales.

In 1997, then-CEO Richard Kovacevich launched an initiative with the goal of having an average of eight banking products per customer. Employees who were in charge of selling these products and surpassed that quota would be rewarded with raises or promotions.[1] It seems like a straightforward and effective incentive, right? Wrong.

The sales quotas were often virtually unattainable, leading employees to cheat in order to keep their jobs. From 2009 to 2016, thousands of bank employees nationwide ordered fake credit cards, opened unauthorized accounts, and issued unwanted insurance products for existing clients without their knowledge. By the time the scheme was exposed, the number of fake accounts totaled three and a half million. When the fraud was discovered, fifty-three hundred employees were fired.[2]

Can you imagine the daily routine of these employees over that seven-year period? They would arrive at the office in the morning, drink some coffee, turn on the computer, and . . . create and manage one fake account after another! In such an environment, it would be incredibly difficult for the average employee to remain honest.

Why did the employees spend their time cheating? Because that was the signal their bosses sent them. Management encouraged and even protected the fraud: employees who informed Wells Fargo's ethics department about the fraudulent behavior later reported being retaliated against.[3] While the official mission statement of the bank stated that ethics is important, the incentives and the backlash to reports of fraud sent a very different message.

The total cost to the bank was, and still is, substantial. The biggest damage was to its reputation—a blow from which Wells Fargo is still recovering. And to think, all this could have been avoided had management thought more carefully about the potential adverse effects of its incentive's initiative.

Where did the bank go wrong? As we discussed in chapter 5, if you design incentives for quantity, you must build in a mechanism that will check for quality. This system achieves two goals: making it costly for the workers to produce low-quality products because of punishment and consequently sending a signal that management cares about quality. In the Wells Fargo case, this could have been accomplished with a good audit system that could catch employees who make up accounts and punish them. Audit and punishment for cheating would reduce the incentives to cheat. This direct effect is called "deterrence." Importantly, such an audit system would also send a signal to the employees that management cares about honesty, not just having a perfunctory mission statement about the importance of ethics. Investing resources in protecting the interest of clients sends a strong message: we care about our clients and are willing to spend money to protect them. This signal would have been in line with the official message the bank was sending and would have changed the workplace culture. The quantity of products and services would have been lower, but in turn, the quality would've been higher. That is, employees would have opened fewer accounts, but those accounts would have been real and profitable.

Wells Fargo reacted to the scandal by profusely apologizing in public and eliminating all internal incentive schemes. I've since learned through occasional consulting that incentive schemes are now a no-go in the entire banking industry. But removing incentive schemes from a company's arsenal altogether is a costly overreaction. Introducing the right audit mechanisms in the first place to counterbalance incentives that reward quantity would have sent the right signal and prevented the failure.

A Fine Is a Price

Picking up your kids from day care on time is important. Back when my daughters were toddlers, I remember getting stuck in traffic one day and driving like crazy to get to their day care on time. The day care closed at 4:00 p.m. I pulled up at 4:02 p.m. I raced in, mentally rehearsing the profuse apology that I had scripted during my drive. I was met with the teacher's disapproving stare, and the words immediately got stuck in my throat. It wasn't a great experience.

A couple of weeks after this incident, the day care's owner introduced a fine of ten New Israeli shekels (this took place in Israel; the value of ten shekels was about US$3 at the time) for parents who arrived after 4:10 p.m. "Oh," I thought to myself, "only $3? All right." The next time I was running late, I didn't drive like crazy. It wasn't worth risking my life for $3.

Inspired by this experience, Aldo Rustichini and I designed a field experiment to test the effect of fines in day cares on late parent pickups.[4] We started with ten fine-free day cares. For the first four weeks, we simply recorded the number of late pickups in each. Then, in six of the day cares, we introduced a $3 fine for late-coming parents. It turns out that I wasn't the only one who changed their behavior in reaction to the fine—the average number of parents who were late doubled! The fine, originally introduced to discourage parents from being late, actually promoted late pickups. Why?

Before the policy, parents felt bad when they arrived late. This could send a bad signal to the self, as well as a bad social signal. By introducing a small fine for being late, the owner of the day care signaled that it is not that bad to be late. Parents learned that lateness wasn't as frowned upon as they had originally thought—after all, they were only getting fined a mere $3. The fine allowed them to arrive late while avoiding the feeling of guilt. In this way, it served as a price: it allowed parents to decide whether the price was low enough for a "late pass." A support for the claim that the small fine signals that being late is not that bad comes from the last part of our study, in which we removed the fine and observed what happened. Well— behavior stayed the same as when the fine was in place. The parents learned from the fine's price tag that it's not that bad to be late.

It's not just small day cares with their $3 fines that send such signals. Large organizations can make similar policy mistakes. The Welsh government learned this lesson when it issued a policy that fined parents £60 for taking children out of school during the school term.[5] Parents often did this in order to take family vacations when travel prices were lower and destinations were less crowded. Like the $3 late fine at the day cares, the £60 acted as a price: it allowed parents to decide if the price was worth pulling their children out of school for a couple of days. A report found that the number of unauthorized family holidays increased after the introduction of such fines. Some parents explicitly said that they found it more financially desirable to pay the £60 fine than to travel during the more expensive holiday season. Savvy travel agents even started offering to pay the fine as part of a package deal!

In addition to illustrating how a fine can act as a price, these two examples also tell us that the size of the fine serves as a strong signal. Some day cares in the US impose a $5 fine for every minute the parent is delayed. Some fines are even steeper. A mother from New Zealand posted on Facebook that she was fined $55 for being one minute late. Her kid's day care has a flat fine of $20 for being late to pick up the child, plus $35 for being one to thirty minutes late and then $85 for being thirty-one minutes to one hour late. How effective is this large fine? According to the day care, only two parents were charged under this policy in one year. Most day cares I know of can only dream on such statistics.[6] Han van Dissel, the dean of the Faculty of Economics and Business at the University of Amsterdam, told me what might be the best example of a steep penalty: in some day cares in Paris, if the parents are late to pick up their kid, the manager takes the kid to the local police station, and the parents need to pick them up from there. This severe punishment makes it extremely costly to be late and signals that lateness is heavily frowned upon. Similarly, if the Welsh government had made the fine for taking kids on vacation during the school term large enough, it would have been effective. Remember that incentive size serves as a signal.

A Nail to the Chest

The image on the next page represents a fundamentally bad incentive.

As a passenger on a motorcycle or moped, the last thing you'd want is for your driver to have a helmet while you don't. It's dumb to ride without wearing a helmet in the first place, but it's not just that: think about the risks you take while driving—maybe you speed a little on the highway or sip a Frappuccino while in traffic. We often take more risks than necessary, and the safer we feel, the more risks we are willing to take.

The driver in the picture is wearing a helmet, making her feel relatively safe. That probably causes her to take more risks. If you are the helmetless passenger riding with her, you're in a bad spot. As Sam Peltzman argued in 1975, once seat belts and other safety regulations became mandatory in the US around the late 1960s, the number of car accidents may actually

NAIL TO THE CHEST

Do you want your driver to feel safe?

increase.[7] Drivers might have taken more risks because seat belts reduced the likelihood of severe or fatal injuries in the case of a crash. The new regulations weakened the incentive to drive safely by signaling to people that even if they were involved in an accident, they would be fine.

The rising number of AIDS cases further illustrates this point. Before treatments were developed, contracting AIDS was a death sentence, and people were extremely careful about its spread. Now that AIDS has a treatment and is viewed as a chronic disease rather than a death sentence, people find it less threatening and take more risks, such as having unprotected sex, thereby increasing the number of infected people. The availability of the new treatments reduced the incentive to be careful.

To be clear, I am not saying that having safety measures in cars (or developing lifesaving new treatments) is a bad idea. Giving a driver a sense of safety *while allowing the passenger to go helmet-free*, on the other hand—that's a bad incentive.

Steven Landsburg, author of *The Armchair Economist*, took this signaling approach a step further and offered the following brilliant insight: you, as a passenger, shouldn't want a seat belt for your driver. Rather, you might consider installing a long, sharp nail to the steering wheel of the car, such that your driver will be abundantly clear on the consequences of an accident.[8] You can tell the driver that you don't want them to drive too fast and that safety is your number-one consideration; but build this nail into the car, and you can rest assured that your driver will understand the signal: you want them to drive as safely as possible!

The Hanoi Rat Massacre

Back in 1897, Paul Doumer was appointed as the governor of French Indochina, an area based in what is now known as Hanoi, Vietnam. In a truly French fashion, he immediately set out to modernize the city, with the crowning achievement being the introduction of toilets.

Unfortunately, the delicate French colonists weren't the only ones who liked this addition to the city's infrastructure—the rats of Hanoi did too. The sewer system that ran under the town was quickly overtaken. Resilient and innumerable, even professional rat hunters failed to stop their proliferation. Something more drastic had to be done, effectively and quickly.[9]

Doumer and his team got together and came up with an innovative solution: deputize the citizens of Hanoi by offering one cent per rat as a reward. The citizens were required to submit the rats' tails to the government offices as proof; there, a poor fellow was tasked with counting them and paying out the rewards. Tails started to pour in.

Just as Doumer and his team were ready to call it a success, intriguing reports started coming in: tailless rats running amok in the city. As it turned out, enterprising citizens had realized that cutting off a rat's tail and letting it live and breed made more financial sense than killing it. A rat without a tail could have rat babies with tails that could then be cut off and submitted for a reward. The citizens' creativity didn't stop there. A new, profitable profession came into existence: farms dedicated to the breeding of rats. Some especially innovative citizens began importing rat tails from faraway places![10]

The incentive failed because it solely targeted quantity and ignored quality. The governor wanted people to kill the local rats to stop their proliferation, but that wasn't what the incentives actually rewarded. As is the case in the Wells Fargo example, the mistake was targeting quantity instead of quality. A simple fix could have been to pay for rats, not just their tails.

Funny Houses

On a much lighter note, incentives can create odd sights when extended into architecture. I love visiting the charming land of Puglia, located at the base of Italy's boot and known for its olive trees, spectacular beaches, and amazing food. In the breathtaking Valle d'Itria lies one of Puglia's particular draws—at least for the economist in me: trulli. "Trulli" is the name of the structures that were commonly inhabited by peasants, who were incentivized to build them in a unique style.[11] Look at the roofs in the figure below—you won't see them anywhere else in the world.

How incentives shape roofs

How incentives shape windows

A typical trullo (the singular of "trulli") was built to be conical, with a cylindrical base made of dry stone and a limestone-tiled roof. Constructed without mortar or cement, the trulli could be dismantled quickly.[12] In fact, these houses were built with that very intention in mind: remove the top-most stone of the roof, and the entire roof would cave in.[13]

Why would anyone want to live in such a precarious structure? At the time, King Robert of Naples (1309–1343) collected taxes based on the usage of a structure. If it had a roof, it was considered a home and was thereby subject to heavy taxes.[14] The peasants of Puglia thus had to innovate: whenever they spotted a tax collector approaching their town, they quickly dismantled their roofs, so that their homes would not be subject to the tax. Once the tax collector moved on to the next town, they rebuilt their roofs and carried on.

Similar architecture-shaping taxes incentivized unforeseen building behavior in other places as well. For example, can you guess why some of the windows in the building shown in the figure above are blocked with bricks?

The now notorious Window Tax was created in England in 1696 and was used in the eighteenth and nineteenth centuries by governments in France, Ireland, and Scotland.[15] At the time of the tax's introduction, windows were considered reflective of the owner's prosperity: wealthier individuals had larger homes and thus more windows, as the logic went. The authorities wanted to create a progressive property tax, such that wealthier people would pay higher taxes.

At some point, officials noticed a decline in the revenue raised by the Window Tax. It turned out that property owners were blocking windows with bricks, and new houses were being built with fewer windows.[16] To fully grasp the cleverness of this workaround, it is important to first understand the makeup of the tax: six pence per window in a house with ten to fourteen windows, nine pence per window in houses with fifteen to nineteen windows, and one shilling per window in houses with more than twenty windows. Close examination of tax records from that period shows that nearly half of the houses magically just happened to have the tax-efficient number of windows: nine, fourteen, or nineteen.[17] This design again reflects the creativity of citizens when it comes to finding loopholes around bad tax incentives.

Interestingly, the very wealthy did the opposite: the tax made it possible for them to show off by installing more windows than they needed! This represents an example of how incentives can make it easier to send signals to others; in this case, they helped to signal the wealth of the homeowner.

The Window Tax was eventually abolished in 1851, after years of complaints that lack of windows created environments in which disease and health issues could run rampant. The boarded-up windows that are still seen around parts of Europe today serve as a reminder of how bad incentives in the form of taxes can be, going so far as shaping how the world looks.

The houses along Amsterdam's canals are yet another example of this dynamic. It's obvious what the bad tax incentives inadvertently encouraged: narrow houses.[18] Built on naturally soft soil, the foundation of houses in the

Netherlands needed the help of large, load-bearing stakes that were pushed deep into the ground. The citizens of Amsterdam would often cut costs by reducing the length of the stakes, resulting in leaning houses. In an attempt to fix the problem, the government mandated that only sanctioned officials could install the stakes. To cover the cost of this new labor, the government introduced a tax based on the width of the house that was built (wider houses required more stakes).[19]

The result stands beautifully to this day: tall, skinny houses with extremely steep stairs. If you ever visit Amsterdam and find yourself climbing endlessly steep stairs with heavy luggage, you should blame the tax incentives. It should also be easy for you to spot which houses were built by the people who wanted to signal that they were rich enough to pay the tax.

Stakes without Mistakes

Less fun maybe, but not less informative, are examples of incentives that worked. Here are two examples of small changes in incentives that had a big impact on the world.

For the first, imagine that you need to fly from San Diego to San Francisco for a friend's birthday celebration. The figure below shows what comes up in your search. You'll likely choose the Alaska Airlines option.

Now, imagine that instead of flying for fun, you're traveling to San Francisco for work, and your company is paying for your ticket. You frequently

8:00pm - 9:39pm	1h 39m (Nonstop)	$185	Select
⚖ Alaska Airlines	SAN - SFO	one way	
8:55pm – 1030	1h 37m (Nonstop)	$339	Select
▧ United	SAN - SFO	one way	

Which option do you go with? Probably the Alaska Airlines option.

fly with United and care about your "Mileage Plus" status. As such, you might choose the United flight instead. After all, someone else is paying for the flight, and you get the benefits that come with mileage points.

All major airlines today have frequent flyer incentive programs. For every mile flown or dollar spent, customers earn points that can later be redeemed for air travel, upgrades, or various other benefits. These programs incentivize us to stay loyal by increasing the switching costs. An ingenious part of this incentive scheme is that, in many cases, the person who makes the flight choice and enjoys the loyalty program benefits is not the one who pays for the ticket. Your typical business traveler thus has an incentive to choose the airline that they have a frequent flyer account with, regardless of cost. They're less likely to simply choose the cheaper option—why would they? By choosing the airline they always fly with, they get more miles and hence more rewards, all without having to pay a single extra dollar themselves. This brings me to a major rule that incentive designers should abide by: know who pays for the product and who enjoys the incentives, and keep in mind that the two may be different.

The second example of smart incentives takes us to 1978 China, with a simple contract between local farmers and government.[20] The story of this contract begins with eighteen farmers in Xiaogang, a small, impoverished Chinese village with a population hovering in the low hundreds. In 1978, China was at the height of communism. Working in collectivized fields, the farmers received a fixed food ration for their labor—whatever they grew went to the government. To get this ration, farmers needed to meet a minimum quota. Regardless of how long or hard they worked beyond that, they would receive the same meager allowance, usually barely enough to survive on.

This system of incentives gave the farmers no reason to produce more than the quota. Why work harder than you have to when the crops would be taken away? As one farmer put it, "Work hard, don't work hard—everyone gets the same." The signal? No need to work harder than the minimum required.

In the winter of 1978, hungry and defeated, the farmers banded together and came up with a revolutionary idea: instead of farming as a collective, each farmer would get their own plot of land to tend to. A certain share would be turned over to the collective and the government to meet the quota, but they would secretly keep the rest. Yen Hongchang wrote out the contract, and the other farmers signed. The next morning, all the farmers woke up earlier than usual and worked past sunset. Just by changing the incentives, the farmers produced much more than they had in years.

Eventually, the local officials figured out what the farmers were doing. Instead of punishing them, the newly anointed leader, Deng Xiaoping, decided to model the rest of China's economy on the incentive scheme that the farmers had created. Allowed to own what they grew, farmers all over China began to reap higher yields. Economists and historians see this small change in incentives as the first step in a series that has carried hundreds of millions of Chinese peasants out of poverty since 1978. Today, the contract and the story behind it are something that Chinese children learn about and are a perfect example of how smart incentives can change the game.

TAKEAWAY: Bad incentives could be worse than no incentives. Make sure to align your signals.

9

Mental Accounting

Choosing the Incentive's Currency

Glenn Kelman, the CEO of the real estate brokerage firm Redfin, was proud of a gift the company gives its customers. In a video of a board meeting, he discusses a partial refund of commission that real estate agents give to their customers. Even though the company had discovered that the hundreds of millions of dollars given in commission refunds actually had zero effect on the demand for Redfin services, Redfin decided to double down on the refunds. In Kelman's words, they were "just giving money away." The video was meant to be inspirational and to demonstrate how Kelman ignored "the rational thing to do" by continuing to offer refunds despite their ineffectiveness in increasing demand, thus proving Redfin to be true to its mission of looking out for the consumer.[1]

The video is puzzling, not because Kelman made the decision to keep offering the incentive but because he decided to keep offering the incentive in the same way. Incentives aren't all created equal; small differences in incentive programs' framing and structure can greatly impact their effectiveness. Yet often too little attention is paid to making them "work."

The money that Redfin gives to its customers should make its service more attractive to home buyers, who can get rebates of several thousand dollars. But, as Richard Thaler has demonstrated, people consider savings in the frame of the entire deal.[2] For example, you're about to buy a new computer screen that costs $200. The salesperson tells you that the same screen is 25 percent off at another branch of the store twenty minutes away. Would you drive there to save some money? Most of us would make the drive; $50 off a $200 purchase is a big deal. But what if instead of buying a $200 screen, you are buying a new computer for $2,000? Again, the salesperson tells you that the store twenty minutes away is offering the same computer for $1,950. In this scenario, while still saving the same amount of $50, most people wouldn't opt to go to the other store; $50 off a $2,000 purchase may not seem to be worth the drive.

In Redfin's context, although the thousands of dollars it offers in incentives are a significant amount of money, they become less impressive when compared to the overall purchase price of a house. Take the story of Katie as an example. She had recently purchased a house through one of Redfin's agents. The experience was good, but when she thought back on the refund, the details were a bit fuzzy. She remembered receiving a discount but couldn't recall the amount. Katie is a bargain shopper who's always on the lookout for great deals, so her lack of detailed memory on a discount of a few thousand dollars is problematic for Redfin. Not only was the refund amount small compared to the house price, but it was also lost in a swarm of numbers in the stack of mortgage documents that she had to sign.

Changing Perception

Katie Baca-Motes, who is currently a senior director for strategic initiatives at Scripps Research Translational Institute, and I worked on such a reward system with Edmunds.com, a large online company that offers information, reviews, and prices on auto purchases. Say you Google "2019 BMW X3 review." One of the top options you'll see will be from Edmunds .com. Click on it, and you'll see all the information you may need to make a decision: reviews, specs, prices, comparisons, and such. Once ready to buy a car, you'll be asked for your zip code and be directed to an inventory at various dealerships in your area that offer the car you're interested in. Dealerships pay Edmunds.com to display these ads for their cars. Showing dealerships that a customer purchased their car due to an ad on the website is valuable to Edmunds.com, so it decided to give its customers a discount—a cash discount averaging $450 on used vehicle purchases—if they choose to purchase a car that they first see on its website. This discount helped Edmunds.com show the dealerships the value they receive from placing ads. While the discount influenced demand, it didn't work as well as management had hoped.

When Katie and I were asked to help make the incentive more effective, we theorized that the reason the current discount didn't work as well as expected is similar to that in Redfin's case. While for most of us $450 is a lot of money, it is less impressive when it is compared to the purchase of a $20,000 car.

The problem we tried to solve was how to change buyers' perceptions of the discount, making the incentive more effective at no additional cost. The solution we tested involved a different form of incentives: prepaid gas cards. While $450 doesn't feel large relative to a car's price, it does when used toward gas purchases. The psychology is simple: it is easy to imagine reaching for the pump and spending money on gas; $450 in gas is going to make us happy each time we fill up the car knowing that we earned it by being a smart consumer. It just "feels" more significant than a discount on a car's price. This phenomenon is called "mental accounting."

Richard Thaler won the Nobel Prize in 2017 partly because of this concept of mental accounting, which he defines as a set of cognitive operations that individuals and households use to organize, evaluate, and keep track of financial activities.[2] The human brain contains multiple mental accounts, often with separate budgets. For example, housing and dining could be two separate accounts with different budgets. You might have a set budget for dining out every month as well as a separate one for housing, and you would be sensitive to overconsuming in either budget. Even within dining, not all expenses feel the same. While you may spend half an hour looking for parking to avoid the restaurant's valet fee, you probably would not think twice about spending this amount on dessert. Even if the total expenses for the night out are the sum of parking, dessert, and all the rest, it is very annoying to pay for parking, and you'd make more of an effort to avoid it.

These separate mental accounts violate the economic principle of fungibility: that money in one mental account should be a perfect substitute for money in another account. Parking fees and dessert prices of the same magnitude should be treated the same, but they're not.[3] By exploiting the violation of the fungibility principle, Katie and I posited that targeting incentives at a specific, highly desirable mental account could be more powerful than a simple discount on the overall purchase.

To test the impact of mental accounting on discounts, we conducted a field experiment on the Edmunds.com platform. Field experiments are close in nature to the A/B testing done by most online companies, in which companies are trying different options on their customers. The main difference is that we try to use findings from psychology and behavioral economics to guide our tests. Once you learn how to do it, it's easy to run such tests online, especially when you work with a company like Edmunds.com that has mastered the art of running such experiments. When starting the search, customers were randomized into different framings of discounts, and then we followed their behavior on the site. Just as in A/B testing, these customers didn't know that they were taking part in an experiment.

Our main interest was to see how the different framings of discounts would affect purchase decisions. Consistent with our mental accounting hypothesis, we found that $450 off a vehicle had much less of an impact than $450 offered as a prepaid gas card. The shift in framing from a cash discount to gas cards more than doubled the success rate of the incentives. In further testing, we found that the effect was maintained even when the gas card had a lower value than the car discount: car shoppers responded more favorably to a $250 gas card than to a $450 discount on a vehicle purchase!

There are purchases that most of us consider irritating: paying for parking, Wi-Fi, checked bags, and so on. Likewise, no one looks forward to visiting the gas station, so free gas feels great. Crafting an incentive around something that people dislike paying for can improve its effectiveness.

Here's another example using the same concept. Together with three professors in Singapore, Teck-Hua Ho, Marcel Bilger, and Eric Finkelstein, we worked with a taxi company in Singapore that was interested in improving its employees' health.[4] Physical inactivity is quite problematic, as the fourth leading risk factor for mortality, and it also imposes significant costs on governments, insurers, and employers through increased medical expenditures and reductions in work productivity.

When designing incentives to change behavior, taxi drivers are a good target population for such an increase in physical activity, because given their long work hours and sedentary work environment, most taxi drivers are physically inactive and are at high risk for chronic disease.

The Singaporean company we worked with was willing to pay $100 a month in cash incentives to motivate the drivers to exercise more. We suggested a small variation on this: as in the gas card example, we looked for something that the taxi drivers really don't like paying for. We learned that taxi drivers in Singapore do not own their taxis; they pay a rental fee of approximately $100 per day to the company that owns the taxis. This electronic transfer of payment is done daily via an automatic deduction from a driver's bank account. This daily rental fee is highly salient and aversive to the drivers. It's always fresh in drivers' minds, and many will report working part-time on their "off" days to offset the financial loss. Therefore, to invoke this mental account, we chose to frame the reward as a rental credit equal to the value of one day's rental fee.

To monitor exercising, the taxi drivers who participated in our experiment received a Fitbit and were paid to wear it. In the first period, we simply measured how many steps they walked each day. Then, for four months, we paid them a reward if they reached a target number of steps. Finally, in months five to seven, we stopped paying the reward but kept measuring the number of steps each driver walked.

The drivers were randomized into two groups, and the difference between them was the framing of incentive: for one group, we called it a $100 cash reward for every month they met their monthly goal, and in the other group, we called it a $100 to cover the daily rental fee of the taxi.

The result of this small change in framing was strong: drivers increased the number of steps they took in both incentive treatments when compared to baseline, in which no incentives were given. For example, in the first month of incentives, the cash group walked about fifteen hundred steps more, but the drivers in the free-rent treatment improved by about two thousand steps, which is significantly more than that of the cash group. The simple cash incentive motivated drivers to exercise more, yet the "free rental" incentive worked significantly better. Our hope was that getting drivers into the habit of walking would change their long-term exercising behavior, such that they will walk more even after the incentive program is over. Hence, we measured the change in steps both during each month of the four-month intervention period and in the three months after the rewards were removed. And, while smaller, both the improvement and the difference between treatments were there even in months five to seven, after we stopped paying them.

Remember when I said that sometimes people find that their incentives failed and conclude mistakenly that incentives don't work? In this case, we can see that even when incentives work, using some simple behavioral changes can increase the return on the investment significantly. The question about incentives shouldn't be limited to whether to offer one but should also include whether it's being offered in the best way.

What Does Mental Accounting Mean for Companies Like Redfin?

Going back to Redfin's example, simple creative thinking could increase the effectiveness of the incentives as well as the company's profits while simultaneously making the customers even happier. Can you think of framing methods that can improve Redfin's incentives? One example is to offer the refunds in the form of costs that come with a new home, like the money that will undoubtedly be spent at the local home-improvement store in the months after moving in. If Katie were using the refund credit card on her trip to Home Depot, she would have appreciated it much more!

Facts are dry: "$450 discount if you buy the car through us" is storyless. Leaving it open for interpretation might end up with a story that consumers don't like. You should actively shape the story your incentives tell.

Case Study: "Losses Loom Larger than Gains"

Imagine being a teacher in the city of Chicago Heights, located thirty miles south of Chicago. Chicago Heights is made up of primarily low-income minority students who struggle with low achievement rates. You are proud of teaching these kids and are doing your best to make them successful. One day, a team of researchers shows up at your school with an interesting incentive offer.[5] They will pay you money if the kids in your class improve their performance by the end of the school year, on the basis of a percentile rank improvement in test results.[6] The researchers promise you a maximum possible reward of $8,000 for your students' performance improvement over the school year. You also know that under this program, the expected value of your reward is $4,000, which is equivalent to approximately 8 percent of your salary.

The structure of the incentives is a bit unusual, however: you get $8,000 transferred into your bank account at the beginning of the school year. The catch is that you would have to return some or all of it depending on whether your students can reach certain performance targets by the end of the school year. Would you be able to improve your students' tests results? You are a bit insulted, as giving you financial incentives to improve students' performance implies that you are not doing a good enough job at the moment. You know that research shows that some teachers are more effective than others; but could incentives make you a better teacher? Given the amount of money offered, you are willing to give it a try.

A field experiment by Roland Fryer, Steven Levitt, John List, and Sally Sadoff tested the effectiveness of "loss aversion" incentives relative to the traditional "gain" incentives, in which teachers receive bonuses at the end of the year based on the same achievement criteria. "Loss aversion" is a psychological principle coined by Amos Tversky and Daniel Kahneman. According to their theory, rewards are evaluated relative to a reference point, such that the outcome is coded in our brain as either a gain or a loss, and losses loom larger than equal gains.[7] That is, people are affected more by trying to prevent a loss than by trying to gain. Hence, framing a reward as a loss would have a greater effect on behavior than framing it as a gain would.

Loss aversion, therefore, predicts that teachers who receive the $8,000 at the beginning of the year will work harder to avoid losing it than will teachers who are promised to gain this reward at the end of the year. This prediction is interesting because it is all about the framing of rewards: teachers with the same student performance in both the gain and loss groups will receive the exact same final bonus.

Do you think you would work harder to avoid returning money that was deposited in your account at the beginning of the year than if you were standing to gain the reward at the end of the year?

The field experiment's results show that indeed the teachers who were primed for loss aversion incentives had significantly more success, whereas the teachers' performance in the gain treatment did not improve relative to that of the control group, which received no incentives. That is, promising rewards to teachers if their students improved their test scores had no effect on students' performance. However, framing the incentive in terms of losses led to sharp improvements in students' academic outcomes: the students in the loss treatment gained as much as a ten-percentile increase in their scores compared to students of the teachers who didn't receive any incentives. For comparison, the increase in students' performance was roughly the same order of magnitude as increasing average teacher quality by more than one standard deviation.

The loss aversion experiment with teachers is a great example of how using traditional incentives may lead you to conclude that "incentives don't work"; after all, the students' test scores didn't improve with the gain-framed incentives. The right conclusion, however, is that you need to understand the psychology behind the incentives to make them work.

This result shows the importance of framing. The same magnitude of rewards is more effective when you frame them as a loss rather than as a gain. This loss framing story is applicable in other settings too. Simply put, people work harder to protect what is already "theirs."

Imagine that you are a factory worker at a high-tech enterprise in China focusing on the production and distribution of consumer electronics. On top of earning an average weekly base salary of between RMB 290 and RMB 375 (roughly equal to $42.50 and $54.96), you are also incentivized by a weekly bonus when your team's production reaches a certain threshold. You are notified of this bonus via a company letter: "The company is rewarding productivity. You will receive a salary bonus of RMB 80 for every week when your team's weekly production average is above or equal to 20 units/hour."

Nice—your additional hard work will be noticed and rewarded accordingly. With the bonus being more than 20 percent of your weekly salary, you are motivated to work hard toward the production goal.

Now, what if you received the following letter instead? "The company is rewarding productivity. We will grant you a provisional bonus of RMB 80 before the start of every work week. For every week in which your team's weekly production average is below 20 units/hour, the bonus will be taken away."

Loss aversion predicts that you would probably treat the provisional bonus as yours already and work even harder to reach the production goal and keep the bonus in your salary. This is exactly what was found in a Chinese high-tech manufacturing facility field experiment.[8] Two groups of workers received the same bonus incentives framed in two different ways: as a gain (first letter) and as a loss (second letter). While workers' productivity increased in both groups when compared to the baseline, the team of workers incentivized by the loss framing significantly outperformed the team of workers who were motivated by gaining rewards. The observed treatment effects persisted throughout the span of the entire four-month experimental period, suggesting that the framing of incentives can affect long-term growth of productivity in firms.

The workers' experiment tells us that psychological insights are applicable to labor markets, where a simple change in the framing of employee contracts can boost long-term worker productivity. Your signal will become stronger and more effective as you frame the incentives with proper psychology.

Incentives frame the story, and the story "I'll work hard to win the reward" is less motivating than the story "I'll work hard to avoid losing the reward." Whenever you can control the narrative, make sure to make people feel that they've already won the reward but might still lose it if they don't meet the goals.

TAKEAWAY: Targeting incentives at a highly salient mental account could increase the return on investment by changing the story.

10

Regret as Incentives

A righteous man prays every week before the lottery outcomes are announced: "God, please bless me with a win for once in my life. I've always been good, and I have seven kids to feed." For years, every week, once the results are announced, the man cries for hours: "Why? Why not me?" One of these crying days, the man finally hears a voice telling him, "How about buying a lottery ticket first?"

Here's a personal story about regret. My family immigrated to Israel from Budapest after World War II; in case you are wondering, they never regretted that. At the end of a long journey, they arrived in Tel Aviv in 1948. My father's parents were in their late forties and, like most survivors of the Holocaust, had no possessions and no jobs. They were given a small apartment in a public housing block that was built quickly to accommodate the large wave of immigrants to the new country (Israel was officially established in May 1948). My grandmother started a small tailoring business from their tiny apartment, and my grandfather worked a variety of temporary jobs until he landed a good job at a bank. They were poor, but they were happy.

My maternal grandparents had a very similar story. The two families knew each other from Budapest and ended up living in the same block in Tel Aviv. My parents knew each other as kids in Budapest and had met again on this block in Tel Aviv as young adults. They fell in love, got married, had children, and lived happy and full lives until they passed away. As far as I know, there were no regrets there either.

A few years into my parents' marriage, they arranged a party to celebrate their anniversary. One of my mother's aunts earned her living selling state lottery tickets. At this anniversary party, the lotto sister and my paternal grandfather started discussing the state lottery, in which a ticket had six numbers on it. If all six numbers came up in the weekly lottery, you'd become rich. Convinced, my grandfather bought a ticket.

After that party, my grandfather kept buying the ticket with the same numbers week after week, until he became hooked. For decades later, till his death, he kept buying a ticket with the same six numbers every week. Even when on vacation, he made sure to have someone else buy it for him. Why? Here, the regret finally enters. If my grandfather had stopped buying the ticket and the numbers came up as the winner, he would have regretted it immensely. He knew that this would be devastating for him. The cost of weekly tickets wasn't worth the dreadful feeling of regret. He didn't want to live with the fear of this happening, so he kept buying the tickets mostly to avoid this fear of regret.

My grandfather was not unique in liking the lottery. According to Statista, US lottery sales totaled $91 billion in 2019, with more than half of the adults in the country participating that year.[1] The large presence of lotteries in everyday life indicates that they are attractive to many people. There could be many reasons for the desirability of lotteries, such as overweighing of small probabilities, according to which people put disproportionately large weight on small-probability events, thereby making the psychological impact of such events large relative to that of the event's actual likelihood.[2]

Because of lotteries' popularity and learning from the experiences of people like my grandfather, the Dutch cleverly created the Postcode Lottery. In this lottery, the "winner" is a postcode: every week a different postcode (with nineteen addresses on average and up to twenty-five addresses in it) is randomly selected as a winner.[3] If you live in the winning postcode area, you very quickly learn about your win, as do your neighbors and friends.

The catch is that in order to win the prize, you have to buy a lottery ticket for that week. If you do, good for you. If you don't, you will probably regret it for a long, long time.

To make not buying a ticket even more painful, apart from prize money, the winners would also get a brand-new BMW. What could be more motivating than thinking about passing by your neighbor's fancy BMW in your street, knowing that you could have had one just like that if only you'd made the small investment of purchasing a lottery ticket?

In a normal lottery, unless you buy the same ticket every time, like my grandfather, you don't know the counterfactual: whether you would have won if you had bought the ticket. In the postcode lottery, however, you would know.

We try to avoid the painful emotion of regret when we make decisions. In behavioral science, we call this behavior "regret aversion." The Postcode Lottery's creators push this feeling further. In their ads, they state, "You didn't buy any tickets? That means your neighbors will win everything. Buy some now, before it's too late!" Another ad says, "Sour—that is how it feels when you miss out on at least 2 million [euros] by just an inch. Because seeing a multimillion prize awarded to your own address and winning nothing because you did not buy a ticket, that is something you do not want to experience."[4]

Regret aversion influences how we make future choices—trying to minimize future regret. This "anticipated regret" is an important motivator. We anticipate that some decisions will lead to regret, and we don't want to experience this feeling—so we make choices to reduce the chances of risk or regret. Importantly, anticipated regret is stronger when it is easier for the individual to learn about the outcomes associated with their decision.[5]

In my grandfather's case, he anticipated that if "his" numbers came up and he didn't have the ticket, he would regret it. So he kept buying the tickets. In the Dutch Postcode Lottery, people anticipate that if their postcode comes up and they don't have a ticket, they will regret it, so they choose to buy the lottery ticket every week. As demonstrated in both stories, regret can strongly influence individuals' decisions.

Could strong motivators like anticipated regret be used as incentives for behavior change in the field? A few years ago, I visited the Bill & Melinda Gates Foundation to talk about incentives. The foundation had just opened its new Seattle headquarters campus. The city welcomed this new campus, but there were worries regarding the impact that the campus—which had a capacity of more than a thousand employees—might have on traffic in the area. To reduce this negative impact, I was told, the foundation introduced some incentives for its employees to reduce car use. Specifically, it provided free access to public transportation and made employees pay $9 a day for parking if they chose to park in the foundation's facility.

One additional element of this incentive really interested me: employees were paid an extra $3 for every day they came to work without their car. Since approximately five hundred employees a day didn't use the parking garage when they came to work, the $3 incentive cost to the foundation adds up to about $1,500 a day. These kinds of incentive schemes are being used by many organizations. Given the high daily cost, the foundation asked me, could it design a more effective incentive scheme and either spend less money for the same participation or use the same budget and get more people to switch to public transportation?

Leveraging the power of regret, I did offer a different way of using the $1,500 incentives: have a "regret lottery" that pays $1,500 every afternoon. The lottery will randomly pick one name in a little ceremony broadcast on the internal net. The lottery will pick a name, the name will be announced, and then the system will check whether the employee parked their car in the parking facility that day. If not, we have a winner. If the employee did park in the facility, sad music will be played, and a new name will be picked as a winner. The process repeats until a nonparker gets picked. The people whose name were drawn but who parked their car would regret driving immensely. This should create a buzz in the office!

While the foundation didn't want to test my proposal, referencing fear of negative feedback from employees as a reason, another company was interested. This company has a large office space with classrooms that host different types of workshops. The company provides free parking for participants of the workshops at a nearby parking facility by validating their parking tickets. Since the company pays the parking facility per ticket validation, management knew the precise cost of each car parked and was willing to experiment with incentives that would simultaneously reduce parking and save the company money.

The study started with a pilot that was conducted as a "proof of concept" to the management, in order to convince it that using incentives can increase the company's profits without creating tension with unhappy participants. The pilot was a success, and the company learned that it could profit from incentives without upsetting the participants (as revealed by a postclass survey that found no difference in satisfaction relative to regular workshops). The company was convinced by the pilot and agreed to launch the full study.

So the study began. It took place during a week in which 240 participants came for a five-day workshop (Monday to Friday) and were taking part in different classes. They were promised free parking for the week. On Monday, each group of participants was offered a different incentive.

After all parking tickets were validated for the day, a representative of the company came to each class and asked participants to avoid using their car for the rest of the week if possible, citing traffic and environmental considerations. The company and I then randomly split the participants into four groups with sixty people in each:

- *Control:* There was no mentioning of incentives for this group.
- *$5 fixed:* Participants were promised $5 for every day in which they would come to class but would not need to validate a parking ticket.
- *$500 lottery:* Participants were promised that on Friday there would be a lottery for $500. For every day that a participant didn't need a parking

validation, a ticket with their name would be entered into a box. One name would be randomly drawn out of this box on Friday, and the lucky winner would be called to receive the $500 they earned.

- *$500 lottery with regret:* The procedure was similar to that of the $500 lottery group, but every name that entered into the box each day had a mark showing whether this person needed validation or not. On Friday, after the "lucky" ticket was drawn, the name of the person was called. If the ticket indicated that they did not validate parking for the winning day, they earned the $500. If they did validate parking for that ticket, then the procedure would be repeated by taking a new name out of the box. This would continue until an eligible ticket was drawn.

This design allowed the company to have a simple cost-benefit analysis for the different incentive schemes. It also precisely measured the relative effectiveness of the incentives, avoiding a situation in which the company might use incentives that "work" but are less effective than other payment schemes.

While people like participating in lotteries, it's unclear whether lotteries are useful in behavioral interventions. Some studies find that paying people cash incentives yields a higher response rate than providing either a lottery option or no incentive, while others find the opposite result.[6] Promising recent work—mostly in the health-care domain—has found that lottery incentives work better than a "sure-thing" prize.[7] It seems like the devil is in the details of the way the lottery is framed. That's why it's important to study the effectiveness of such incentives in the relevant industry that wishes to use them.

The results of our study indeed showed that different incentives had a different effect. While all incentives were more effective than the control group, some were more impactful than others. Which incentive do you think would be the most cost-effective?

The $5 fixed participants used parking 10 percent less than control. However, this reduction came with a high price, because every nondriver (including participants who wouldn't have used the parking facility anyway) had to be paid. On average, the incentive cost per one additional no parking was $36, which was way more than the amount the company was willing to pay.

As expected, the $500 lottery did better. It reduced parking by 18 percent relative to control, with a lower cost. The average incentive cost for the marginal no parking was $12, which was below the cost of parking, so the company was already happy with this. Lo and behold, the results of the $500 lottery with regret were even better. It reduced parking by 26 percent, and the incentive cost was only $8 for the marginal no parking.

The $8 cost of reducing parking in the lottery with regret was way below the cost of validating a parking ticket, so the company ended up choosing to implement this incentive scheme. The experiment demonstrated to management that simple incentives can increase profits. It also testifies to the lesson that even when incentives are profitable, as in the case of simple lotteries, we should keep looking for ways to improve them. A small change in the incentive framing and implementation, like adding a regret component, could reshape the story and make a larger impact.

TAKEAWAY: Anticipated regret is a powerful emotion that could be used to motivate people.

11

Prosocial Incentives

Most of the incentive schemes that we've discussed so far use direct compensation to motivate effort. However, sometimes our actions are driven by other reasons, such as helping others. Consider the following two scenarios in which a company wants to motivate its employees to quit smoking:

Scenario 1: A smoking employee is rewarded with $5 for every week of abstinence.
Scenario 2: A smoking employee gets to donate $5 to a local charity for every week of abstinence.

Which incentive design do you think is more effective at motivating employees to quit smoking? Notice how the incentive levels are low in both scenarios. Evidence suggests that small monetary incentives may be ineffective and may even lead to adverse effects when the rewards are low, as in the case of Scenario 1.

Aldo Rustichini and I investigated this issue in our paper "Pay Enough— or Don't Pay at All" back in 2000.[1] In one of our field experiments, we gathered 180 high school students to collect donations for charity in a door-to-door fund-raising campaign. The students were randomized into one of three treatments: the no-compensation group, in which students were only motivated by a speech expressing the importance of the donations; the small-compensation group, in which in addition to the speech, the students were promised 1 percent of the dollar amount collected; and the high-compensation group, in which the students got the speech and were promised 10 percent of the dollar amount collected. Which group ended up collecting the most donations? You might expect that those who received a higher commission rate would collect more donations, but as the paper's title hints, students in the no-compensation group invested more effort and had a higher average amount collected than those in the 1 percent treatment. While the students in the high-compensation (10 percent) group collected more money than those in the low-compensation group, they still performed worse than those without any compensations. What constitutes small and large incentives depends on the case, but the crowding-out effect demonstrated by this experiment supports that Scenario 1 may not be as effective as Scenario 2.

Why, then, is the incentive scheme in Scenario 2 effective despite its equally low incentive level? Well, by donating to a charity, not only does our altruistic giving improve the overall outcome of the beneficiaries, but we also derive private value and experience, what my colleague at UC San Diego Jim Andreoni has called the "warm glow" effect: a sense of joy and satisfaction resulting from doing our part to help others. The warm glow effect is a great example of self-signaling: by helping, donating, or volunteering, we signal to ourselves that we are good people and hence get a positive boost to our self-image. Evidence suggests that the source of this warm glow is mostly dependent on the effort exerted to help others, rather than the magnitude of the outcome. As long as we recognize that we put in effort to help others, we can experience the positive self-signal produced by the warm glow, no matter how much we've actually helped.

The prevalence and success of volunteer fire departments reflect such intrinsic motivation's power. As the name suggests, most volunteer firefighters work for free and are expected to respond to emergency calls. Many of them have other jobs in addition to working shifts at the fire department. Why volunteer? Ron Roy, the division chief for Douglas County Fire District and a volunteer firefighter with forty-seven years of experience, explained, "It is about our communities and the hometowns in which we have elected to live and raise our families. We should care about all of those around us and recognize their needs. . . . That pride [of volunteering] is a valuable commodity on which the community can't put a price. It's about personal reward from those who deeply care."[2] Indeed, putting a price on helping communities could crowd out the volunteers' motivation and pride. Roy represents the majority of American firefighters: about 67 percent of all the firefighters (1.11 million) in the US in 2018 were volunteers.[3] This figure is even more drastic in some other countries: 80 percent of Argentinian firefighters are volunteers; 100 percent of firefighters in Chile and Peru are unpaid.[4] Evidently, people are very motivated by volunteering and the signaling power of altruism.

Does this mean that prosocial incentives are always better than monetary incentives? When should we utilize prosocial incentives versus monetary incentives? My former PhD student Alex Imas designed a clever experiment to test these questions.[5] He recruited university students to test whether they exert more effort under a prosocial incentive design or a monetary incentive design. To measure effort, he used a hand dynamometer that recorded force output in Newtons for the students to squeeze. All students were asked to squeeze the device for sixty seconds first before the experiment to obtain a baseline measurement. The device measured on average how hard they squeezed over the minute. Afterward, the students were asked to squeeze the hand dynamometer in a second round with an incentive involved.

The students were randomized into a control group or one of four treatments. These treatments manipulated how much they were paid for squeezing harder in the second round (low versus high amount) and who received the money (them versus a charity).

Consistent with the previous intuition, when the incentives were low, the students exerted more effort when they worked for charity than when they worked for themselves. However, when the incentives were high, the students no longer worked harder under prosocial incentives than under monetary incentives. This effort gap closed: the students worked harder when they were paid more, but they didn't work harder with higher pay when the payment went to charity.

These findings tell us that prosocial incentive designs are better when the reward is small, because we are generally insensitive about the magnitude of charitable contribution and care more about the fact that we contributed. On the other hand, self-benefiting incentive designs are better when the reward is large, because while small monetary rewards can crowd out our motivation, we are very responsive to large amounts of money.

There's a wide range of practical applications of these psychological insights. Pret a Manger, an international sandwich chain, leveraged this concept to motivate its employees and promote a positive work environment. After having established hundreds of stores in Britain, the successful franchise slowly expanded into major US cities like Manhattan and Chicago in the 2010s and was being praised for its welcoming employees and intimate customer service. What's Pret a Manger's secret? The *New York Times* reported multiple company strategies such as hiring, paying, and promoting employees on the basis of qualities such as cheerfulness. One specific strategy worth noting is how the company hands out bonuses: employees receive at least a £50 bonus in vouchers when they are promoted or reach training milestones. Instead of pocketing the bonus as in traditional company incentives, the employees must give the voucher to their colleagues who helped them.[6] This incentive design results in the giving employee getting a "warm glow" and the receiving employee being appreciative of the gift, thus improving the working environment and consequently customer satisfaction.

While traditional monetary incentives are often effective, they're not always the best option. Sometimes making a self-benefiting incentive prosocial could transform the meaning behind the reward, reshape the story, and achieve greater results.

TAKEAWAY: When rewards are small, prosocial incentives may be more effective than self-benefiting incentives.

12

Awards as Signals

"Slowly the time went by until there were just 60 seconds before his battalion must start its 'suicide job' in Okinawa."[1] That's the beginning of an article in the *Knoxville News-Sentinel* describing the actions of Desmond Doss, a US Army corporal and combat medic, as well as a conscientious objector who was opposed to carrying weapons.

On May 5, 1945, after a month of back-and-forth battles in Okinawa, Doss's unit approached the Hacksaw Ridge, tasked with ascending and securing it.[2] The Japanese army waited until the US troops reached the ridge's plateau and then began its counterattack. When the US troops were desperate for medical attention, Doss was there, treating US soldiers one at a time amid the endless gunfire and bombardment, knowing that without him, these soldiers would either be left for dead or captured and tortured. Doss carried the wounded soldiers one by one to the escarpment's edge, where they could be sent to a safe location for further treatment. It was estimated that Doss saved seventy-five soldiers that day.

Most of us can agree that what Doss did is incredible and deserves recognition. And indeed, on October 12, 1945, he received the United States' highest personal military decoration, the Medal of Honor. The emotional ceremony was held at the White House, where President Truman personally gave him the medal.[3] Doss lived to the age of eighty-seven, always proud of his actions and the medal.

Awards come in various forms: they could be big prizes such as the Medal of Honor, the Oscars, or the Nobel Prize. They could also be more modest, such as Employee of the Month, Most Valuable Employee, Customer Service Awards, or Perfect Attendance Programs.

While awards are utilized as incentives, they are different from traditional monetary incentives. Imagine, for example, that instead of the ceremony at the White House, Doss was mailed a $10,000 check with a thank-you note. It would have been nice to receive the check, but it would have carried a very different signal from that of the medal. While monetary awards are acceptable in many cases, they are frowned on in others. Awarding $10,000 to Doss instead of a medal not only would violate the social norm of not being paid to risk your life for the country but might also be insulting. The monetary aspect is not what makes an award for bravery valuable, and it puts a price tag on the award, which could psychologically backfire. Do recognition and money add up here, such that Doss would have been happier receiving the medal as well as a check? Or would the check "crowd out" the recognition, as it potentially makes an official stance that the act of risking one's life on the battlefield is only worth $10,000?

How can you use awards to your advantage? How can you leverage signals to strengthen your incentives and shape the story that your awards convey? This chapter is based on work I did with Sandy Campbell and Jana Gallus.[4] In chapter 1, we discussed social signaling—how a person's actions can reveal credible information about them to others. Awards often have a social signaling dimension that can greatly increase their perceived value. Doss's receiving a medal for bravery credibly signals to others that he was courageous, even without knowing the details of his actions. Winning a Nobel Prize in physics signals to others academic ability, even to those of us who cannot understand or appreciate the contribution itself.

Awards signal not only the recipient's abilities and qualities but also the award giver's values. In chapter 5, for example, we talked about companies that value innovation but don't incentivize taking risks. Using awards to encourage risk-taking is a great opportunity to effectively signal the company's values to the employees. If you recall from chapter 5, Tata, the Indian multinational conglomerate holding company, does exactly this and recognizes innovative ideas, attempts, and failures by giving out a "Dare to Try" award that encourages employees to try risky ideas.[5]

The success of awards depends on self-signaling as well. In chapter 2, we discussed how buying a hybrid car could signal to yourself that you care about the environment. In contrast, people cannot choose to win an award. A valuable award is usually not something that can be bought; it's something that is bestowed on a person to recognize a significant accomplishment. Say you just won the Employee of the Month award in your company. You probably had been showing up earlier or trying harder at work. Receiving the award affirms the belief that you have been doing well and that your effort was noticed. In this way, awards reinforce signals to oneself and may serve to validate and even change beliefs about oneself.

An award is multifaceted, and different aspects of an award can change the self- and social signals being sent. The success of an award thus relies on the details in these design aspects. Let's take a look at some crucial award features that can affect signaling and shape the story.

The Audience

When a tree falls in the forest, does it make a sound? When awards are given in private, do they have an effect? They do, but less. No audience means no social signaling value.

Think about the annual Oscars ceremony. Part of the value of the Oscars ceremony is in the fact that so many people watch it. Receiving an award in private with only few people who know about it has less social signaling value. However, sometimes the audience doesn't have to be present at the ceremony for the award to have social signaling value; it's enough that they see the plaques or small statues sitting on office shelves. Who's watching is also important: it could be peers who can evaluate what you do, your friends and family whom you'd like to impress, or a group of strangers whom you'll never meet again. The identity of your audience contributes to the social signaling power carried by the award.

Contrast Doss's medal with another bravery story. On August 9, 2009, a US military base in Afghanistan was the target of a coordinated attack. Right away, an enemy sniper wounded the US unit's medic, and a rocket-propelled grenade sparked a major fire in the unit's arsenal. As the fire grew larger, a disastrous explosion seemed inevitable. As the unit was about to abandon the base, an unnamed Navy SEAL acted. He directly faced fierce gunfire and dragged the wounded medic from the hot spot to safety. The SEAL then ran head first into the arsenal and dragged out crates of explosives. This unnamed SEAL ended up receiving a Navy Cross, the US Navy and Marine Corps' second-highest decoration awarded for valor in combat and extraordinary heroism.[6]

The unnamed SEAL is not alone. Almost one in five recipients of the US highest honor medals go publicly unnoticed or unnamed to protect the secrecy of stealth missions.[7] Without an audience, as you can imagine, the social signals that a Navy Cross sends are significantly diminished—only a few people involved in the classified mission know about their exceptional heroism.

While the social signals are lacking without an audience, the unnamed Navy SEAL probably still experienced strong self-signals regarding his bravery. The private ceremony further proved to him the value of his sacrifice and bravery and boosted his patriotic and courageous self-image.

Scarcity

Another important aspect of awards is their scarcity. The scarcer the award, the more social and self-signaling value it has, as giving the same award out too often or handing out too many different awards in a given field diffuses attention. The Nobel Prize attracts much attention in part due to the rarity of the event. If the prize were awarded once a week rather than once a year, its prestige and reputation would suffer; or imagine a weekly Oscars ceremony.

Wikipedia is a good example of how to apply the scarcity of awards in the field. As a free domain, with its operation entirely dependent on volunteer contributors, Wikipedia needs to continuously attract and hold onto valuable contributors. After the biggest online encyclopedia reached its peak number of volunteer editors in 2007, there was a worrisome slump in the number of contributions and edits on the website.[8] Without these valuable editors, Wikipedia would cease to survive in the turbulent online competition.

To change the trend, Wikipedia founder Jimmy Wales designed the Wikipedia Awards.[9] These awards vary by scarcity, giver, and significance: ranging from Editor of the Week, a recognition award from the community that is frequently handed out to thank editors for their work, to Wikimedian of the Year, an annual award presented at Wikimania, the official Wikimedia annual conference, to celebrate major achievements of an individual Wiki-pedian. The top award is the Order of the Day, which is awarded, rarely, to a Wikimedia developer for exceptional service to the community. These intangible awards ended up being a great success. Jana Gallus, who studied Wikipedia Awards in 2017, reports that they increased newcomer retention by 20 percent, and this effect lasted for more than one year after the initial award was given.[10]

Sometimes the organization takes it too far, however. Take the Triple Crown Trophy as an example. It is arguably one of the most difficult and thus rarest sporting accomplishments. As the greatest achievement in horse racing, it has been forty-two years since a horse has received the honor of this award.[11] To earn the trophy, the champion horse must win three different races located in three distinct tracks with unique lengths. Racehorses, like humans, tend to specialize at certain distances: some are good at sprinting, while others excel at enduring long distance. Because of the award's extreme difficulty and scarcity, most horse owners don't focus on pursuing the Triple Crown Trophy. Many of them shy away from training their horse to be versatile in various distances. They recognize that the odds of training a horse to win the Triple Crown Trophy are so slim that they are better off focusing on specializing in one distance.

On the other hand, having awards that are too common can backfire as well. Attendance awards are one of the most common educational awards. From kindergarten to high school, teachers of all sorts hand out attendance awards to motivate students. However, contrary to common assumption, attendance awards don't appear to work, as they send unintended signals to the students: if so many students can get it, why should I care?[12]

Who Gives the Award, and How Do They Decide?

Marlon Brando, the legendary actor and film director, experienced a steep career decline in the 1960s. In 1972, he made his comeback in a big way, by starring in *The Godfather*, which grossed $135 million nationwide and is to this day critically regarded as one of the greatest films of all time.[13] Brando's phenomenal acting as the original Don Corleone, ruthless yet full of humanity, propelled him to the Oscars.

On March 5, 1973, all eyes were on actors Liv Ullmann and Roger Moore, who were on stage announcing the forty-fifth Academy Awards' Best Actor recipient. The crowd went wild as Moore declared Marlon Brando as the winner. What came after became a classic that is still amazing to watch: to everyone's surprise, Sacheen Littlefeather, a Native American woman, walked onstage. She extended an open palm and declined the Oscar statuette. As the atmosphere intensified, Littlefeather introduced herself as an Apache and the president of the National Native American Affirmative Image Committee. Representing Brando, she stated that though Brando was very honored, he could not accept the generous award because of the treatment of Native Americans by the film industry and in movie reruns on television.[14]

The crowd started booing. Then the booing became overshadowed by a united applause, as Littlefeather said that she hoped that in the future "our hearts and understandings will meet with love and generosity."[15] Brando, the second person ever to reject an Oscars Best Actor award, indicated that accepting an award fundamentally shows tolerance toward the organization's actions and values.[16] Despite facing much backlash, Brando and Littlefeather stood by their values, refusing to support an organization that facilitates a discriminatory film industry. Their actions under the international spotlight brought public awareness to the film industry's mistreatment of Native Americans and inspired future boycotts of the Academy Awards.

Brando's boycott demonstrated what happens when the award giver's values don't align with those of the recipient. In most cases, however, the award giver's prestige and status lead the recipients to infer that they share the giver's goals, which may evoke an increased identification with the giver. Doss was awarded the Medal of Honor by the president of the United States in the name of the US Congress, two institutions that he had the utmost respect for. Having that intimate physical moment with the president was part of the honor. In the case of Wikipedia, the founder, Wales, personally bestows the Order of the Day award in order to emphasize its importance and appeal to a connection with the recipient. Jana Gallus suggests that increased self-identification as a "Wikipedian" was one of the main mechanisms behind the award's persistent positive effect.[17]

What if the giver's status is unclear (e.g., because the awarding body is new)? In these cases, and in contrast with the example of paying $10,000 for bravery in the battlefield, adding a significant tangible element can serve to establish the award as meaningful, thus making it a valuable self- and social signal. The significant monetary sum that is attached to the Nobel Prize, for example, most likely contributed to its establishment early on as an important award, despite the controversial legacy of Alfred Nobel himself. With time, the prize gained importance far beyond its monetary value.

I hope you're convinced that *who* provides the award is important; it's also important *how* they select the recipients. Is it an elaborate selection process, which begins with nominations and involves a thorough evaluation by peers and vetting by experts? Does it have some technical requirements, such as attendance? Or is it maybe a corrupt process?

Doss's Medal of Honor falls into the category of subjective evaluation, in which others assess the recipient's qualification on the basis of opinions and recommendations. Subjective evaluation may be necessary when the performance is difficult to objectively measure, as is the case for "breakthrough discoveries" or "artistic accomplishments." Think of the music industry: while there are objective evaluations such as *Billboard*'s streaming numbers, the Grammys, BET Awards, and Rock and Roll Hall of Fame serve as subjective committees that provide community validations.

However, subjective evaluations can be gamed. In 2016, Denzel Washington had the honor of winning the Golden Globe Cecil B. DeMille Award, which is bestowed on actors who have made "outstanding contributions to the world of entertainment."[18] The Hollywood Foreign Press Association (HFPA) only presents one individual annually with this honor. Notable winners include Walt Disney, Morgan Freeman, Jodie Foster, and Robert De Niro.[19] Most established actors want a shot at this honor, which would cement their status as legends in the film industry.

During Washington's acceptance speech, he said that his friend Freddy Fields, an American film producer, confidently predicted his win that year. With an award this competitive, it's quite hard to predict which actor will win. How did Fields know that Washington was going to take the crown over other accomplished actors?

The foresight was simple: Fields invited Washington to that year's first Hollywood Foreign Press luncheon, telling Washington, "[The HFPA is] gonna watch the movie, we're gonna feed them, they're gonna come over, you're gonna take pictures with everybody, you're gonna hold the magazines, take the pictures, and you're gonna win the award."[20] Washington followed Fields's plan and attended the lavish lunch and movie party, and he personally befriended and took pictures with the Golden Globe voters.

Washington's acceptance speech exposed the behind-the-scenes partisanship of the evaluation process as a joke. Needless to say, while the crowd was entertained by the story, the HFPA was not. Washington's story is just the tip of the iceberg. It might also not be a coincidence that *The Muse*, a movie with a 53 percent rating on Rotten Tomatoes, was nominated for a Golden Globe after Sharon Stone, one of the main cast members, had her representative send eighty-four gold watches to each of the voters in the HFPA.[21]

The audience is becoming more aware of the existence of partisan votes that don't represent the legitimate quality of the artists and their work. An evaluation process in which the authority or integrity of the evaluation committee is in question, like the one Washington exposed, can lower the social signaling value of the award.

The conclusion is simple: well-executed awards can send powerful signals and be a strong incentive for people. Shape the story that your award conveys by carefully considering each aspect of the award. Use awards wisely!

TAKEAWAY: Audience, scarcity, status of the award givers, and selection process affect the award's signaling value and can promote identification with the organization.

PART FOUR
Use Incentives to Identify the Problem

● ● ●

A man goes in to consult his doctor regarding his wife of thirty-seven years. "You see, doctor, I'm worried. I think my wife is developing hearing problems," he says. "But I don't know how to approach her and recommend that she gets checked. Any suggestions on how to do it without upsetting her?" His doctor calms him down, telling him it's often the case that hearing deteriorates with age. He suggests a simple test he can do with his wife. "Next time the two of you are together, and she has her back to you, call her from the other side of the room in a low voice. If she doesn't hear you, get a couple of feet closer to her and try again. If this doesn't work, try getting even closer to her." The man waits for the first chance to follow his doctor's suggestion. That evening, he sees his wife sitting on the living room sofa. He calls her from the other end of the room in a low voice. "Jane?" No reaction. He's now even more worried and gets closer to her, whispering, "Jane?" Again, no reaction. So he gets even closer and tries again: "Jane?" His wife turns to him and says, "For the third time, WHAT?"

This old joke has always been both funny and insightful to me. The man was fundamentally wrong in his diagnosis of the problem. Oftentimes, so are the people who study human behavior. It's humbling, to say the least. Like the man in the joke, economists and psychologists in my field often think "people" are the source of a problem, when in reality, it's us. We regularly decide that people make mistakes, calling it "irrational" behavior (which is just a fancy scientific way of saying "stupid"). However, it is often the researcher who makes the mistake by not understanding the underlying reasons behind a behavior.

Such misdiagnoses are not unique to social scientists. They happen often in the medical field—more than one would like to think. In the US, approximately twelve million people who seek outpatient medical care are misdiagnosed each year.[1] That's one out of every twenty patients! When the misdiagnosis is corrected quickly, no harm, no foul. When it's not, it has the potential to result in severe injury, both physically and financially. After all, in order to effectively treat a disease, the doctor needs first to know what it is—hence the procedural battery of tests such as scans and blood draws.

PERSPECTIVE TAKING

What's the problem? Depends on who's asking

These do not directly cure the patient but rather help to diagnose the problem. Then, and only then, can a doctor begin treatment. If the problem is diagnosed incorrectly from the get-go, the doctor will treat the wrong problem.

Much of the work I've discussed with you thus far has involved using incentives as a solution to a problem. Incentives can also be used to help diagnose a problem from early on, much like blood tests can help diagnose a disease. When companies or governments try to solve the wrong problem, you can imagine the consequences that could reverberate not only financially but also socially through changed policies that may not be appropriate or effective.

Solving the wrong problem could also be the result of a wrong perspective (see the deer in the figure).

This part of the book uses four examples to discuss how incentives can be used to better understand why people do what they do. Use incentives from the start to correctly diagnose the problem, and then you can begin to work toward a solution.

13

Are US Students Really So Bad?

Monday morning, 8 a.m. Fifteen-year-old Tyler strolls into his tenth-grade class to see thirty desks with closed packets set on top of them. His yawn turns into a groan. This can't be good. Walking over to the back row, he plops himself down into the hard plastic seat and slouches, waiting for everyone else to trickle in. He sees Mr. Grossman at the chalkboard, writing "Start Time" and "End Time," but Tyler holds onto the hope that it's not what he thinks. No such luck. As soon as the last student arrives, Mr. Grossman announces that their school had been randomly selected to participate in the Programme for International Student Assessment (PISA). The test will take three hours. But then, Tyler learns that the results will not affect his grades at all. No one he cares about will ever know about his performance on the test. He will not get his score back, and neither will his parents nor his school. Mr. Grossman starts the clock. *Let's get this over with*, Tyler thinks.

Tyler's done long before the three-hour mark. After all, he has absolutely no incentive to want to take this test or to do well on it. He's *fifteen*—the US national ranking on standardized tests means next to nothing to him. He's zoned out by the time you get to the word "rankings." Tyler's apathy toward the PISA is probably shared by many of his peers.

Nonetheless, so much weight is put onto these standardized tests in the field of education. They're regarded as an accurate measurement of student learning. Policy makers are increasingly interested in using student assessments as a way to evaluate the success of the education system. The fact that students in the US perform so poorly on them has been a concern for many years now.[1]

The PISA is a triennial international survey conducted by the Organisation for Economic Co-operation and Development (OECD), which aims to evaluate education systems worldwide by testing the skills and knowledge of fifteen-year-old students.[2] More than half a million students in seventy-two countries take the test, which assesses knowledge in science, mathematics, reading, collaborative problem solving, and financial literacy.[3]

Like the US, many countries shape parts of their education policy decisions on the basis of the results of standardized tests. As we discussed before, Finland, for instance, performed unexpectedly well on the 2000 PISA; analysts have noted that its school practices are now a model for the world. Germany, on the other hand, surprisingly underperformed; then it convened a conference of ministers and proposed urgent changes to improve its education system.[4]

On the 2012 PISA, among the sixty-five participating countries and economies, US high school students ranked thirty-sixth for mathematics performance, with scores declining since 2009.[5] In response to the poor performance on such assessments, the US secretary of education at the time, Arne Duncan, quipped, "We have to see this as a wake-up call. I know skeptics will want to argue with the results, but we consider them to be accurate and reliable. . . . We can quibble, or we can face the brutal truth that we're being out-educated."[6]

Many explanations popped up around the topic in the US. Some suggested that the problem was the school system, whereas others pointed to socioeconomic factors (e.g., high rates of inequality and disadvantaged students), culture, or the way parents in the US raise their children.[7] But no one stopped to ask, Can we really conclude from this test that US students' academic ability is low? My colleagues John List, Jeffrey Livingston, Sally Sadoff, Xiangdong Qin, Yang Xu, and I explored an entirely different explanation: What if the students are just not trying as hard as students in other countries?[8]

See, test scores are based on two factors: the students' ability *and* the effort they put into the test. The common interpretation is that the results reflect differences in ability; we suggest that they also reflect differences between countries in students' effort level. If students in different countries have different levels of intrinsic motivation to perform well on the assessment test, the unmotivated students might be just as smart and capable, but their scores wouldn't necessarily reflect that on a low-stakes test. If so, the poor US performance relative to other countries may be partially explained by a difference in effort exerted on the test itself, rather than differences in actual ability. In other words, Tyler and his friends may feel no motivation to do well on a test that they don't care about, but that lack of concern doesn't mean they're not as smart and knowledgeable as their counterparts in China (who score among the top of the list) or Finland. It just means they're not putting in as much effort on the test.

To investigate whether public policy makers were wrong in their diagnosis of the problem, we set up an experiment with incentives in high schools in both the US and Shanghai, China. We chose Shanghai specifically because it was ranked first in math on the 2012 PISA, whereas the US was ranked thirty-sixth on that same test. We conducted an abridged version of the official test, with twenty-five math questions collected from previous PISA tests, and gave students twenty-five minutes to solve them.

Our manipulation was simple: In the control groups, students were simply asked to answer as many questions as they could within the twenty-five-minute time frame. These control groups mimicked the conditions students faced on the actual PISA test, in that students had no external motivation to do well on the test. The game tree shown here represents the decision

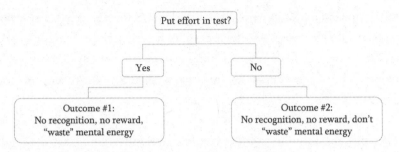

When there's no incentive to put effort into test

that students in the control groups faced. They could put in effort and get absolutely nothing extrinsic (Outcome #1 in the game tree), or they could take the test quickly and carelessly, without expending too much effort on it (Outcome #2).

Outcome #1 is no exaggeration in the US. Somewhere, somehow, someone thought teenagers would put in maximum effort on a test just for the heck of it. To reiterate, the students who are randomly selected to take the PISA test don't even get their test results back. They don't get the chance to feel proud or to be shamed into doing better. No one would tap Tyler's shoulder a year later and say, "Hey, remember that test you took when you were fifteen? You did poorly, and now the US is ranked thirty-sixth. Thanks a lot, Tyler." The fifteen-year-olds probably forgot about the test minutes after they took it and would probably never hear about it again. It should come as no surprise to any of us that many fifteen-year-olds in the US would go with Outcome #2. Reflecting on my fifteen-year-old self, I'm sure I would have.

However, for our hypothesis to be validated and to demonstrate that the problem was effort and not ability, we needed something else. Again, public policy makers tend to attribute the difference in test scores to a difference in *ability* between the Shanghai and US students.[9] Our hypothesis, on the other hand, was that Shanghai students are more likely to invest effort in low-stakes tests simply because they are asked to. Why? One reason could be that Chinese culture stresses effort, whereas US culture emphasizes innate ability. In China, the effort is additionally inspired by a sense of community and pride: students knowing that they're representing their country's academic ability on a test like the PISA motivates them to try harder in order to demonstrate their patriotism. The teachers might also underscore the significance of representing the country in such an exam and further encourage the students to try their hardest. This difference amounts to a cultural difference in attitudes, but we needed to show that in an experiment. To do so, we used—you guessed it—incentives. So, what did we offer the students to make them put in the effort that simply wasn't there before?

Monday morning, 8 a.m. Lucas strolls into his tenth-grade class to see all thirty desks with two closed packets set on top of them. He's midgroan when he notices a green edge peeking out from one of the packets. He rushes to his seat, and his suspicions are confirmed: the second packet is stuffed with twenty-five crisp $1 bills. His eyes widen. As soon as the rest of his class trickles in, Mr. Fitzgerald announces that their school has been randomly selected to take part in an experiment. The test has twenty-five questions, and for each question they answer incorrectly, $1 will be taken away. If they answer all twenty-five questions correctly, all $25 will be theirs to keep. Mr. Fitzgerald starts the clock. *Let's begin,* Lucas thinks with a determined grin.

That's right—we offered them money. In the treatment groups, just as students were sitting down, they received $25 and were told that we would take away $1 for every question they didn't answer correctly. (The Chinese students faced incentives of equivalent cash in Yuan.) With these incentives, we employed the psychological phenomenon of "loss aversion," discussed in chapter 10. Physically having the money in your hands and potentially losing it is more painful than thinking about not receiving money that is

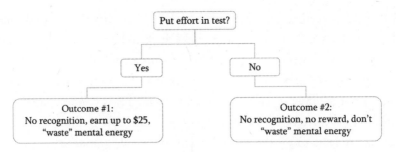

When incentive to put effort into test is added

intangible in the first place (i.e., thinking about being paid a couple of dollars less at some point in the future). Because of loss aversion, this incentive scheme is also more motivating than having the students gain $1 for every question that they answer correctly.

Our experimental design gave us four groups to compare: the US versus Shanghai students, each with or without incentives. Notably, we wanted to ensure that the incentives would influence only effort on the test itself and not preparation for the exam. To isolate effort, the treatment groups learned about the monetary incentive just before they took the test, so the only thing the students could do differently was try harder on the test itself.

Now, our token high school US students faced two very different sets of incentives when making their decision. They could put in more effort and get up to $25 (Outcome #1 in the game tree above), or they could take the test quickly and carelessly and get very little money (Outcome #2).

The students now had strong motivation to put in effort, because they had the potential to earn money by doing so. Were the incentives large enough to make Outcome #1 more attractive than Outcome #2 in the game tree? Yes.

The results confirmed our hypothesis: in response to the incentives, very little about the performance of the Shanghai students changed. Apparently, the Shanghai students were already trying as hard as they could without incentives, and the introduction of an additional incentive could not change that.

The scores of the US students, however, rose dramatically. With the incentives, the US students tackled more questions and were more likely to answer those questions correctly. We estimate that if US students received incentives on the actual PISA test, the US would cut its ranking gap with Shanghai roughly in half, improving from the current thirty-sixth place to nineteenth place.

Billions of dollars are spent based on the assumption that standardized tests such as the PISA reveal true student ability and reflect the effectiveness of the way education systems are structured in different countries. The US policies influenced by these standardized tests assume that the ability of US students is lower than the ability of students in other countries. In reality, although the results of these tests are partly influenced by ability, they are also heavily influenced by intrinsic motivations and cultural differences in attitudes toward low-stakes tests. Using incentives exposed that it is indeed not all about ability.

The PISA experiment demonstrates the importance of identifying the problem correctly by using incentives as a diagnostic tool. Note that I am not suggesting here that we should pay students to work hard on tests; I just say that incentives for a small sample can help us diagnose the problem. The first stage in solving the problem is to correctly diagnose it, as is the case when visiting your doctor. Remember the joke about the guy who thought his wife was losing her hearing? Don't simply assume you know what the source of the problem is; use experiments to test your intuition whenever and wherever you can.

TAKEAWAY: The assumption that low-stake tests reflect only differences in students' ability is rejected by the data. Public policy based on this assumption could be wasteful.

14

Overhead Aversion

How Nonprofits Get a Bad Rap

At a conference last night, you were swayed by an emotional speech from the CEO of a prominent charity for impoverished children, and you decided to donate $1,000. You wire the money in the morning, feeling a certain sense of warmth. Then you head to the airport for your flight home. When you check in, you're still feeling pretty good. You walk through the doorway of the plane and look for your economy-class seat. As you're making your way down the aisle, you pass someone familiar sitting in first class. It's the CEO of the charity you just donated to. How do you feel?

After seeing the CEO sitting in first class, you'd probably feel resentful and maybe a little mad. You might even regret sending in that check, because you feel like all you did was help pay for the CEO's first-class seat. You're not alone. Many people don't like charities with high levels of *overhead costs*—expenses that aren't directly attributed to the primary objective, including the CEO's travel expenses. With a tunnel vision on overhead costs, we often don't think about how effective the donation will be to the cause when making the decision to donate. With little time and energy for research, we base our decision largely on one question: What percentage of my donation will go to overhead? This concern highlights another question: Why are people so averse to paying overhead costs in the first place? The answer to this question is this chapter's topic. Some background is needed first before we dive in.

I feel so good for donating money so the CEO will have more leg room!

Philanthropy has always emphasized the enormous potential and impact of giving. Many of us believe in the power of giving to create meaningful change. In the US alone, individuals donated close to $300 billion to charity in 2019.[1] Even in the market of good intentions, however, it's important to provide some economic incentives to drive organizations.

In a 2013 TED Talk, the activist and fund-raiser Dan Pallotta called out the double standard that drives our broken relationship with charities. He argued that when it comes to nonprofits, we equate frugality with morality—we closely scrutinize nonprofits' spending, rewarding them for how little they spend instead of what they get done. We seem to have one rulebook for the nonprofit sector and another for the rest of the economic world. We don't judge CEOs of regular companies by how modest they are in their spending but by outcomes, such as the company's profit. This rulebook discriminates against the nonprofit sector and keeps nonprofit organizations from realizing their full potential, Pallotta argued.[2]

The double standard is especially prevalent in employee compensation. Making millions of dollars selling books or weapons in the private sector is okay, but if you made millions in personal income through your nonprofit trying to cure cancer, you'd be vilified and chastised from all sides. In the general population's view, an MBA graduate making $400,000 a year working at a bank is okay, but the CEO of a charity making that much? No way—completely unacceptable. This skewed public perception drives talent away from the field of charity. People who could make a huge difference in the nonprofit sector end up choosing the for-profit sector because they're unwilling or unable to make this lifelong economic sacrifice.

Back to overhead aversion—one of the reasons I like this topic is that as an economist, I understand that when giving, I should care about the overall impact of my dollars and not the overhead of the charity. However, as a human being, I would feel bad passing the CEO in first class on the way to my economy seat. In other words, although I understand that I should care about impact rather than overhead, in practice, I care about both. And I'm certainly not alone: studies have shown that donors strongly prefer charities with low overhead regardless of cost-effectiveness.[3]

Two reasons are typically used to explain why people don't like charities with high overhead costs. The first is that high overhead might imply that the organization is inefficient and that the people who run it are bad at their jobs. The second is that high overhead might suggest corruption within the charity, either through high consumption or embezzling. We've all heard of examples of these two types of problems in charities. Donors may therefore be wary and use a charity's overhead spending as a signal of how much the charity is actually doing for its cause.

Although I recognize the first two reasons, I also propose a third one directly related to the donor's feelings and inspired by our first-class CEO thought experiment: donors want *their* money to have a direct impact on the cause they support. They might feel that they've made a greater impact when they know their contributions went directly toward the kids' meals as opposed to the CEO's first-class seat. In other words, thinking their money went entirely to the kids amplifies their self-signal and reassures them that they are good people for helping the needy.

Ayelet Gneezy, Elizabeth Keenan, and I asked ourselves: Could this feeling be why people are averse to paying for overhead?[4] Which one of the three reasons just described is the primary driver of overhead aversion? Apart from simple curiosity, we thought a better understanding of the reason behind this overhead aversion might lead to a new way to increase donations. Our idea was motivated by a simple thought experiment: Imagine you are the CEO of a charity who just secured funds from a generous private donor to help launch a new fund-raising campaign. How would you use this initial donation as an incentive designed to maximize contributions from other potential donors?

This isn't just a hypothetical—board members in charity organizations ask this question all the time when they receive large donations. Traditionally, charities have used these initial financial gifts to solicit additional donations in two primary ways: (a) describing the initial donation as seed money ("a generous donor already gave us $10 million for the cause") or (b) using a matching model in which the charity uses the initial funds to match every new dollar donated. These two uses of initial donations—seed money and matching grants—have been studied and proven to be effective in increasing donor contributions.[5] In our experiment, we wanted to use incentives as a diagnostic tool, offering a new fund-raising approach that will reveal *why* people hate paying for overhead. To do this, we proposed a third alternative incentive: telling donors that their donation would be overhead-free.

Think back to when you walked past that CEO in first class, and imagine instead that at the conference, he and his charity promised you that 100 percent of your dollars would go toward covering meals for the needy kids. Someone else had given the nonprofit the money necessary to cover all the overhead expenses, including compensation, travel, and other administrative costs. Now when you pass the CEO in first class, you don't feel quite as bad—it wasn't your money that put him there. Your money was put directly to good use. Would that knowledge help alleviate your negative emotions?

We thought it would. And if it does indeed help, it could test our assumptions that people are averse to paying for overhead costs and are more willing to donate when they believe their money will be directly used to solve a problem. Verifying this intuition could guide us in how to better use initial funds to attract more donations and how to increase charitable giving by circumventing overhead aversion. To test this incentive in our experiment, we used the initial donation to cover the charity's overhead costs, thereby allowing all subsequent donations to be overhead-free and go directly to the cause.

Just as in the PISA example, we ran a field experiment to systematically diagnose the reasoning behind overhead aversion and test whether the standard two explanations were missing something crucial—in this case, the emotional aspect associated with the donor's own contribution. We tested the idea with a foundation specializing in education. The foundation purchased the right to send a one-time donation-request letter to forty thousand potential US donors who had donated to similar causes in the preceding five years. All participants were informed about the foundation's new initiative, were told that the cost of the new program was $20,000, and were asked to donate toward this goal.

Together with the foundation, we secured the funds needed for the incentives and created four different groups; each received a different type of incentive to donate. Specifically, each group, consisting of ten thousand individuals randomly sampled from the list of forty thousand past donors, was sent one of the following incentives:

- *Control group*: No additional incentives were offered.
- *Seed group*: Participants were told that the foundation had already secured $10,000 for the project from a private donor.

- *Match group*: Participants were told that the foundation had already se-cured $10,000 for the project from a private donor that would be used as a matching grant. This grant would match every dollar donated up to $10,000.
- *Overhead-free group*: Participants were told that the foundation had al-ready secured $10,000 for the project from a private donor that would be used to cover all overhead costs. Thus, every dollar collected would go directly toward the program.

This field experiment allowed us to learn more about what dissuades donors from making charitable contributions to companies with large over-head costs: Is it the size of the overhead cost that turns donors off, or is it who pays for it? It's important to diagnose the root cause of overhead aversion before we rush to come up with a solution. We hypothesized that if we covered all the overhead costs associated with the project, we would incentivize donors to give, because they would have the assurance that every dollar *they* give would go directly to the cause.

The figure on the next page presents the overall donations collected from the ten thousand appeals in each of the four groups. The seed and match treatments were effective in increasing the donation amount above the control, but the overhead treatment proved to be even more effective.

The result was mainly driven by the fact that more people were con-vinced to donate in the overhead-free group. Incentivizing potential donors by informing them that overhead costs would be covered by an initial dona-tion significantly increased the number of people deciding to donate and the total donation amount compared with the seed and matching incentive approaches.

These results helped us diagnose the reason behind overhead aversion; they showed that the alternative explanation was important: donors care not only about helping the cause but also about how doing so makes them feel.

Understanding the reason behind overhead aversion is not just a theo-retical exercise; it can also help increase giving. One approach would be to

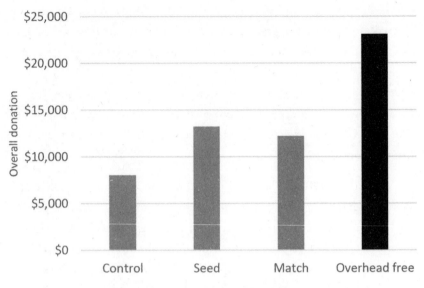

Overall donation in four types of donation incentives

"educate" small donors who give $100 on why they shouldn't care about overhead and instead concentrate on impact. However, given that there are typically many small donors, this approach would be very challenging. Furthermore, measuring a charity's impact is hard.[6]

Imagine instead that, as the person in charge of development in a hospital, you are facing a big donor who is about to give $5 million to your institution. You could tell the donor how the money will be used—on a new building or some state-of-the-art machines. Alternatively, you could try to convince the donor to use the donation to cover the overhead costs of raising money for hospital development. This conversation may allow the hospital to offer an overhead-free campaign for the smaller donors, all of whom care about whether they're giving directly to the cause. Our research suggests that this approach—using the donation as an incentive in the form of overhead-free donations for smaller donors—may help increase the number of donations and the total donation amount. By allotting the money to cover overhead, the $5 million could go much further than if it were simply put toward a new building.

A prominent example of this approach at work is a nonprofit called charity: water, which splits into two separate organizations: "charity: water," which accepts donations that go entirely to the cause, and "The Well," which consists of a dedicated group of private donors who pay for all the overhead expenses.[7] This approach addresses individuals' desire for direct impact as well as overall giving. It allows organizations to focus their efforts on convincing a handful of big donors that their money is best spent on overhead, which supports the development and maintenance of strong infrastructure. Members of the general public, on the other hand, get to feel good as they partake in overhead-free donations—a win-win solution!

More generally, the relative efficiency of paying for overhead demonstrates again how important it is to control the framing of the story. The three incentives we tested in this field experiment were exactly the same from a traditional economic point of view. However, just as in the Coca-Cola example in the introduction, the way you tell the story is important. Find the frame that people care about, and your incentives will go further than ever.

TAKEAWAY: The source of overhead aversion is not just worrying about corruption, inefficiencies, and overspending. Emphasizing donors' personal impact is important.

"Pay to Quit" Strategy

Making Employees Put Their Money Where Their Mouth Is

Imagine that you are a project manager at a midsize company over-seeing dozens of employees. Often, you assign straightforward tasks to in-dividual employees expecting well-polished results but end up receiving lackluster material. You don't doubt your workers' capabilities given their qualifications and past achievements. What could be the cause of their poor performance? There are many plausible explanations, such as a shortage of time to complete the task, health issues, and a lack of motivation. While it's easy to rule out some of the external explanations by checking in with your workers, it's almost impossible to dig out the truth when it comes to their motivations.

This is true from the first moment the employee sets foot on the com-pany premises. There's one case in negotiations when it's acceptable to lie: when interviewing for a new job, you should act excited about the pro-spective company, regardless of your true feelings. In most negotiations, the right strategy is to play it cool and try to convince the other side that even though you'd like to make a deal, it doesn't matter that much to you. Imagine walking into a used car dealership saying, "Wow! I've been looking for this model for over a year now. This is an amazing and unique car— I want it! What's the price?" You'll probably walk out paying way more than you should. However, in a job interview, the opposite is true. An enthusiastic candidate is more valuable to the company. The best strategy is to show as much excitement about the job as possible, even if it means exaggerating a bit.

Since everyone has incentives to show enthusiasm, how can you, as an employer, tell who's faking? There is no point in asking employees how excited they are to work at your company, because they're going to say, "I'm thrilled!" While some employees would tell the truth, there's no way to differentiate between the people who are truly motivated and those who aren't.

How can you determine if the problem of an employee's poor performance is motivational? To diagnose the problem with incentives, one of the strategies that we implement in behavioral economics is to create situations in which it's "incentive compatible" to tell the truth. Instead of asking people questions that will probably yield answers catered to please you, we want to motivate them to show us their true preferences with incentives.

As an employer, how can you create an environment in which employees will reveal how much they want to work for you? A few companies used an interesting "Pay to Quit" strategy. It started with Zappos offering $2,000 to their employees to quit, followed by Amazon offering up to $5,000. The video-game company Riot Games upped the ante even more, offering its employees $25,000 to quit—no strings attached.[1]

Here's Amazon CEO Jeff Bezos explaining the Pay to Quit strategy in his annual letter to shareholders:

> Pay to Quit is pretty simple. Once a year, we offer to pay our associates to quit. The first year the offer is made, it's for $2,000. Then it goes up one thousand dollars a year until it reaches $5,000. The headline on the offer is "Please Don't Take This Offer." We hope they don't take the offer; we want them to stay. Why do we make this offer? The goal is to encourage folks to take a moment and think

about what they really want. In the long-run, an employee staying somewhere they don't want to be isn't healthy for the employee or the company.[2]

A Pay to Quit strategy is a clever way of putting employees' excitement to the test by forcing them to put their "money where their mouth is." The company no longer has to rely on asking employees about their true feelings—it simply gives them a choice and observes. In most companies, disgruntled employees have no motive to reveal their true feelings. The extra monetary incentive makes hiding these true feelings costly to the employee. Pay to Quit makes lying expensive, particularly if the employees really are dissatisfied. It might be enough to make some employees choose to move on. This incentive not only serves as a diagnostic tool that reveals if the employee has motivational struggles but also brings a solution to the table: the unmotivated employee can leave happily, which is a win-win for both the employee and the company. The unmotivated employees can move on while accepting a considerable bonus; and the company benefits because the remaining employees who turned down the temptations are more committed to strive toward long-term goals.[3]

Zappos, the innovator of Pay to Quit, grew from $70 million expected annual sales in 2003 to more than $1 billion in 2008, right before it was acquired by Amazon in 2009. Bill Taylor, at *Harvard Business Review*, partially credited Zappos' success to its outstanding customer service. The company is "bursting with personality," and the exit bonus is a crucial factor in selecting the engaging and entertaining call-center employees who make their customers happy.[4]

Pay to Quit is a drastic strategy, but as a manager, you can look for signals demonstrating that your employee is staying with your company not because they have no other choice but because they prefer you over some other very attractive options.

I worked with a large consulting company that was interested in implementing the Pay to Quit incentive. The holy grail for the company's workers is to become a partner. Most of the employees who start at the company do not end up achieving this goal. They get experience and knowledge and then switch over to work at other companies, benefiting from the experience they acquired. This process is good for both the company and the employees, who usually leave on good terms and appreciating the experience.

The consulting company had a specific concern: it was pushing to make a major technological change in the way the company operated, and this change required the employees to invest time in learning the new technology, thus drastically shifting the way they worked. While some were excited about this opportunity, others didn't want to deviate from the status quo. However, the company was facing adverse selection: it couldn't know which employees wanted to make the change and which didn't. Simply asking would result in everyone saying that they're excited about the change.

Say that the company evaluates employees at the five-year mark. As discussed earlier, asking an employee whether they are happy at the company would probably be answered with "Sure!" Even if the employee is not very motivated and plans to leave soon, they wouldn't reveal this. The company can learn much more about the true preferences of the employees at this stage if it offers them a nice exit bonus. To illustrate this situation, an employee's decision process is plotted in the game tree shown here.

Employee decision when facing Pay to Quit offer: utility of employee.
If motivated enough to commit for the long haul, then Outcome #1 < Outcome #2 →
rejects exit bonus. If not, then Outcome #1 > Outcome #2 → accepts exit bonus
and leaves the company.

If the employee does want to quit, it would probably be good for the company to learn it at this stage and send that person away with a nice bonus, as a good ambassador who will have only nice things to say about their time at the company. In Outcome #1, with the unmotivated employees taking the offer, Pay to Quit helps the company avoid the cost of low-quality employees, which adds up significantly in the long run.

In Outcome #2, those who will choose to give up the bonus will show their dedication to stay and try to make it to the partner position. The result of this selection process would be that the employees who choose to stay will be the more motivated ones and those who are better at their jobs. Research in online labor markets shows that the workers retained with the Pay to Quit offer had a mean task accuracy of 28.3 percent over that of the workers in the control group, who didn't have any incentive offers.[5]

Moreover, the psychology of the situation suggests that sunk opportunity costs can affect subsequent behavior. By giving up the bonus, the employees will signal to themselves that they are serious and motivated. They will feel a need to justify to themselves that it was worth it to give up the bonus and stay by working harder and being committed to a long-term goal. A field experiment at a University of Amsterdam gym reflects this insight. Some new members of the gym were offered a full refund plus a cash payment of 10 percent of the initial subscription price to quit the gym. When compared to the control subjects, the members who received and rejected the offer of refund and cash payment were statistically more likely to visit the gym by 0.29 times a week, to resubscribe by 4 percent, and to earn higher posttreatment grades by 0.76 (on a ten-point scale).[6]

TAKEAWAY: Offering employees money to quit can filter out unmotivated employees and keep determined employees on the job longer. The signal "I'm motivated" is now credible.

16

Bribing the Self

Cheating and Self-Signaling

Have you ever gone to the mechanic with what you thought was a minor problem with your car and ended up receiving a large bill with "important repairs" that you didn't understand? I have. Have you ever gone to your physician with back pain, only to hear that the best solution for your problem was back surgery? I have. But like most of the general population, I don't have the expertise needed to judge whether these recommendations were the best for me.

As consumers, we have limited knowledge and often rely on experts' advice and recommendations to make decisions. These recommendations, however, aren't always the best for us. What can often be seen in these situations is an information asymmetry between the advisor and the consumer: the mechanic knows much more than I do about fixing cars, and the physician knows more than I do about alleviating back pain. Hence, trust is an important component of such relationships. Think about your physician: they worked hard to earn a medical degree so that they can help, not to rip you off. While the medical field is full of information asymmetry and conflicts of interest, you trust the physician to put your health at the top of their priority list.

Yet, partially due to doctors recommending unnecessary procedures for which they are directly compensated, overtreatment in the medical field is estimated to cost $210 billion in wasteful annual spending in the US.[1] Back surgery for pain, for example, isn't an anomaly. There is a growing number of surgical options available as solutions for back pain, many of which have been shown to be unnecessary and even harmful.[2] In addition to unnecessary surgeries, a large portion of medical waste comes from the overprescription of drugs. Studies have shown that doctors who receive payments from the medical industry tend to prescribe drugs differently than their colleagues who do not.[3] How could physicians live with putting their own financial interest before their patients' health?

It's not only physicians. Financial advisors are also often directly compensated for certain products. While some advisors may ignore their own incentives and give an unbiased recommendation to their clients, many give biased advice to increase their own profits—sometimes at the expense of their clients' best interests. As with physicians, the compensation structure of the financial advisor is important. The two that are most common are fee-only and fee-based structures. Advisors with a fee-only structure are compensated solely for their advisory services, usually as a percentage of assets, and not for the financial products they recommend. On the other hand, advisors with a fee-based structure are often affiliated with registered broker-dealers or insurance companies, so they earn commissions based on the products they recommend.[4] These commission-earning advisors often try to conceal this behavior from their clients. What is behind the advisors' decision to recommend a financially selfish product while sacrificing their clients' benefits? How can they reconcile monetary gain and the threat to their professional integrity?

Experts might feel bad if they give bad advice; in our terminology, they could receive a negative self-signal. Upon reflection, the advisor could think that they're not a great person for deceiving the consumer.

"Fortunately," there is a solution. To attenuate this conflict between monetary gain and self-image, advisors may *self-deceive* by convincing themselves that their advice is ethical. A physician may convince themselves that a surgery doesn't only maximize profits but is also the best course of action for their patient.

The trick for successful self-deception is to have room for ambiguity or subjectivity in the recommendation. With respect to whether a surgery is needed, for example, it is often a subjective assessment whether surgery is the optimal method to alleviate a patient's back pain, and there's usually no counterfactual to suggest that the surgery is excessive. Using this ambiguity, experts have their ways to convince themselves that their recommendations—which maximize their own material gains—are actually the best course of action for their clients, salvaging their otherwise-damaged self-image.

My colleagues Silvia Saccardo, Marta Serra-Garcia, Roel van Veldhuizen, and I wanted to understand how this self-deception works and use incentives to diagnose the psychology behind biased recommendations—how people can give selfish advice based on their own incentives while still believing that they have behaved ethically.[5] To do that, we created a simple Advice Game in which advisors are tasked with recommending one of two investment options, A or B, to an uninformed client. We systematically manipulated the advisors' ability to self-deceive—that is, how well the advisors can justify to themselves their profit-maximizing recommendations, and measured the magnitude of the bias in their advice.

The Advice Game we created is simple. The advisor sees two options. Investment A is a 50-50 lottery between $2 and $4. Investment B is a 50-50 lottery between $1 and $7. We created these two lotteries such that the expected payoff of B ($4) is higher than that of A ($3). However, B has a higher variance. Think for a second: Which investment would you choose for yourself?

Our advisors in the game were asked to choose which investment to recommend to the clients. We didn't inform the clients about the investment, so only the advisors knew about them, and the clients' only available information was the advisors' recommendation.

And here comes our manipulation to test for self-deception. In the first treatment, the advisors had no incentives to recommend either of the investments. This group was the control in the experiment. In this case, 31 percent of the advisors recommended investment A, and the rest recommended investment B. Evidently, investment B is preferable to most advisors.

We then contrasted this result with two treatments in which the advisors had a $1 incentive to recommend investment A. That is, if the advisors recommended investment A, then they would automatically receive a bonus of $1. Would that be enough to bias their recommendations? Turns out that it depends on *when* they learn about the extra incentive.

In one treatment, called "before," we first told the advisors about their incentives and only then told them about the investment details and asked them for their recommendations. In contrast, in the "after" treatment, we changed the order of information. We first told the advisors about the investment options, asked them to think (not tell us, just think) which one they believe is better, and only then told them about the extra incentives to recommend A.

The figure below presents the flow of the experiment for the advisor.

Why did we vary the time when the advisors are informed about the incentives? If the advisors are informed about the incentives *before* having

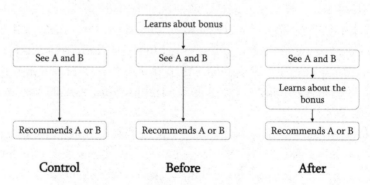

Three types of advisor decision timeline

a chance to evaluate the investments, they can engage in self-deception. They can distort their beliefs by convincing themselves that recommending A, and earning the incentives, is also the best option for the clients. Knowing that they'll receive a bonus if they recommend A, they are already biased when they read the investments' description. They look for ways to justify choosing A and convince themselves that the client would actually prefer A. They can, for example, justify the benefits of A by claiming that it is ambiguous which option is better because it depends on the client's risk preference, and since A has a lower variance, it's a safer option for the client.

If we reverse the order and tell them about their incentives only *after* they make this evaluation (which is probably that B is better for the client), they can't go back in time and convince themselves that A is better. If the advisor privately evaluates the investments before learning about the incentives, engaging in self-deception becomes harder. In such a case, the advisor can no longer recommend the incentivized investment while preserving a positive self-image.

Here's what we found: as mentioned earlier, only 31 percent of the advisors recommended A in control, when they had no incentives to recommend it. This percentage almost doubled to 61 percent in the before treatment, in which we first told them that they will earn more money if they recommend A. However, in the after treatment, they ended up choosing A only 33 percent of the time—which is not a statistically significant difference compared to the rate of choosing A in the control. Using incentives, we successfully diagnosed the dilemma of "ethical" biased recommendations and uncovered the psychological process in which advisors engage in self-deception in order to maintain a positive self-perception in the face of selfish advice.

To tie these results back to physicians who recommend unnecessary treatments, it might be that they really believe that this is the right way to go. They know about their incentives before they make the recommendation but don't think that this self-interest affects their choices. Data support these kinds of biased beliefs. For example, when a reporter asked doctors to comment on findings regarding overtreatment, "several doctors who received large payments from industry and had above-average prescribing rates of brand-name drugs said they are acting in patients' best interest."[6] Our research shows that they might really believe that they act also in the best interest of their patients. But they are probably influenced by their incentives and use self-deception to avoid the negative self-signal and protect their self-image.

This finding sheds a light on the decision process behind biased recommendations and presents a challenge to people who create systems in which informed advisors can bias their recommendations and thus results. One solution is to create or partake in systems in which advisors don't have a financial stake in the choices a client makes. For example, you might consider asking a different physician who has no financial ties with your decision for a second opinion. Another solution is to design procedures that reinforce the role of self-image costs to reduce unethical behavior by ethical-but-biased individuals.

TAKEAWAY: Self-deception allows advisors to recommend the options that benefit them at the expense of the clients without feeling bad about it.

PART FIVE

How Incentives Lead to Behavior Change

● ● ●

It has been my experience that folks who have no vices have very few virtues.

—*Abraham Lincoln*

"10, 9, 8, . . . 3, 2, 1. Happy New Year!" As the clock strikes twelve, Sandra and her friends shout and jump in unison, celebrating the beginning of a new chapter. Sandra, with a determined look in her eyes, announces to her friends, "This is the year! I'm going to get in shape and lose at least fifteen pounds." Her supportive friends cheer with encouragement. Inspired by Sandra's declaration, many share their own New Year's resolutions, ranging from saving more money to eating healthier. Everyone leaves the party feeling energized and motivated. Fast-forward a couple of weeks into the year, however: Sandra has already canceled her new gym membership, claiming that work is getting too busy and it's a waste of money to continue subscribing.

It doesn't have to be a New Year's resolution. Consider fifty-five-year-old John, who goes in for his annual doctor's appointment. One look at his doctor's face, and John can already tell there's bad news. His doctor tells him that he's thirty pounds overweight, prediabetic, and at high risk for a stroke.

The doctor advises John to take a prescribed medication, eat healthier, and walk for at least thirty minutes a day. John leaves his doctor's office with this new resolution, determined to change. Flash-forward to just two days later, and John's on the couch, watching reruns of *Friends*. The only steps he's taken are the ones on the short path from the couch to the fridge, for a cold bottle of beer.

It's easy to dismiss Sandra and John, to scoff and say they're weak willed or lack self-control, but it's not just them. Many of us have experienced short-lived resolution. While it's easy to declare "new year, new me" and set ambitious long-term goals, it's hard to follow through and stay committed. US gym data reflect this phenomenon: more gym memberships are purchased in January than any other month, representing around 11 percent of the total annual memberships purchased.[1] Many people, however, are like Sandra; they aren't good at keeping the momentum going. Around 50 percent of new US gym-goers give up their memberships by the end of January, and only 22 percent of them make it to October.[2]

It seems as if people are overconfident about their future self-control and therefore overestimate their ability to change their behavior, such as visiting the gym more often. This overconfidence could be very costly. For example, Stefano DellaVigna and Ulrike Malmendier, both professors at UC Berkeley, analyzed the contractual choice of 7,752 US health-club members over three years and found that the members with monthly subscription fees of over $70 only attend on average 4.3 times per month, equivalent to paying more than $17 per visit. According to their calculations, 80 percent of these members would have been better off using a ten-visit pass, paying $10 per visit instead. Throughout their membership, the average foregone savings added up to $600; DellaVigna and Malmendier called this behavior "paying not to go to the gym."[3]

There are two possible reasons for this overpaying behavior. As I already mentioned, the first is overconfidence: when signing up, I'm overly optimistic and think I'm going to use the gym much more often than I do later. The other reason could be a sort of game that I play against myself. I know that in the future I'll be tempted not to get off the couch and go to the gym. And if I opt to purchase the individual visit passes and they cost me $10 every time I visit the gym, I'll be more likely to end up staying on the couch. So I prefer to pay the subscriptions in advance to ensure that my future self will have less excuse not to go.

Going back to John's time on the couch just a couple of days after his doctor's visit, this type of behavior illustrates the challenge that behavioral economists and policy makers face when trying to use incentives to change habits. Can you think of a stronger motivation than the one John faces? His situation is quite literally life or death. John's failure to change his behavior is probably not due to a lack of information or motivation. The terrifying information that he is prediabetic is probably still fresh in his mind, and the motivation at stake is already so much stronger than anything else that can be offered by others. After all, John doesn't need to run a marathon to be considerably healthier; he just needs to walk for half an hour a day.

In this space, where motivation for change is already so strong, behavioral scientists try to enter with our extrinsic incentives. A growing effort to try to find what works and what doesn't is on its way. A notable group in this space is the Behavior Change for Good Initiative, led by the economist Katherine Milkman and the psychologist Angela Duckworth, both from the University of Pennsylvania. Milkman and Duckworth create interdisciplinary teams of academic experts, introduce them to large organizations, and go out together to test what works at scale in behavior change. They conduct large studies, simultaneously testing the scientific team's best ideas for changing a target behavior. I find this approach, which includes behavioral interventions and incentives, very promising.

Academic knowledge can also be translated into economic success. A few years ago, a then twenty-two-year-old Samantha Pantazopoulos, who had just graduated from college, asked to meet with me to discuss an app she had in mind. We spent an hour in my office during which Sam described her idea. I often meet people with interesting ideas, but this was different. The idea was interesting, but more than that, it was clear that Sam is a force of nature. She convinced her cousin Dylan Barbour (from season 6 of ABC's *Bachelor in Paradise*, for those who follow) to join her to cofound Vizer.[4] Their idea is simple: create an app that tracks fitness activity via smartphone, Apple Watch, or Fitbit, and use this data to incentivize users to complete daily fitness goals. One part of the incentive they offer is social: each time a user meets the goal, a meal is donated and distributed by Feeding America. We discussed this kind of social incentive in chapter 11. The second part is a more traditional incentive: when members meet the goal, they earn a point, which they can later redeem for a healthy reward for themselves. That was four years ago. Dylan and Sam keep developing their app and are becoming an important player in the wellness world.

But before we discuss how incentives can make a difference, there is one point to clarify: Is the fact that people fail to change their behavior a mistake? Is the fact that John doesn't walk half an hour a day or that Sandra can't accomplish her exercise goal a mistake? According to traditional economists, yes: people are assumed to be perfectly rational creatures who can seamlessly incorporate and react to new information. My approach is different. I'm not here to judge whether something is a mistake. I ask a much simpler question: How can I help? I don't know if Sandra and John are being irrational and making mistakes; I just know that they want to change their behavior, but for one reason or another, they fail. The challenge is to find a way to implement behavior change in such a way that people like Sandra and John would choose and successfully commit to it.

This part of the book discusses the psychology behind people's inability to sustain behavior change and how incentives can be leveraged to promote desirable habits and reduce maladaptive habits in the long run. The fundamental question is how can we motivate people to change a behavior that they want to change and to do so with the lowest cost possible. Our money can go a long way, particularly if the incentives also help to form habits in the long run. Good interventions result in behavior change that sticks even after the incentives are removed. In this part I outline four channels through which incentives can impact behavior change. This part is based on work I did with Agne Kajackaite and Stephan Meier.[5]

A large amount of effort is devoted to trying to create long-term behavioral change in various domains, and incentives may help. Understanding how incentives interact with other motivations is key to the success of efforts such as increasing health outcomes, productivity, environmental protection, and savings.

17

Creating Habits

Change Happens One Step at a Time . . . Literally

John wants to exercise for an hour a day. When he first visits the gym, he has a rough time. He struggles to exercise for even ten minutes and goes home sweaty and spent. He wakes up the next day extremely sore, still more flab than ab. But if he keeps going to the gym, he'll build up his "habitual stock," which is a fancy way of saying that he'll get some practice and experience. Exercising may become more enjoyable (or at least less painful) as the benefits become tangible, visible, and clear—he will feel better and stronger in daily life, lose a couple of pounds, and be able to see the faint outlines of leg muscles. Evidence suggests that starting is the hard part.

Incentives can help in getting people to start something new, which helps build up this stock of behavior. If John earns a reward each time he visits the gym, he will have stronger extrinsic motivation to actually start going to the gym. Even if he suffers a lot at the beginning, he will eventually suffer less, or even start enjoying it, and be more likely to continue even after the incentives are removed. In the next sections, we'll discuss experiments using incentives to promote exercising, showing that paying people to start going to the gym pays off even after the incentives are removed. This evidence supports the notion of habitual stock, suggesting that exercising slowly becomes enjoyable for those who get off the couch and continue to exercise more. The general rule we've learned is that incentives can help

Habit formation

people start an activity, build up that habitual stock of behavior, and hence begin to sustain long-term behavior.

Paid to Sweat

For researchers like me, a paper is a bit like a child: the details of its development are always vivid in my mind. The story of how my interest in "incentives to exercise" developed starts at a conference in Tucson. My friend Gary Charness and I were in a hot tub near a pool, admiring the bountiful Arizonan mountains and chatting about incentives. This conversation happened after I had published papers on how incentives can destroy one's intrinsic motivation to do things simply because they're good and not because one's paid to do them. In particular, we discussed whether we can "bribe" our kids to change their behavior. In some cases, it was clear that we can do so with no long-term problems.

If you try to get your kids off diapers, for example, giving them a reward every time they go to the toilet might speed up the process. Then, once they're off diapers, you can stop bribing them, probably without having to worry that they'll revert to using diapers. In general, such behavioral changes that are "one and done" are easier to influence with incentives. The harder change is the one that needs a repeated action: for example, it is easy to get children to read a book, but it's harder to make them regularly enjoy reading books.

Gary and I then started discussing exercising, a hard behavioral change that probably requires repeated action. Why are there periods in our lives when we are more likely to exercise and then other periods when we can't get ourselves to move? We thought that giving people incentives to start exercising and keeping them for a while might create a habit that will stick after we stop paying them. So we designed a field experiment to test whether incentives can indeed create exercising habits.

We had a few different treatments in our experiment; I'll discuss the more interesting ones here. In the experiment, we offered university students incentives to attend the campus gym.[1] Students came to our lab, read some material about how important it is to exercise, and then were promised $25 to visit the gym at least once during the next week. We verified their attendance using the gym's entrance records. When the students returned to the laboratory in the following week, we randomly divided them into two treatments. One was simply a control group. The students in the second treatment were promised an additional $100 (paid upon completion) if they visited the gym eight more times during the next four weeks. We were able to observe the students' gym attendance before, during, and after the intervention.

Did paying students to visit the gym work? Of course it did. Our students would do almost anything for $100, but that wasn't what we were after.

We wanted to see what would happen to gym visits *after* we stopped paying them to go to the gym. Our hypothesis was that getting people started and accumulating this "stock of behavior" would make them more likely to keep exercising, because within a short time after starting the exercise routine, going to the gym would become less painful and more enjoyable.

We were testing the idea that the first few gym visits are costly and not so much fun but that after four weeks, this cost-benefit changes and people keep going even without incentives.

As expected, we found a very large spike in gym visits for the incentives group that lasted until week five, when we stopped the incentives. The interesting part is what happens after: during weeks five to twelve, after we stopped paying participants in the incentivized group, they were twice as likely to visit the gym, on average. This improvement in gym attendance was entirely driven by the changes from people who had not been regular gym attendees previously. In other words, students who already visited the gym regularly before our study weren't especially encouraged by our incentives.

Our experiments indicate that it is indeed feasible to promote the formation of good habits by offering monetary compensation for a sufficient number of occurrences. As we discussed before, doing so appears to move some people past the threshold of stock of behavior needed to engage in consistent exercising. By establishing that incentives to exercise work, the paper based on the study sparked a conversation about using monetary interventions to promote exercising and habit formation. Let's look at some subsequent studies that replicated and furthered our experiment and provided additional insights on habit formation.

Naive Mistakes

Our study left open questions that were investigated in follow-up studies. First were Dan Acland, a professor at Berkeley, and Mathew Levy, a professor at the London School of Economics.[2] Their main question was, What do people who are incentivized to exercise think about their future gym visits? Do they believe that after such intervention, they'll become frequent gym-goers? And are they right in their predictions?

Acland and Levy also incentivized participants to attend the gym for a month and used a similar experimental design to ours. We have established that incentivized students continued to attend the gym more than the non-incentivized students for weeks after the incentives ended, but does this exercising habit decay over time? Acland and Levy were able to collect longer attendance data, stretching from thirty-seven weeks before to thirty-three weeks after the intervention. The entire period included three full school semesters as well as summer and winter breaks, which paints a fuller picture for monitoring habit formation and decay. This study replicated our findings: incentivizing gym attendance indeed encourages short-run habit formation. However, good things don't last forever: the effect largely decayed over the course of the four-week winter vacation. This suggests that while incentives can lead to habit formation after an intervention, their effect has an expiration time. It also suggests that in order to achieve a long-term effect, we need more than just a jump-start.

To answer the main question regarding participants' beliefs about future attendance, Acland and Levy elicited the participants' pre- and post-treatment predictions of their attendance after the intervention. The participants were asked, before and after the incentive period, how often they would continue to attend the gym after the intervention had ended. Acland and Levy found that the participants had self-control problems that were generated by present bias (a concept that we'll explore fully in chapter 19) and, more importantly, that the participants were partially naive about their self-control problems: they substantially overpredicted their future gym attendance. This result shows that people are not fully aware of their lack of self-control and tend to overestimate their future selves when it comes to committing to exercising.

These kinds of beliefs can explain people's short-lived resolutions and the aforementioned finding that people purchase monthly and yearly health-club memberships when they should instead stick to single-visit passes, given their actual attendance: they naively believe that they will use the gym much more than they actually do.

Tie Me to the Mast!

Given self-control problems, how can we make sure people like Sandra and John follow through, using incentive programs? One way is to use commitment devices, a way to lock oneself into committing to a plan that is otherwise hard to follow through using willpower alone. One of the oldest examples comes from Greek mythology: The Sirens were dangerous creatures who specialized in luring nearby sailors with their charming music and voices. Odysseus, the legendary hero and king of Ithaca, came up with a strategy to avoid disaster: he tied himself to the ship's mast to prevent him from being entranced and jumping overboard after hearing the song of the Sirens.[3]

In 2015, the economists Heather Royer, Mark Stehr, and Justin Sydnor utilized commitment devices in a field experiment to treat gym attendees' self-control problem. The participants in their experiments were one thousand employees at a Fortune 500 company.[4] The employees were randomly allocated to one of two groups: one group was the control, with no incentives; in the other, incentivized group, participants were offered $10 per on-site exercise facility visit for up to three visits each week.

As expected, the incentives worked, showing a positive effect of incentives on forming exercising habits. Replicating the results of the experiment that Gary and I conducted, the positive effect was also only for people who did not go to the gym at all prior to the experiment. People who had gone to the gym before reverted to their previous level of gym attendance after the incentives were removed.

The main intervention in the experiment happened after the incentive period was completed. Half of the participants in the incentivized group were offered a self-funded commitment device: they could choose to put up their own money. Willing participants pledged that they would continue to use the on-site fitness facility and not skip more than fourteen days of exercising in a row over the following two months. The deposit would be donated to charity if the users didn't meet the declared exercise goal. Basically, users were offered to "tie themselves to the mast" and commit to reaching the exercise goal they have set for themselves. They had nothing to gain by risking their money, apart from convincing their future selves to go to the gym—otherwise they would lose their own money.

In addition to the financial loss aversion at play, the participants also experienced the power of self-signaling: breaking the commitment goal after formally pledging to stick to it would negatively signal to themselves that they are weak-willed and damage their self-image. Being able to keep their promises to themselves, on the other hand, positively signals that they are determined individuals, thus boosting their self-image and encouraging them to continuously exercise. Was the commitment device effective? Yes! It led to habit formation and improved the habit formation's lasting impact. Over the two months after the original incentive ended, the group that took up the commitment contract retained half of their incentive-induced increase in exercising. In other words, the "expiration time" of the incentive program was significantly extended with the help of a commitment option, which comes with no additional cost. This long-run effect on habit formation lasted even after the commitment contract period had ended, which suggests that commitment devices can be leveraged to urge individuals to continue to exercise after the intervention.

Better Together

Imagine two scenarios, both taking place on lazy Sunday afternoons: In the first, while you have promised yourself to go to the gym today, your couch is feeling extra comfortable. In the other, you're also relaxing on the couch but suddenly receive a text from your friend saying that she is on her way to the gym. You remember that you have talked about working out together with her. In which situation are you more likely to get your butt off the couch? Can friends encourage gym attendance and facilitate exercise incentives and potentially habit formation?

In 2010, the economists Philip Babcock and John Hartman investigated this question by focusing on the social effects of exercise incentives in their field experiment.[5] They surveyed and incentivized college students to go to the campus recreation center. In order to test the social effects, Babcock and Hartman had the students fill out a friendship survey prior to the experiment. In this survey, students marked, from a list of names of students participating in the experiment, the names of the people they knew. The experimenters were thus able to elicit a detailed friendship network from the participants, all of whom lived in the same residence hall. The students were then randomly assigned into either a treatment or a control group. Those who were selected into the treatment group were promised $80 if they visited the university gym at least eight times in the next four weeks.

After randomization, individual participants were naturally exposed to a random number of treated and untreated peers. To analyze the social effects of exercise incentives, Babcock and Hartman then looked at how this random variation in the numbers of treated and untreated peers to which the participant was exposed influenced the effectiveness of the incentives. In line with the reasoning illustrated by our initial scenarios, their intuition was that an incentivized participant would visit the gym more if they were friends with more incentivized peers.

Knowing more people who were incentivized to exercise increased gym attendance. The authors found that the participants who had been incentivized to exercise increased their gym attendance more if they had more friends who had also received incentives to exercise. On the other hand, incentivized students attended the gym less if they had more friends in the unincentivized control group. It seems that people's exercising behavior was very much influenced by that of their friends.

If like-minded friendships could boost gym attendance, could a dependent partner motivate gym-goers? In 2017, Simon Condliffe, Ebru Işgın, and Brynne Fitzgerald, economists at West Chester University, designed an experiment to test whether teamwork increases exercise.[6] They recruited college students to visit the student recreation center on campus in a similar way to the experiments described earlier. The most interesting comparison in this experiment was between an individual treatment, in which students participated in the experiment without a partner, and a treatment in which each student was randomly assigned a partner. In the partner treatment, the two participants were tied together financially: each team was only eligible for the incentive if both teammates met the required goal. The researchers found that when students were incentivized as a team, they attended the gym significantly more.

These findings suggest that social networks and a peer's presence can enhance the effect of incentives for habit formation. The implications are also interesting regarding when you want to pick up your exercising routine: coordinate with a friend, and you might end up being more successful in actually exercising. This network effect might also act as a commitment device, which we discussed in the previous section. You might not want to go to the gym now; but you know your friend is waiting for you, and you don't want to disappoint them.

This commitment not to disappoint your friend reflects the power of social signaling. If you cancel your exercise plans with your friend at the last minute, you signal to your friend that you're not reliable, which damages your social image. On the other hand, consistently keeping your promises and sticking to the plan boosts your social image, thus motivating you to exercise more. My friend told me a story that demonstrates this nicely: He wanted to go to the gym but couldn't get himself to do it. His wife got him a voucher for three months of biweekly fitness classes with a personal trainer.

He never missed a class. The personal trainer served as a commitment device; if my friend couldn't make it, he had to explain to the nice trainer why. To sum up, doing it together might be more successful than doing it alone.

Routine or Flexibility?

Stable habits are developed from routines. By consistently following a set pattern of repeated behaviors, there is less cognitive effort required for an individual to engage in the desired behavior. Think about your morning routine: for years, you've had a more or less regular morning routine that's developed into an efficient process. With the fluid mental association in place, eventually the performance of the routine behavior becomes largely automatic.[7] Now, while the previously mentioned experiments incentivized regular gym attendance, the participants all had a flexible incentive schedule: they had to attend the gym multiple times a week to be eligible for financial compensation, but there wasn't any specification on a particular time window for exercising. Could enforcing strict routines of gym attendance lead to more persistent exercising than offering flexible incentives does?

Recently, a team of economists from Harvard and Wharton (John Beshears, Hae Nim Lee, Katherine Milkman, Robert Mislavsky, and Jessica Wisdom) investigated this question in a field experiment with 2,508 employees at Google, which, like many other companies, is interested in getting its employees to utilize its workplace gyms more regularly.[8] At the start of the experiment, participating employees all selected a daily, two-hour window that was best suited for exercising, and they would receive daily exercising reminders at the beginning of this window on every weekday. To test the effectiveness of routine incentives compared to that of flexible incentives, the participants were then randomly assigned to one of three types of treatments: a control group with no incentives; flexible groups, in which participants were paid if they exercised at least thirty minutes at a workplace gym on any weekday; or routine groups, in which participants were only paid if they exercised for at least thirty minutes within their chosen two-hour window at a workplace gym on any weekday. The difference between the second and third treatment is whether the participants had the flexibility to choose when to exercise each day.

To an economist, it seems obvious that flexibility is better. After all, it provides more options. As just discussed, psychologists, however, might guess that fixing the time would help in creating a routine. So, what was more effective at getting the employees to the gym, strict routines or a flexible schedule? As it turns out, participants who had the flexibility to choose when to exercise each day exercised significantly more than the participants who had to follow the prespecified exercising windows. This result continued after the incentives were removed. Contrary to past psychological theories and to our intuition, this finding suggests that when people follow an exercise schedule at an equal frequency but with a restricted routine, they tend to exercise less and form weaker long-term habits.

Before you reactively abandon your exercising routines and start visiting the gym during spontaneous free time, however, it's important to note that this result is quite context dependent. The Google working environment is fast-paced, and the work schedule can be very uncertain and shifting. It is, therefore, hard for its employees to stick to a preidentified narrow two-hour window of free time that won't be disrupted by unexpected agendas, even for $7 per gym visit. Routine incentives may very well be effective for habit formation when utilized by people with more stable and consistent schedules and work environments.

TAKEAWAY: Incentives could jump-start gym visits and build up a long-term exercising habit. When possible, add other psychological reinforcements, such as commitment devices and social networks, to enhance incentives and prolong the habit.

18

Breaking Habits

Kicking Bad Behaviors to the Curb

In the same vein as creating habits, incentives can help *break habits*. John may be exercising more now, thanks to the help of incentives, but his beer consumption hasn't changed, and his doctor isn't happy about it. If past consumption can help create habits by building up a stock of behavior, could reducing consumption "kill" habits by reducing the stock of behavior?

Yes, indeed. Good and bad habits are both created by continuous consumption. Just as increasing consumption can create habits, reducing consumption can "kill" habits by reducing the stock of behavior. Think back to the exercising example: enjoyment from going to the gym today is probably influenced more by gym visits from the past month than by gym visits from a year ago. Thus, the best predictor of whether you'll go to the gym next week is if you have been there this week, not a year ago. Similarly, the best predictor of whether you'll smoke cigarettes today is if you smoked yesterday. If the habitual stock of behavior decays over time, incentivizing people to stop a certain activity for a while reduces the probability that they will return to their old habits once the incentives are removed.

How can incentives help break John's beer-drinking habit? If John were to receive an incentive for each day that he drinks only water, he might stop drinking beer or at least break the habit of drinking a can as soon as he comes home from work. In other words, a potential way to kill a habit is to incentivize quitting that activity *for a while*. That way, the habitual stock will begin to decrease. The goal is to deplete this stock such that by the time the incentives are removed, the stock will have decreased to the point where the activity is discontinued. Later I'll discuss a practical way in which John can incentivize himself to quit drinking beer.

This chapter focuses on an incredibly prevalent yet harmful habit: smoking. About one of every five deaths in the US each year is caused by cigarette smoking.[1] In addition to about half a million deaths annually, smoking-related illnesses accumulate billions of dollars in health-care costs and unmeasurable physical harms. Most smokers are aware of these negative consequences, and as many as 70 percent of smokers want to quit smoking, but only about 3 percent of them succeed every year.[2] Why is it so hard to quit smoking? Unlike exercising, the pleasure of smoking is immediate, whereas the painful consequences come in the future. Here's how incentive cessation programs try to help.

Paid to Quit Smoking

In 2009, Kevin Volpp and colleagues ran a field experiment at a multinational company in which they paid employees to quit smoking.[3] Companies that are interested in getting employees to exercise more have a direct economic motivation to get their employees to quit smoking as well: smoking leads to increased health-care costs and decreased worker productivity.

The first step in the experiment was to randomly assign 878 employees to either the control condition, in which employees only receive information about smoking-cessation programs, or the treatment condition, in which employees receive the same information about programs plus financial incentives.

To receive the incentives for quitting, the employees in the incentivized group had to pass biochemical tests. They were promised $100 for completing the smoking-cessation program, $250 for quitting smoking within six months after study enrollment, and another $400 for staying abstinent for an additional six months after the initial cessation. The payment timing was chosen that way because most relapses happen within the first month of a quitting attempt, and about 90 percent of relapses happen within the first six months.[4]

The money was enough to get the employees to drop smoking. The incentivized participants had significantly higher rates of enrolling in the smoking-cessation program, completing the program, and quitting smoking within the first six months after study enrollment. As you probably understand by now, we care about the long-term effects. Previous literature on smoking cessation suggests that once a smoker quits for one year or longer, they have a 95 percent likelihood of staying abstinent over a twenty-month period.[5] The incentives were effective at getting smokers over this momentous yearlong hurdle. Incentivized participants had significantly higher rates of smoking cessation than did the unincentivized employees in the control group nine to twelve months after enrollment, as well as fifteen to eighteen months after enrollment, after the incentives concluded.

While the results are encouraging, the long-term cessation rate of the incentivized participants was only 9 percent. It is still a success given that the unincentivized group had a significantly lower cessation rate of 3.6 percent. This suggests that financial incentives not only can motivate people to join smoking-cessation programs and get them to quit smoking in the short-term but can also help smokers to avoid relapses and break the habit in the long run, even after the incentives are removed.

Save the Baby

While I have continuously emphasized the importance of long-term effects, sometimes short-run success can be an achievement in itself. For pregnant mothers, for example, quitting smoking during their pregnancy is important, even if they relapse postpartum. Smoking during pregnancy is the leading preventable cause of poor pregnancy outcomes in the US, as it leads to tissue damage in an unborn baby's lungs and brain, a higher chance of miscarriage and preterm delivery, and lower birth weight, just to name a few.[6]

While many interventions have experimented with informational strategies, such as receiving advice from health-care professionals and learning about smoking-related hazards in self-help materials, they didn't work that well in changing cessation rates.[7] This isn't particularly surprising, since pregnant mothers probably know and understand that smoking could harm their babies, but any damage caused is invisible until the distant future. Amanda, a pregnant smoker, talked about her experience; when asked about her smoking habits as a mother, she confessed, "I knew that babies were born with poor health issues because of smoking. I also knew a lot of people who smoked while they were pregnant, who all had healthy babies." She thought that "it won't happen to [her]" and she "wasn't able to stop."[8] Could financial incentives, then, carry smoking mothers safely through their pregnancies? If so, what kind of incentives should we offer?

In 2012, a team of health researchers led by Stephen Higgins investigated this question by using incentives in the form of vouchers redeemable for retail items.[9] They randomly assigned fifty-eight pregnant mothers to one of two conditions. Both groups received vouchers. For the control group, the voucher was simply a gift, regardless of whether the participants smoked. Mothers in the contingent condition, on the other hand, earned a voucher only when their smoking abstinence was verified biochemically.

The abstinence-monitoring frequency was initially daily and gradually decreased to every other week throughout the pregnancy. On the basis of these tests, the contingent vouchers' value started at $6.25 and escalated by $1.25 per abstinence verified, until it reached the maximum value of $45. If the mothers failed a biochemical test, the value of contingent vouchers would reset back to their initial low level, but two consecutive negative tests would restore the voucher value back to the pre-reset level. This incentive structure slowly builds up a positive monetary momentum that rewards continuous abstinence, and failures are punished while still allowing redemption. Smoking mothers were thus financially encouraged to stay abstinent for as long as possible and bounce back if they relapsed. On the other hand, women in the control group received noncontingent vouchers with a constant value of $11.50 per visit before childbirth and $20 per visit after childbirth.

Which form of voucher is more effective? As you might've intuited, the contingent vouchers increased seven-day abstinence at the end of pregnancy to 37 percent, which is significantly greater than the 9 percent for the noncontingent voucher group. What about the long-term effects? For mothers twelve week postpartum, the increased abstinence was 33 percent in the contingent group compared to 0 percent for noncontingent vouchers. In the twenty-four-week postpartum assessment, which was twelve weeks after the voucher incentives stopped, the mothers in the contingent voucher condition still had a seven-day abstinence rate of 27 percent, compared to 0 percent of mothers in the noncontingent group.

Put Money (Instead of Cigarettes) Where Your Mouth Is

As we've seen in the case of pregnant smokers who received unconditional incentives, relying solely on self-control to quit smoking does not work that well. In fact, none of the participants in that study were successful in staying abstinent in the long run. How, then, can smokers deal with their limited self-control? Remember the commitment device that gym attendees used to effectively pressure themselves to commit to exercising? The same strategy can help smokers quit by putting their money at stake.

In 2010, the economists Xavier Giné, Dean Karlan, and Jonathan Zinman tested whether such a voluntary commitment product can help smokers quit.[10] Two thousand employees, all smokers, at a Philippine bank were randomly assigned into one of two groups: participants in the control group received wallet-sized cue cards illustrating visually aversive pictures that are shown on cigarette packages (such as smoke-damaged lungs), while smokers in the treatment condition were offered the opportunity to sign a commitment contract to help them quit. During the six-month intervention period, the voluntary commitment contract required a bank employee to collect weekly self-determined deposits from a smoker. If the smoker passes a urine test six months later, they will get all of the money back; but if they fail the test, the money will be donated to charity. This weekly deposit contract design applies continuous and escalating monetary pressure to the employees, which enforces their abstinence effort to stay on track throughout the six months.

Similar to the commitment device that incentivizes exercising, this smoking-cessation deposit contract also carries self-signaling power. Breaking the contract not only causes the smoker to lose the deposit but also signals to the smoker themselves that they lack determination. The smoker is therefore motivated to stay clean to avoid the negative self-signal and protect their self-image.

Social signaling is another layer of commitment factor packaged in this design. Think about being a client of this contract: every Saturday afternoon, you must get ready for a visit from a bank employee who comes to collect a deposit from you. If you put $0 into this week's deposit, it probably implies that you failed to stay abstinent; thus, you signal to a fellow bank employee that you are weak-willed. Your social image would be damaged, and you would feel embarrassed. This additional layer of social pressure tied into the contract can generate higher deposits and better enforce abstinence.

One problem that commitment devices usually face, however, is low take-up rate.[11] Not many people want to test their self-control against their own money, even if they know that putting money at stake can help them quit smoking. In this experiment, only 11 percent of smokers who were offered the contract signed up. Those who did sign up, however, were considerably committed to their contract: the average deposit by the end of the six-month-period was 550 pesos ($11), which is contextually significant, as it is equal to about 20 percent of an employee's monthly income.

With this limited take-up in mind, putting money at stake was indeed shown to be an effective strategy to get smokers to quit. At the end of the six-month contract period, participants who were offered a commitment contract were 3.3 to 5.8 percentage points more likely to be clean than those in the control group were. Similarly significant results for the commitment device were replicated after twelve months, when the smokers were administered a surprise test six months after the intervention ended and free of any financial incentives. Despite the effectiveness, 66 percent of smokers who committed to the contract ended up failing to quit smoking. This tells us that while some smokers acknowledge their need for a commitment device to compensate for their self-control issues, they nonetheless are overconfident in and erroneously project their future selves' ability to resist temptations.

Quit Together?

We all know about the power of peer pressure. When your friends smoke, it can be tempting to follow suit and join them. On the other hand, peer pressure could also be used as a tool to help you quit smoking. Having a group of friends who are dedicated to quitting smoking together could motivate you to stay on track. That was the idea that a team led by Scott Halpern from the University of Pennsylvania investigated in its study of group effects on smoking cessation in 2015.[12] CVS Caremark employees and their friends and relatives were invited to participate in this field experiment and were randomized into a control group or one of four treatment groups. Participants in the control group received "usual care," which consists of the American Cancer Society cessation guides, local smoking-cessation resources, and for some of the CVS employees, free access to nicotine-replacement therapy and a behavioral-modification program. As for the four treatment groups, two of them offered incentive programs targeting individuals, whereas the remaining two groups offered incentive programs targeting groups of six participants.

In addition to testing social effects, the researchers were also interested to see if deposit contracts are more effective than reward programs. As we've seen in the commitment contracts for bank employees, smokers were very motivated to avoid losses. But are smokers more motivated to avoid losing their own deposited money than they are motivated to seek gains from reward programs? To answer this question, one of the individual incentive treatments and one of the group incentive treatments offered reward programs granting about $800 for successful smoking cessation. The two remaining individual and group incentive treatments offered deposit programs requiring a refundable deposit of $150 plus granting $650 in reward payments for successful smoking cessation. The four treatment groups are then group reward, group deposit, individual reward, and individual deposit. Similar to the previously mentioned incentive design, the $800 bonus in all groups ($150 deposit included for the deposit-based program) is spread out as $200 given out three times, at fourteen days, thirty days, and six months after the participants' target quit dates.

In the group-reward treatment, group members were rewarded for collective success: at each of the three reward time points, if only one participant successfully quits, they would receive $100; but if all six participants quit, they would each receive $600. By making payouts increase with group success rates, this incentive design leverages social signaling and interpersonal accountability to motivate smokers. Imagine that you are the only person who failed to quit in your group. Your failure would socially signal to your group members that you lack determination; thus, your social image within the group would be damaged. You might feel embarrassed and guilty that your failure caused others to miss out on more rewards. Success would promote your social image within the group. This way, collaborative efforts, such as monitoring and encouraging other team members, are incentivized.

On the other hand, in the group-deposit treatment, group members are pitted against each other: the total reward of $3,600, which includes $150 deposit and $450 bonus from each of the six group members, was redistributed among the members who successfully quit at each of the three checkpoints. Each time point, therefore, has a reward pot of $1,200. Let's say four out of six members successfully quit at fourteen days; they would split the total reward of $1,200 for that time point and receive $300 each. The group members were anonymous to avoid potential undermining efforts. This incentive design leverages loss aversion in a group setting: seeing your own money and bonus being split by others in the group because you failed to quit smoking could be devastating.

To keep the total expected value and bonus of all treatments equal, participants in both the group-reward and group-deposit treatments were also given a $200 bonus if they successfully stayed abstinent through the six-month period.

The results reflected the aforementioned take-up rate concern of commitment incentives: 90 percent of participants who were assigned to reward programs accepted them, whereas only 13.7 percent of participants who were assigned to deposit-based programs decided to join. As for rates of sustained abstinence through the six-month intervention period, all four of the incentive programs significantly outperformed the control group. The expectation was that group cessation incentives would outperform individual incentives. However, group and individual incentive programs turned out to have very similar six-month abstinence rates, at 13.7 percent and 12.1 percent, respectively. The fact that group incentives didn't outperform individual incentives suggests the social effects weren't as strong as hypothesized. What about reward versus deposit programs? Reward programs had significantly higher abstinence rates than deposit-based programs, with a five-percentage-point lead. However, it turns out that this lead was mainly due to the difference in acceptance rate between the two types of programs. When this differ-ence was accounted for, the results flipped: among the participants who accepted the deposit-based programs, the rate of abstinence was 13.2 per-centage points higher than that of those who accepted the reward-based programs. The result suggests that commitment devices like deposit-based incentive structures can be effective for those who are sophisticated enough about their limited self-control to join the program.

Poor Smokers

Back in the 1940s, the smoking rate was higher among people with more years of education. In the following decades, however, as smoking-related health risks became more apparent and widely accepted, the tobacco in-dustry started transitioning their marketing strategy to target lower-income communities. Tobacco companies handed out free cigarettes to residents of housing projects, along with tobacco coupons for prevalent low-income goods like food stamps and prepaid debit cards. Partly as a result of these efforts, 72 percent of smokers today are from lower-income communities.[13] Despite the least affluent people being disproportionally burdened by smok-ing habits, there isn't much evidence regarding the effect of incentives on helping low-income smokers who are outside clinical or workplace settings quit smoking.

In 2016, Jean-François Etter and Felicia Schmid from the University of Geneva recruited 805 low-income smokers in Switzerland to investi-gate this issue.[14] Participants were randomly assigned to one of two condi-tions. Those in the control group received educational booklets and access to a smoking-cessation website. Those in the treatment group received the same informational content plus financial incentives, which were offered six times after biochemically verifying abstinence at one, two, and three weeks and one, three, and six months into the intervention. The incentive scheme also utilized escalating rewards to promote sustained abstinence.

The maximum sum of financial rewards was $1,650, which started at $110 at week one and escalated to $440 at the end of the six months. All participants had a taxable income lower than $55,000, so this reward was quite significant. If the participants failed a biochemical assessment, the value of the next reward would be reset to the value of the last reward they received. Again, this type of design punishes failures but still leaves hope for participants to strive for future abstinence rewards. To avoid the low-income participants spending their abstinence reward on cigarettes, the incentives were paid in the form of gift cards at a large supermarket chain that doesn't sell tobacco or alcohol.

To further motivate the smokers, they were all asked to sign a contract during the enrollment visit stating their commitment to quit smoking by a target quit date set by themselves. This contract was then countersigned by a research assistant and by an optional social supporter, who could be a family member or a friend of the smoker. This social supporter was then asked to support the smoker during their abstinence journey.

As mentioned earlier, the power of self- and social signaling is at play with this commitment contract design: by signing this contract, the smokers formally signal to themselves their commitment, and keeping their self-agreement is a powerful motivation; by having a social supporter sign the contract, the smokers socially signal to their friend or family member their commitment. Having a social witness can be quite influential because breaking a promise to a supporter and disappointing a helper who had faith in you could be more devastating than breaking a promise to yourself.

The results indicated that financial incentives are indeed effective in getting low-income smokers to quit smoking and stay abstinent in the long run. Rates of seven-day abstinence were significantly higher for the incentivized smokers than for the nonincentivized smokers at months three (54.9 percent vs. 11.9 percent), six (44.6 percent vs. 11.1 percent), and eighteen (18.2 percent vs. 11.4 percent). Additionally, the main metric for long-term cessation—rates of continuous abstinence between months six and eighteen—was also significantly higher in the incentive group than in the control group. With continuous and escalating financial incentives, 9.5 percent of incentivized smokers were able to stay abstinent for twelve months after the incentives were removed.

The insights derived from cessation programs and their incentive structures are not limited to encouraging smoking cessation, as they can also be utilized to tackle other bad habits, such as excessive fast-food eating and watching too much TV.

TAKEAWAY: When stretched in the long run, incentives can slowly eliminate habits and sustain long-term change. To strengthen the effects of incentives, add other psychological reinforcements, such as deposit-based commitment devices and social supporters.

19

I Want It Now!

What else could we do to help John break his beer-drinking habit and exercise more? Keeping in mind that John's health benefits are far in the future, providing up-front incentives may help in overcoming one of the most fundamental problems in behavior change: the cost is typically now, whereas the benefit is only in the far future. For instance, some of the benefits of exercising are far in the future and intangible, but the satisfaction of sitting and drinking a beer is immediate.

It's 2 p.m. on a Saturday. You finish another episode of your new favorite show on Netflix and are about to click "continue watching" and dive right back into the action, but you remember that you should go to the gym today—you promised yourself that you would work out at least twice a week. What would you do in this situation? We all face temptations daily, whether it's watching TV, playing video games, or eating unhealthy food. When facing the difficult choice between something you *want* to do and something you *should* do, we often opt for the former.

Is there some way that you can promote desirable habits while also reducing the guilt and wasted time from tempting activities? Katy Milkman from Wharton, Julia Minson from Harvard, and Kevin Volpp from the University of Pennsylvania suggested a clever method—they call it "temptation bundling."[1] The concept bundles the immediately gratifying "want" activities (watching the next episode of your favorite show) with "should" activities that have delayed benefits and require willpower (going to the gym).

For many years now, I've allowed myself to watch my favorite TV show only while I'm exercising on the elliptical machine. This combination solves two problems: first, it increases the desire to exercise by making the immediate experience of this "should" behavior less painful; second, it reduces the guilt associated with the indulgent activity by exclusively pairing this "want" activity with a beneficial behavior.

This bundling idea is exactly what Milkman, Minson, and Volpp tested in their field experiment at a large university fitness center. They used page-turner audio novels ("want" activity), coupled with exercising ("should" behavior). Participants were randomized into three groups:

- *Control*: Participants were given a $25 Barnes and Noble gift card at the start of the study.
- *Full*: Participants were given access to an iPod containing four audio novels of their choice that they could only listen to at the gym.
- *Intermediate*: The same as the full treatment, but the audio novels were loaded onto their personal iPods instead, which they could access at any time.

As predicted by the temptation bundling insight, the participants in the intermediate group visited the gym 29 percent more frequently than those who were in the control group. This result suggests that merely encouraging people to restrict audiobook enjoyment to the gym significantly promotes gym attendance.

Even more effectively, participants in the full group had a significant 51 percent increase in gym attendance relative to the control group. This increase highlights the effectiveness of a commitment device that fully limits the access of a "want" activity to a "should" activity. While the treatment effects did decline over time, there was nonetheless a significant demand for a commitment device like this at the end of the experiment: as many as 61 percent of the participants opted to pay to have gym-only access to iPods with audio novels. This demand for commitment suggests that people are aware of their limited willpower and are willing to pay for an effective temptation bundle that forces them to commit to a "should" activity.

Knowing the power of temptation bundling, you can leverage it to help facilitate various beneficial behaviors beyond exercising. If you recognize your lack of willpower to eat healthier, for example, you can restrict yourself to watch your favorite show only when you're eating healthily; or if you're procrastinating on chores, you can allow yourself to listen to a desirable audiobook only when you're doing dishes or laundry. If you recognize your limited willpower in some beneficial behavior and find a tempting activity that can complement such "should" behavior, you can create your own temptation bundle.

This temptation bundling is designed to overcome *present bias*. Consider two scenarios:

Scenario 1: Choose between $100 today and $110 tomorrow. Many people might prefer getting the $100 bill immediately, so they can go ahead and spend it today rather than waiting for tomorrow to come. "Now" is strong.

Scenario 2: Choose between $100 a year from now and $110 a year and a day from now. If you waited a full year for the money, you might as well wait another day and get the extra $10. Since both options are in the distant future, you wouldn't mind waiting an extra day, right?

Notice how in both scenarios you're offered the option to wait an extra day to receive $10 more, but you're more impatient to do so in the first scenario. This tendency of people to settle for a smaller present reward rather than to wait for a larger reward in the future is called *present bias*. The idea is simple: "now" is very strong and hard to resist.

But this kind of behavior can lead to funny reversals. Remember that in Scenario 2 you chose to wait a year and one day to receive $110? Well, exactly one year has passed, and I'm going to change things up for you. Originally you chose to wait another day to receive $110, but now I allow you to change your mind and offer you to take the $100 immediately instead. This new option is the same as Scenario 1, and we know what you prefer there: you don't want to wait another day, so you change your mind and simply take the $100. This kind of reversal is called *dynamic inconsistency*, because people make an initial choice in advance but change it when the time to act comes.

Present bias and dynamic inconsistency are major reasons for our struggle with behavior change. This failure to achieve our goals is not due to a lack of motivation or bad planning. As mentioned before, the costs and benefits are temporally separated: the costs are now; the benefits are in the future. Too often we fail to realize how strong these forces are. We make commitments for the future and are overconfident about our ability to stick to them. We're going to start our diet, exercise, or quit smoking tomorrow. But when "tomorrow" actually arrives, we're lured again by our old habits.

Here's a fun example: The psychologists Daniel Read and Barbara van Leeuwen surveyed participants about their snack choices. Participants could choose between a healthy but less tasty snack or a less healthy but tastier one. The interesting part came from comparing what people chose for now versus what they chose for next week. When asked what they want to eat next week, 49.5 percent of their participants chose the healthy snack. But when asked what they want to eat now, 83 percent chose the unhealthy one.[2]

Present bias doesn't just affect people's food preferences; it could also lead to quite significant financial consequences. The economists Stephan Meier and Charles Sprenger, for example, studied credit card debt, which is a very bad way of accumulating debt because of the high interest rates that credit companies charge. They started by measuring people's present bias using some experimental techniques and found that 36 percent of their participants had present-biased preferences. They then compared the experimental results with real data and found that these present-biased individuals had a 16 percent higher probability of being in credit card debt.[3]

Present bias and dynamic inconsistency have strong implications regarding how to design incentives that work. If people want to have it now, give it to them now. Make the incentive front-loaded and not too far in the future. If someone changes their behavior in the desired direction, give them an immediate reward.

Another effective and sustainable way to counteract present bias and temporal discounting is to lower the cost of the activity in the present by removing barriers. We'll discuss this solution in chapter 20.

TAKEAWAY: Present bias and dynamic inconsistency make behavior change difficult. When possible, make your rewards immediate to increase their effectiveness.

20

Removing Barriers

Have you ever heard of anyone, from parents to medical professionals to politicians, saying something in the spirit of "Kids should watch more TV and exercise less!"? Physical activity is reputed to have a positive association with health, and many studies cite benefits such as weight control, lower risk of cardiovascular and other diseases, and improved mental and emotional health.[1]

That's why I was disappointed when my daughter came back from school one day and told me that due to budget cuts, her physical education teacher was fired and now she'd have no PE classes at all. Was this a wise decision for the school to make given the budget constraint? Put differently, imagine that all that the school management cares about is academic performance (sadly, this is often true), and it is now required to make a painful trade-off. Say that the students currently have ten hours a week of math and two hours of PE class, and the school management needs to eliminate two hours of class time given the budget constraint. The options that the management considers are either to cut two hours of math or to eliminate PE altogether.

If we want kids to be more successful in school, would the two-hour-a-week PE class help more than the extra two hours of math? Should we let kids spend more time running around in the afternoon instead of continuing to study? It is hard to answer this question depending solely on the available data.

The question of whether regular physical exercise is important for educational achievements is hotly debated as politicians decide which budgets to cut in schools. To inform this debate, my colleagues Alexander Cappelen, Gary Charness, Mathias Ekström, Bertil Tungodden, and I wondered, Do the positive effects of exercise spill over and improve not only health but also academic performance?

Folk wisdom suggests that the answer is yes, with the commonly used catchphrase "healthy mind, healthy body." The Institute of Medicine released a report with evidence suggesting that "children who are more active are better able to focus their attention, are quicker to perform simple tasks, and have better working memories and problem-solving skills than less-active children. They also perform better on standardized academic tests."[2] This is every parent's dream: throw your kids into Little League, and they'll ace their math tests.

These previous findings, however, suffer from the *correlation-is-not-causation* problem: Children who exercise more might do better academically because, for example, they also have more self-control or stronger will-power. That is, they are not doing better academically because they exercise more; rather, they exercise more *and* do better academically because of other character traits. The Institute of Medicine findings observe simple correlation, not causation. We can't conclude from such findings that exercising causes better academic performance.

Free the Gym

Experiments are necessary to establish plausible causation and allow for subsequent policy recommendations. To do exactly this, my colleagues and I incentivized students to exercise more and then observed whether their academic performance improved.[3] We directly investigated the effect of exercising on academic success by randomly assigning people to go to the gym or not.

To test the hypothesis that exercising improves academic performance, we incentivized university students to go to the gym and measured the effect that the increased exercise had on their academic performance. When we run such interventions, we do our best to make them scalable. That is, if someone wanted to actually implement the suggested policy change, it would be realistic and feasible at the practical scale. A major consideration with incentives in education is that whenever we try to implement them, we get a strong pushback from educators, who believe learning should be based on intrinsic motivation and not on extrinsic incentives. Not long ago, I presented my work on incentives to teachers at a high school in Los Angeles. Just mentioning the idea of incentivizing students was enough to get them going—they were not happy with my ideas. Their argument, based on the crowding-out effect discussed earlier, is that if you pay students for educational achievement, they might improve in the short run, but they won't be interested in studying in the long run. With this challenge in mind, we decided that the simple approach of paying participants per gym visit would not be politically feasible and instead opted for an indirect approach based on *removing barriers*. We recruited students from two universities in Bergen, Norway. At these universities, gym memberships cost about $140 per semester. Instead of paying participants for exercising, we gave them free gym membership. We invited students who were not members of any gym and gave them a gym access card, free of charge. By doing so, one main barrier to exercising—shopping for and purchasing a membership—was removed.

Participants who responded to our invitation filled out a survey that could help us learn about their lifestyle and habits, such as hours spent studying, life satisfaction, and self-control. Then, we randomly assigned 400 participants, out of the 778 we recruited, to the treatment group; these 400 participants received the free gym access card. All participants consented to allowing us to receive their gym's scanner data, so we were able to measure their total number of gym visits during the semester. They also gave us permission to inspect their administrative data regarding grades and the number of classes they completed.

As predicted, removing an exercising barrier by giving participants a free gym membership increased the chance they'd use the facilities. Few students in the control group attended the gym at all, whereas most of those in the treatment group—those who had received the incentive of the free gym access card—attended at least once.

But, of course, the goal of the study wasn't to show that giving students free gym memberships would push them to exercise more. We wanted to figure out what effect exercising has on academic success. In line with the folk wisdom, we predicted that incentivizing physical exercise would have a positive causal effect on academic performance. Because we had access to each student's complete data related to their academic performance, we could use this data to answer our question. This plethora of information included records of exams and the grades received on each of them, as well as the number of credits involved.

As we predicted, we found that incentivizing physical activity generated a strong and significant improvement in academic performance by, on average, 0.15 standard deviations. The effect was doubled among students who, before the experiment, struggled with their lifestyle habits and reported fatigue and low self-control. We also conducted a follow-up survey that asked similar questions as in the initial survey and found that the incentive of free membership led to improvements in such lifestyle choices.

Our results show that incentivizing physical activity *caused* a positive change in lifestyle habits (improved diet, longer sleep time, etc.), which ultimately improved academic performance. These results are important for the ongoing debate because they provide a causal link between exercise and academic success, with a lifestyle habit moderator. The findings suggest that policy makers should consider their budget-cut choices carefully. Too often, PE is the first thing to go—good-bye Mr. Hunter, and make sure you take your basketball with you on the way out! There is a growing concern in the US that physical education is no longer considered a critical element of schooling: in some places, half of the students report having no physical education in an average week.[4] Policy makers have been going with the safer route, figuring that an extra hour of math is better than an hour of exercise. The hour of PE may make a bigger difference than the extra hour of math.

The Importance of Removing Barriers

Back to John, who is struggling with his beer drinking and lack of exercise: What else is stopping him from getting to the gym? John will come up with any number of reasons to remain as he is: the gym's too far, it's too expensive, and so on. How can we help? Incentives can help by removing barriers.

As the preceding example showed, for some people, covering the cost of a gym membership might be enough of an incentive to get them going. Barriers can also come in the form of switching costs. Maybe John's problem isn't the membership fee but rather the gym's location. His gym is pretty far away from his home, but he doesn't want to spend time and effort looking for a closer location. His inertia imposes a procedural switching cost: switching would entail doing research on closer gyms, visiting, comparing costs, learning how and when to pay, and so on. Because these switching costs act as a barrier, John has stuck with the faraway gym he pays for but never goes to. Incentives could help here by subsidizing the closer gym enough such that John would be willing to invest in researching and switching.

A recent empirical study demonstrated the effectiveness of increasing gym attendance by removing barriers by subsidizing gym memberships. The economists Tatiana Homonoff, Barton Willage, and Alexander Willén ran a large-scale wellness program at a university that provided one hundred thousand student observations per year and data on one and a half million gym visits.[5] The program offered gym-membership reimbursement for students who attended the gym at least fifty times in a six-month period. While both our and Homonoff and colleagues' studies removed exercising barriers, we provided free memberships for students up front, whereas they offered membership reimbursement contingent on students reaching their attendance goal. Another important difference between the studies is that we conducted an experiment with randomized treatment groups, whereas they used a natural experiment to observe the long-term effects of before, during, and after administering reimbursements without randomizing participants. To do so, they collected individual-level administrative data on daily gym attendance over a five-year period: one year before the incentive implementation, three years during the intervention, and one year after policy termination.

As expected, Homonoff and colleagues found that when the incentives were in place, the program had a significant effect on getting participants to the fifty-visit threshold, which is the level at which they are eligible to receive reimbursement. Additionally, the reimbursing program increased students' average gym visits by about five visits per semester, which is an overall 20 percent increase from the mean. Most importantly, the results show that 50 percent of the program effect persisted after the incentives were removed. This suggests that for people like John, who has stuck with the far gym that he pays for but never goes to, relieving the switching cost and subsidizing a closer gym will probably motivate him to start going to the gym and even form a long-term exercising habit.

The barrier-removal approach is effective beyond promoting exercising, as it has also succeeded in changing behavior to save energy. Opower, a US customer-engagement platform for utilities, sends out a Home Energy Report by mail to millions of US households regularly. The report contains individual tips on how to reduce energy consumption. Instead of using financial incentives like all our previous examples in this part, the intervention utilizes a social comparison: the report displays where the customers stand in their energy consumption relative to their neighbors. This comparison report carries social signaling power. If a household has consumed significantly more energy in a month than their neighbors have, it could signal that the household is wasteful or antienvironmental, thus hurting its image; conversely, a household can be seen as environmentally conscious if it ranks low in relative energy consumption. According to the economists Hunt Allcott and Todd Rogers, the households that received the report reduced energy consumption significantly, and this effect persisted postintervention, after the households stopped receiving the reports.[6] While the positive effect of social comparison decayed over time, it stayed significant.

How did the reports on energy consumption remove barriers for saving energy? After analyzing the Opower data in 2017, a team of economists led by Alec Brandon concluded that the customers' behavior change was mostly not because of their change in habits but rather because of their investments in capital.[7] Here is a likely scenario: Jack receives his monthly Home Energy Report and notices that his monthly consumption is much higher than that of his neighbors. Concerned, he looks around the house to see what he can modify to save energy and money. Jack then replaces his lightbulbs around the house to energy-efficient lightbulbs. Social-comparison incentives motivate customers like Jack to overcome the costs associated with switching to better technologies, such as purchasing more-efficient appliances.

Using incentives to reduce switching costs is not limited to health and energy saving. Many of the promotions we see in stores are based on this concept. Think about shopping habits, for instance. When we go to Target, most of us repeatedly choose the same brand of toilet paper. During the first couple of times that we choose a toilet paper brand, we might invest effort in comparing options and prices and maybe try a few different brands. Once we are happy with our choice, however, we simply repeat it, almost unconsciously. It is costly to deviate from this consumer inertia. The costs can be either natural, such as spending more time and effort to research the competing products, or artificial, such as missing out on repeat-purchase discounts imposed by the firms to keep you loyal.

If Scott (a brand of toilet papers) wanted to override this habit and convince loyal customers of Charmin (a different brand) to try its brand of toilet paper, it might run an attractive promotion, like buy-one-get-one-free, as an incentive to reduce switching cost and remove barriers. The Charmin customers might veer toward the Scott section when they see the promotion. If they buy it, try it, and find they like it, Scott might become their new go-to toilet paper—even after the promotion ends.

There is another type of switching cost that we don't experience when switching from Charmin to Scott toilet paper but do when, say, we switch from Apple to Samsung phones. When switching away from brands like these that carry a distinct identity and powerful brand loyalty, we could experience a "relational" switching cost that imposes a psychological or emotional discomfort when we break the bonds with the identity.[8] To subsidize this relational cost among other switching costs, T-Mobile, for example, had a promotion in which it covered up to $650 switching fees per line if customers decided to transfer from a competitor.[9] Presumably, a customer who switches to T-Mobile because of the promotion will stay with the company for a while after doing so.

To increase markets' competition, legislators often create policies that aim to reduce the market power of companies associated with large switching costs. In the early days of cell phones, for instance, customers couldn't just switch carriers as easily as we do now—they also had to change their phone number. Recognizing this significant switching cost, the Federal Communications Commission (FCC) mandated that all wireless carriers had to offer number portability by 2004. Several years later, Minjung Park investigated the effects of this new policy on wireless pricing. Examining around one hundred thousand calling plans, Park found that the prices of wireless plans dropped by 6.8 percent in the seven months after the FCC ruling.[10] This significant drop in pricing suggests that the lack of number portability had been a significant barrier to switching, and once the FCC ruling removed this barrier, companies had to turn to cutting prices to retain customers.

Be mindful that while incentives can certainly be used to reduce switching costs, they can also be used to create these costs. Many companies leverage this insight to lure customers with attractive up-front deals and then get them "hooked" on a product by creating exclusive convenience and making it costly to switch. Let's say TurboTax, a software package for preparing income-tax returns, is offering $15 off on its product, so you decide to try it out for your taxes this year. You are then asked to enter a sea of personal and financial information, from addresses to workplace names. After investing much time and effort to provide all the required information, you are pleasantly surprised to find out that the TurboTax software can save all of this information for next year. Now, even if you discover that another tax-preparation product is much cheaper in the following year, you are likely to just stick with TurboTax to avoid the annoying switching costs. Similarly, Amazon's 1-Click patent capitalizes on this cost: customers only ever need to enter their shipping and payment information once, and they can shop endlessly without worrying about having to take out their credit card and reenter their home address. Although it's unclear how much money the patent has brought Amazon, estimates indicate billions of dollars annually.

TAKEAWAY: Incentives can help remove barriers to behavior change. Using incentives to reduce switching costs makes activity take-up easier.

PART SIX
Helping Communities Change Harmful Cultural Practices

● ● ●

We've established the power of incentives and witnessed how effective incentives can shape the story to your advantage, identify and solve complex problems, and lead to individual behavior changes in the long run. What about behavior changes on a community level? Are incentives powerful enough to change cultural practices and traditions that are pervasive and deep-rooted in a community's history going back centuries?

This challenge is different from those we've encountered so far, such as motivating a pregnant mother to quit smoking for an extended period of time or an employee to avoid driving to work. To induce cultural change, it's both the individual and the community-wide cultural traditions that need to be addressed. Culture is often resilient and deeply ingrained due to centuries of evolution, involving interconnected causal forces and widespread social influences. All community traditions, however, consist of individual actions, and every individual behavior ultimately depends on incentives. With acutely designed and carefully implemented incentives, we can uproot and replace harmful traditions with long-lasting beneficial practices.

In this part of the book, we are changing the scenery, traveling to Kenya and Tanzania in East Africa, where the Maasai people live. Using incentives, we will attempt to tackle and change some dangerous and harmful cultural practices. Successfully doing so will promote a symbiotic and long-lasting ecosystem within the region and save hundreds of thousands of young girls from misery—and, in some cases, death.

A warning: the following chapters contain sensitive material that may not be suitable for all readers.

21

From Lion Killers to Lion Savers

Changing the Story

Killing a lion with nothing but a spear is quite dangerous, as you may imagine. Meet Samson—he's about to do just that. Samson is a sixteen-year-old Maasai boy, and this act is his rite of passage. It is how he will prove his bravery and prowess to his tribe and how he will become a warrior. He's been preparing for this moment since a very young age, listening to Maasai bedtime stories of heroic warriors spearing formidable lions and saving their villages in the meantime.

You may be thinking that this all sounds just a bit dramatic, but it isn't in the least—killing lions is central to Samson's culture. The Maasai are a Nilotic ethnic group located in Kenya and Tanzania.[1] They don't have bank accounts or luxury cars; rather, all of their capital is invested in their livestock. Imagine a lion going after your bank account—would your attitude be cavalier? Just as you would probably go to great lengths to protect your financial well-being, the Maasai have good economic reasons to go after the lions that kill their cows and sheep and threaten their very livelihood.

At this point, you may also be wondering just how a professor at UC San Diego fits into this story. So let me just give a quick disclaimer: I did not spear any lions during my time in Kenya and Tanzania. I did, however, spend time with the Maasai, learning, among many things, how they were able to alter one of their long-standing traditions of the aforementioned lion killing.

When I mention wild lions, you may imagine them as killers that are eager to mix up their diet with the occasional chubby tourist or careless tribesman. But in reality, lions, like many animals, generally try to avoid humans. Lions will, however, attack livestock from time to time, often as a result of harsh environmental conditions, such as during a drought or when orphaned cubs are not strong enough to hunt wildlife on their own. When such an attack would occur on the Maasai's land, Maasai warriors would chase and spear that lion, for the most part to prevent it from attacking livestock again. The Maasai and the lions have lived in this equilibrium for hundreds of years.

However, over the past few decades, economic development has drastically reduced Kenya's lion population, and the Maasai lion-killing tradition hardly helped matters. In 1928, Kenya's population was a mere 2.9 million people; over the next century, it multiplied over sixteen times: in 2019, the population was over 52 million and growing.[2] Naturally, economic development followed this population growth, and the combination resulted in a loss of natural habitat, further crippling the lion population. At the present time, only an estimated twenty thousand wild lions remain in Africa, down from about two hundred thousand thirty years ago.[3]

This decline in the lion population is detrimental for many reasons, the first of which is simply the loss of these magnificent animals that have done so much to forge Kenya's international image. Additionally, as with any endangered species, the dwindling lion population has disturbed the balance in the food chain. There is the economic perspective to consider as well: lions are key to the tourism industry in Kenya and have produced great economic benefits. When the lion population started declining, some people wondered, Could incentives be used to change the Maasai lion-killing tradition, which itself was rooted in the economic need to save their livestock?

On the flight to Kenya, my friends and I discussed this question, and we were all excited to meet the people who had grappled with this difficult situation firsthand. A small Cessna departing from Nairobi took us to our final destination in southern Kenya, next to Tanzania. Upon landing, we met Luca Belpietro, an energetic Italian with a can-do attitude. Born and raised in northern Italy, Luca first went to Africa as a kid with his father, an avid big-game hunter (an interesting background for someone who grew up to be an adamant conservationist). In 1996, Luca and his wife, Antonella Bonomi, founded Campi ya Kanzi, an ecotourism lodge on a Maasai-owned wilderness reserve with Mount Kilimanjaro and Ernest Hemingway's "green hills of Africa" as a stunning backdrop.

We headed toward the main building of this "Camp of the Hidden Treasure" to join Luca for dinner. Leaning on the fireplace with a glass of grappa in his hand, Luca told us how, as a young teenager, he built a tent outside his family's house in Italy and took up residence inside it in order to convince his father that he was ready to join him on his African expeditions.

It was during these expeditions that Luca fell in love with Kenya and eventually chose to permanently relocate to the Maasai land, where he and his wife have since built their home and their life together. Their children attend school with Maasai children, and their best friends are tribespeople. Yet, when asked about his relationship with the Maasai, Luca replied, "It is still developing. The Maasai world is one of its own; if you were not born a Maasai there are no doors for you to enter it. I am glad some windows open for me to look into it once in a while."[4]

Luca isn't one to just sit back and wait patiently for windows to open, though. Ever the activist, with full respect for and understanding of the Maasai traditions, Luca established the Maasai Wilderness Conservation Trust to help the community. Employing more than three hundred members of the Maasai tribe, the Trust is dedicated to preserving the wilderness, the Maasai land, and the culture.[5] Its most famous supporter is the actor Edward Norton, who fell in love with the people and the place and started a US-based arm of the Trust. Norton invited a few Maasai to join him in running the New York City Marathon to help increase the Trust's visibility. One of the runners was Samson Parashina, the boy you met at the beginning of this chapter. Now thirty-seven and definitely no longer a boy hiding in the grass with his spear, he stood comfortably near Luca, explaining in fluent English how the two of them had met.

While Samson was training to become a Maasai warrior, he also worked as a waiter at Luca's lodge restaurant. Like his peer warriors-to-be, he trained in using his spear to protect livestock and to kill lions if necessary. At the same time, however, he was learning about management as he made his way up the ranks at the lodge. With this East-meets-West experience in hand, he went to study at a university in Nairobi to further his education. Seeing his potential, Luca appointed him to manage the lodge upon graduation, and later, Samson also became the president and chairman of the Trust's board.

Samson explained to me that one of his first tasks in this role was to find a solution to the drastic decrease in the lion population. In the Kuku ranch, where the lodge was located, the lion population was down to just ten when Samson was appointed. In the neighboring lands, the lion population was barely hovering at seventy, down from over three hundred only a decade earlier. Although encroaching developments accounted for some of the loss, the Maasai were responsible for the other part of the problem. More than one hundred lions were killed by the local Maasai in just the start of 2000, and this trend continued.[6] To address this decrease in the lion population, Luca and Samson put their heads together and designed the "Simba Project" (*simba* means "lion" in Swahili), a financial-incentives-based program.

Traditionally, when a lion kills a cow, the elder who owned the livestock would call the warriors, who would then gather to chase and spear the lion. Although this response doesn't compensate the elder for the dead cow, it does succeed in preventing future attacks on livestock by that lion. The Simba Project is an incentive scheme targeted at the elders who own livestock and was designed to change this dynamic, which was decreasing the lion population.

Luca and Samson explained that under the Simba Project, the Maasai elder whose cow was killed can be financially compensated, but only if no lion is killed in the area following this incident.

This incentive scheme changed the reality that the elders faced. In this new reality, if an elder calls the warriors and they chase and kill the lion, the elder is not compensated. Meanwhile, if the warriors do not kill the lion, the elder is eligible for compensation. You can thus begin to see how under the Simba Project, the elder is incentivized to tell the warriors not to kill the lion. Livestock losses due to conflict with other wild animals (e.g., hyenas, leopards, cheetahs, and wild dogs) are also eligible for monetary compensation under the Simba Project. The inclusion of these other animals under the compensation plan is important for solidifying the norm of not chasing predators and keeping the food chain balanced.

The initial decision (before the Simba Project was launched) is presented in the game tree below. Simply put, the lion kills a cow, and the elder has to decide whether to call the warriors. If he decides not to, the outcome for him is not great: he's down one cow, and the lion may come back for another (Outcome #1). If he calls the warriors and they kill the lion, he's still down one cow; but the lion will not come back, and the risk of losing another cow is reduced (Outcome #2). For the elder, Outcome #2 is better than Outcome #1, and hence the elder will call the warriors.

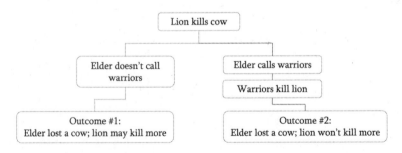

Maasai lion-killing incentives before the Simba Project. For the elder: Outcome #1 < Outcome #2 → the lion will be killed.

The game tree helps us determine where in the process the implementation of incentives would be the most effective by allowing us to consider what the incentive's effect on each "player" would be. In our game tree, the players consist of the warriors and the elder. Note that they don't compete with each other, but each one's decision still affects the other's payoff. The elder's payoff is the life of his remaining livestock, and the warrior's payoff is the rite of passage achieved through the process of hunting and killing lions; now he can become a member of the warrior club.

Luca and Samson decided to focus the Simba Project's incentive scheme on the elders by changing their payoff from calling the warriors. They created a more attractive alternative. In a community meeting, Samson told the elders about the incentive scheme: if the elders refrained from calling the warriors and instead reported the incident to the Simba Project's verifying officers, they would receive compensation for their dead cow. The lion would stay alive, and in the event that it wanders back and kills another cow, the elder would be compensated for that cow as well (Outcome #3 in the game tree below).

As Samson explained the program during that first community meeting, Luca saw the elders' initial looks of confusion and headshakes turn into signs of understanding and acquiescence, as one by one they began to

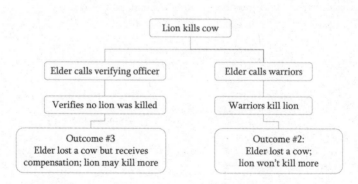

Maasai lion-killing incentives after the Simba Project. For the elder:
Outcome #3 < Outcome #2 → the lion will not be killed.

nod their heads. After the elders left the meeting, Luca and Samson both pondered the same question: Would the incentive be enough to change the elders' behavior and the tribe's long-standing tradition?

An important decision in making the plan work is how much to pay. If the Simba Project were to offer a ridiculously large amount, say, $1 million, to each elder who refrained from calling the warriors, it would undoubtedly work. After all, who would say no? However, the project would be bankrupt with the first dead cow, and the problem would persist.

Instead, the Simba Project considers the market value of the livestock in question and compensates based on that amount. Compared to the economic benefit that tourism involving the lion population brings to the Maasai, the compensation seems to be a manageable price to pay. This financial calculation is extremely important because it makes the project economically sustainable. Luca explained that the project is fully funded by the guests of his Campi ya Kanzi lodge, who pay additional taxes on their lodging expenses, which are in turn diverted toward compensation for livestock losses due to predator attacks. In other words, the tourists who come to the lodge to experience the wilderness are simultaneously helping to fund the program that preserves it.

TAKEAWAY: Incentives can change the culture by changing the payoffs.

22

Insurance Fraud and Moral Hazard

The Maasai Edition

Any program's success relies on its details. You may have already thought of some potential problems in the Simba Project's incentive scheme, as described in chapter 21. The program introduced, in effect, an insurance policy for the elders against lion killing—just as how in Western countries, we insure our cars against accidents. And as with any insurance policy, the Simba Project came with strategic challenges. In this chapter, I discuss two of the main challenges and how Samson and Luca worked together to find solutions to them.

Insurance Fraud

If you thought insurance fraud was invented by Western societies, think again. The elders in Kenya were about to get lion insurance, and Samson was concerned about lion-insurance fraud. He realized that the project's first and most obvious challenge was to ensure that the elders reported incidents truthfully. The Simba Project would fail if the elders were to exploit it.

For example, imagine an elder with a sick cow. With the Simba Project in place, the elder might be tempted to allow the sick "insured" cow to wander into lion territory. The lions, of course, would kill the hapless cow, and the elder could then ask for compensation under the guise of a legitimate incident. Think of this scenario as another game tree, again with the elder as the player. The elder has two options: (1) allow the cow to die of natural causes and go uncompensated or (2) allow the cow to wander close to the lions with the hope that it will be attacked and that the elder will be compensated.

Insurance-type fraud schemes come in a variety of shapes and colors—as do their solutions. You might remember the *Sopranos* episode "Whoever Did This," wherein Tony's beloved but lame racehorse, Pie-O-My, was killed in a mysterious fire.[1] It took Tony only moments to understand that Pie-O-My's co-owner, Ralphie, was responsible for the fire. According to Ralphie's calculations, Pie-O-My had reached the point at which she was worth more money dead than alive, and so he sent an arsonist to burn down the stables—and the horse—in order to collect the insurance money. Tony had his own way of dealing with such behavior; he immediately drove to Ralphie's house, confronted him, and then killed him with his bare hands.

Much less extreme than Tony's solution, Luca and Samson's solution consisted of an enforcement mechanism to deter fraud. My friends and I were able to see their solution in action firsthand the very next day when Samson received a call and invited us along for the trip. On the way, Samson explained how he and Luca had created a group within the Trust called the "Verifying Officers." Overseeing the 280,000 acres of the Kuku Maasai land, these officers were employed to weigh the claims made by the community, much like car-insurance adjusters.

As we neared a boma—a group of small huts made of mud where the Maasai live—one of these officers pulled up next to us on a motorcycle. Together, we walked toward the elder, who was standing outside his boma, anxiously waiting for us. The officer began by asking the elder to explain what had happened, documenting the story as the elder spoke. After this initial interview, the elder led us to the scene where his goat had been killed. The officer needed only minutes to confirm what had happened. He affirmed for our benefit that he believed the elder was telling the truth—a couple of hyenas had attacked the goat, which was starkly evident to him from the paw prints and other tracking indicators. Samson explained that these Verifying Officers were very well trained and could analyze a claim's authenticity with incredible accuracy in a matter of seconds.

The process didn't stop there, however. As the officer took photos and videos of the scene with a GPS-enabled smartphone, Samson explained that the evidence had already been automatically geotagged and fed into a database for a program-wide statistical analysis. The officer's final analysis and conclusion in this particular case were clear: the goat was well within a reasonable proximity to the boma, and the claim was justified. Even so, he entered the claim into the database for the team to further analyze before conferring official approval. As he got back on his motorcycle, he gave the affected elder a credit voucher for reimbursement. Samson told me that when the project first launched, word of this rigorous system spread, and the elders quickly learned that they wouldn't be able to trick these Verifying Officers with false incidents.

Moral Hazard: Why Should I Fix the Fence?

With the insurance-fraud problem taken care of, Luca and Samson had a second challenge to face—something economists call "moral hazard." As the theory goes, whenever a person can insure something like their car or house, they have less of an incentive to keep it safe. Say, for example, that you are not insured and someone steals your car—you'd lose its entire value. You are, therefore, extremely motivated to make sure this doesn't happen. For that matter, car owners without insurance are much more likely to employ extra precautions—such as steering-wheel locks—than are car owners with insurance. If you are insured, the theft may still feel unpleasant, but the blow is substantially softened by the knowledge that, at the very least, you will get most of your money back through insurance. So, although it may initially strike you as counterintuitive, the most run-down cars, such as the one shown in the picture, are commonly protected by extra measures, because these cars are not worth insuring in the first place!

Can you guess why this rusty looking, run-down car has a steering-wheel lock?
No other car in the parking lot has one.

With the Simba Project in place, Samson recognized that the moral-hazard problem could easily occur within the Maasai community. As we walked back toward the car, he pointed out that the boma was surrounded by a circular fence made of thorny bushes, designed to protect families from predators. Within this fence was yet another circular fence; the livestock lived in the ring that these two concentric-circle fences made. Maintaining these fences requires considerable ongoing and community-wide effort.

Luca and Samson initially feared that if the livestock were insured, the elders would have less incentive to work hard to protect them. They wouldn't feel the need to purchase a steering-wheel lock, so to speak. Although they would, of course, still prefer a night without lions, they might feel considerably less pressure to maintain their fences. In contrast to the concern of fraudulent reports, convincing the elders to properly protect their insured cattle does not involve the prospect of fraudulent behavior. From the project's perspective, however, the prospect of carelessness is undesirable because it could lead to compensation for carelessness or neglect.

To deal with this moral-hazard issue, Luca and Samson designed the Simba Project with clear parameters regarding the boma fences. Under the project's requirements, boma fences must be a minimum of two and a half meters (eight feet) in height and have a dense covering with no openings for predators to exploit, and a well-secured gate. The Trust hired Maasai experts to educate the elders on better herding strategies and fence-building techniques. In addition to interviewing the elders and inspecting the scene when a claim is made, Verifying Officers are also tasked with inspecting the construction of the boma. If they determine that the boma isn't properly maintained or that herding is not done according to the Simba Project's standards, the elder may receive reduced compensation reflecting the severity of the problems.

To deal with the moral-hazard problem, the Simba Project offers three types of compensation.[2] Type 1 has the highest compensation and consists of the cases in which the livestock are attacked while being herded using accredited practices or while safely ensconced in a properly constructed boma. In these cases, the elder receives 70 percent of the market value for each livestock lost. Like our automobile insurance, the elder is not fully compensated, in order to keep some incentives in place for him to avoid such incidents, mimicking the reason most insurance policies retain a copay. The next two types of progressively reduced compensation encompass problems with either herding or with boma-based security.

TAKEAWAY: Don't be naive—insurance reduces the incentive to be careful.

23

Changing the Warriors' Story

An elder reminisces,

Being a warrior is exciting and fun; it has many privileges but also
many duties. Many of us look at those times as the best in our
lives—though by no means the easiest. To become warriors, we
have to demonstrate our bravery: we have to undergo circumcision
in front of the whole community, without flinching or squinting
our eyes or giving any other signs showing that we are experiencing
pain. After all, if we cannot bravely withstand that bearable pain,
how can we persuade the elders that we will risk our lives to protect
our livestock and our community?

Thus, from a young age, Maasai boys are trained not only to kill predators but also to endure high levels of physical pain, so that at the age of
fifteen, they can undergo their circumcision ceremony without crying. During the circumcision ceremony, the fifteen-year-old boys in the community
all sit in a row, watching with impassive faces as the circumciser makes his
way down, cutting them one by one. Crying or showing any kind of pain is
considered a grave sign of weakness and a shame to the tribe.

Thus far, the focus of discussion has been on the elders and how to
change their payoff. How might the warriors feel about the project, though?
Would they simply stand back and passively accept the loss of tradition?

Although many people in Kenya now enjoy a modern lifestyle that comes with economic development, the Maasai continue to proudly structure their society according to their ancestral traditions. Although they are more likely to settle down in one place now, they still consider themselves seminomadic pastoralists, in that each person still fulfills a traditional role. Women are in charge of raising children, looking after goats and sheep, and taking care of household chores. The Maasai have an extreme version of a patriarchal society, and you'd learn quickly while visiting them that some of the gender roles are different from what we're used to in the Western world.

When my friends and I arrived at the lodge, the men greeted us, while the women carried our luggage to the tent. In general, women work much harder than men do. Warriors, however, are still young men, whose role is to protect the tribe from predators and enemies. Elders—men who have completed their service as warriors—take great pride in their role of governing the tribe, and that pride is not so easily dismissed, especially given the warriors' tradition.

Samson explained to us how killing a lion served as a rite of passage and, moreover, that a Maasai warrior is defined by his contribution to the tribe's welfare. As one of Samson's friends recalled, "We now belong to an age group, a group of peers with whom we share duties and responsibilities. We have strict rules to follow. We can't eat meat at home; instead, we have to go out in the bush and slaughter an animal with other warriors—this is to prevent us from eating meat meant for the rest of the family. We cannot drink alcohol or take any drugs: we need to be alert at all times and ready to spring into action to rescue our cattle or protect our community." With the weight of the tribe on their shoulders, these young men proudly serve as full-fledged warriors until about the age of thirty, at which point they restyle as elders, take wives, and start their families.

Having been a warrior himself, Samson quickly recognized that getting the warriors on board with the Simba Project was a pivotal challenge that needed to be addressed. Luca and Samson predicted that the financial incentive would be sufficient to push the elders into a departure from tradition, but they realized that the warriors had no incentive to change their behavior; after all, killing a lion with a spear remained their rite of passage and their entrance into manhood.

The Simba Project, therefore, needed to compensate not just the elders for the livestock deaths but also the warriors for the shift in tradition. In an effort to do so, the project created another group, called the "Simba Scouts." While the Verifying Officers deal with claims, the empowered Simba Scouts are charged with a task that's the polar opposite of the warriors' tradition: protecting the lions. This group consists of established warriors, some with copious experience in killing the very animals that they are now tasked with saving. The Trust achieved this change through education: warriors, both young and old, are now taught about the importance of saving the lions. Older and more seasoned warriors assist the Trust in educating younger warriors, who have slowly begun to change their views. Many of these older warriors saw friends die while trying to kill lions and thus have welcomed a way of life that preserves the warrior tradition while saving lives. The Simba Scouts have redefined bravery, the core value of the Maasai warriors, as not to kill lions but to preserve them, thereby preventing unnecessary deaths and promoting a symbiotic environment between the warriors and lions. Simba Scouts also play a valuable role in their communities by informing the herders about the location of nearby lions to prevent livestock losses.

By changing the narrative, the Simba Project created an alternative rite of passage that allows the warriors to retain their pride and traditional warrior roles. They changed the story with new incentives that slowly turned the tide. Gradually, many warriors have begun to apply for the Simba Scout positions, understanding that this duty is now the role of a warrior, both making a decent living and preserving tradition.

During my own time in Kenya, I was able to meet the leader of one of the Scout groups and got a chance to see the Scouts in action. Twenty-three-year-old David Kanai, a charismatic and athletic Maasai warrior, invited us to join his group and search the mountain slopes for lions one morning. With six other Scouts dressed in traditional Maasai clothing, we headed toward the Jeep that would take us up the mountain. Sandals made of old car tires scraped the path, spears ready, and deftly honed knives clinked together on belts. Excited to have company, the Scouts demonstrated their impressive spear-throwing strength along the way (and made fun of my miserable attempts at it).

As we got into the Jeep and drove toward the mountain, David and his Scouts debriefed us regarding their plan and explained how we were to behave. Upon arrival, we stepped out of our Jeep, and their relaxed attitudes all but disappeared as they quickly leapt into formation, scouting the surrounding area warily. David explained that as Simba Scouts, part of their job is to monitor lion movements within the area with the help of special tracking collars. Reaching toward his belt, he unhooked an antenna that detected the signals sent from the collars worn by lions in the area. This was old-school technology that helped the Scouts locate the lions, albeit not with great precision. With a better understanding of the lions' general movements and behavior, the Scouts could protect both the lion population and the Maasai. Their job was to reduce human and wildlife interactions, which was what often led to the killing of livestock in the first place. The Scouts used the data they collected to inform the herders about the lions' locations, which in turn allowed the herders to move their livestock away before conflict could arise.

As we made our way farther up the mountain, we still couldn't see the lions, but David told us they were hiding nearby, watching us. The Scouts followed the tracks and found the remains of a zebra that the lions had eaten just a couple of hours earlier. Although we never came face-to-face with them, the morning wasn't by any means wasted. The Scouts now knew where the lions were and immediately used this information to warn the nearby herders to stay away from the area, proactively preventing any potential conflict.

David, leader of a Simba Scouts group, and
his team member Joseph, in search of lions

The hard work in setting the incentives paid off. Luca and Samson's understanding of the incentives at play drove the ideas behind the Simba Project and eventually led to the program's success. As mentioned previously, approximately ten lions were left in the area when the Project started. Ten years in, that number has increased to sixty-five, the maximum number that this territorial animal can reach within the given area due to natural-resource limitations.

Tradition itself has even evolved within the Maasai community. Elders no longer call for warriors when their livestock are attacked. Young Maasai boys no longer try to kill lions. The lion population in the area is thriving, along with tourism, and the Maasai and Luca couldn't be happier with this result. The Simba Project successfully turned a tradition that had become harmful into a beneficial one: incentives changed the story.

Interested as we were with the Simba Project's success, it wasn't the reason we traveled to Kenya. We had journeyed far for another related purpose: we came to take the lessons learned from the Simba Project and use them to design an incentive scheme to break a horrible tradition within the Maasai community: female genital mutilation.

TAKEAWAY: Use incentives to build a new tradition.

Changing the Economics of
Female Genital Mutilation

The Night Lucy Will Never Forget

Three women joined my mother. One held a long, curved blade, glistening with blood rust. The hand that gripped it was old, wizened, and sure. I backed away, but couldn't tear my eyes from that hand, that blade. I was almost at the door; I could hear the sound of the children playing outside the boma when I bumped into a hard, unyielding figure. One of the women, my favorite aunt, had moved to block the entrance. The other grabbed my arms and pinned them so that I could not move. She pushed me down onto the hard dirt ground, and my aunt walked over to help. The last woman, the circumciser, approached and behind her, my mother. I looked towards her, pleading with everything I had. She was my mother—she would protect me, right? With sad but determined eyes, my mother said, "This is what must be done." And with that, they began to cut—and I began to scream.

This account by Lucy Nashaw describes what happened to her when she was nine. She bled for nearly a month, spending sleepless nights writhing in pain. When the bleeding finally stopped, she was immediately married off to a forty-year-old Maasai man with two other wives.

It is estimated that the vast majority of women in the Maasai tribe in Kenya and neighboring Tanzania have been circumcised (or "cut").[1] Girls customarily experience the cut between the ages of twelve and fifteen. Much like how killing a lion was seen as a Maasai boy's rite of passage, undergoing circumcision is seen as a girl's rite of passage into becoming a mature woman in the Maasai culture.

The Kenyan government has a vested interest in stopping what Lucy and thousands of unfortunate girls like her experience every year: the practice of female genital mutilation (FGM). In 2011, Kenya joined other countries in Africa to outlaw FGM, defined by the World Health Organization as "the partial or total removal of the external female genitalia, or other injury to those organs, for non-medical reasons."[2] The tradition is routine among five of Kenya's forty-two tribes but is most prevalent within the Maasai.

It is too late to change things for Lucy but not for the thousands of Maasai girls going through FGM every year. Let me assure you that this is not an example of rich Westerners traveling to a Third World country to insert themselves into people's culture and traditions without invitation. FGM, often compared to raping young girls, is a practice that should be stopped, and many people have tried to do so. There are some basic human rights violations that cannot and should not be dismissed as part of a culture that we don't understand.

You might be wondering why there is such a huge pushback against FGM when circumcision is common among male babies all over the world, and, as we ourselves have described, Maasai boys are also circumcised between the ages of ten and fifteen.[3] Without justifying male circumcision, female circumcision is entirely different in many respects. Whereas male circumcision rarely leads to complications, FGM is one of the most persistent, pervasive, and silently endured human rights violations in the modern world. The victims experience severe physical and mental health consequences for the remainder of their lives, as well as adverse effects on secondary education, underage marriage, and family planning. With part of the clitoris and much of the labia cut, many girls are forced to drop out of school for months at a time because of medical complications. They are never able to enjoy sexual intercourse; infections become a common, recurring issue; and they often have problems controlling urination. Complications during childbirth due to scars are also a huge issue, endangering both the mother and the baby.

With so many negative health consequences, how did this practice become a tradition? The story goes that long ago, Maasai husbands used to leave home for a year to hunt or protect the tribe, only to come home and find their wives pregnant with another man's child. FGM was developed as a solution to this concern. Circumcision ensured that sex would not be enjoyable for their wives and hence reduced the chance of infidelity. Over time, it became a tradition and began to serve as a girl's required rite of passage into womanhood and marriage.

Unfortunately, the efforts by governments and nongovernmental organizations to change the Maasai tradition of FGM through education and legal action alone have been largely unsuccessful. Education campaigns about FGM in particular have been around in Kenya for a while, even before the 2011 law, but they bring about change very slowly—too slowly to alter the social norm.[4] Education may convince the occasional mother to save her daughter from being cut, but that family then risks being ostracized by the community. To achieve long-lasting change, the social norm must change. Relying only on slow-moving educational efforts would result in girls continuing to suffer every year, an outcome that simply must not be accepted. The team (Alexander Cappelen, Ayelet Gneezy, Ranveig Falch, and Bertil Tungodden) and I were in Kenya to propose a different approach to stopping FGM—one based on incentives.

The FGM tradition has economic implications. A bride is "worth" more in the marriage market if she is cut; the parents get a larger dowry (more cows) for her, and the girl can find a higher-status husband.[5] In the face of these economic incentives and the massive social pressure to follow tradition, risking a daughter's health is a price a large majority of Maasai parents are willing to pay, even after the mother has undergone the same tragic tradition.

Deep-rooted tradition is particularly difficult to change, no matter how harmful. When economic incentives are also at play, this effort becomes even harder. Yet, as we've seen in the previous chapters, other Maasai traditions are no longer practiced, demonstrating that change is indeed possible. One of the reasons we were optimistic regarding the ability to change the FGM practice is the Simba Project's success, which used economic incentives to break the lion-hunting tradition. Our question now is this: Can we use economic incentives to help end female circumcision among the Maasai? Our team is currently working on an intervention with the goal of changing the incentives faced by the decision-makers, thus creating an economic incentive *not* to cut the girls.

A Suggested Intervention

To understand how we designed our proposed intervention to reach this goal, begin by visualizing the current incentives in place, which are outlined in the game tree on the facing page. The decision-maker in this game tree is the mother, because mothers are the enforcers of FGM within the Maasai; thus, they decide whether to have their daughter cut. If the mother decides against it, her daughter will probably be unable to find a high-status husband, the family will not get a high dowry, and the daughter will probably be shunned by her peers (Outcome #1 in the game tree). If the mother decides to have her daughter cut, on the other hand, the likelihood of finding a high-status husband and getting a high dowry increases, and the daughter's place in the community is solidified (Outcome #2 in the game tree). Outcome #2 is socially and economically better than Outcome #1, and hence the mother would choose to cut her daughter, as the large majority of Maasai mothers currently do.

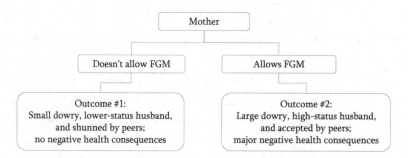

The FGM decision without the proposed incentives

Our job was to determine where in the process incentives would be the most effective in changing the mother's behavior. How could we use incentives to change the outcome so that the alternative to cutting would be preferred? Clearly, the incentive would have to be sizable, but it would also have to be scalable, because we wanted to make the most of our budget and hopefully convince the sponsoring organization to implement it in other places.

After much discussion with members of the community, including Samson and Luca, we learned that typical Maasai parents want their daughter to go to high school. Currently, however, most Maasai girls finish primary school at the age of fourteen and are immediately circumcised and married off. Sadly, the 2011 law had the unintended effect of lowering the age of FGM among girls, because younger girls are less likely to be aware of the illegality of the practice, understand their rights, and resist.[6] Hence, by fifteen, many girls are already starting their families, with their first child on the way.

However, a lucky few have a very different path. Maasai girls who are able to get a high school education have better prospects regardless of whether they are cut, but very few girls are sent to high school, simply because there are no high schools on the Maasai land. To obtain a high school education, these girls must be sent to boarding schools relatively far away. The cost of these boarding schools (up to US$2,000 per year) is too high for most Maasai families. The rare few who get this opportunity and graduate from high school have very different lives from those who are circumcised and married off. Upon returning to the tribe at the age of eighteen, these educated Maasai girls are able to find well-paying jobs. Many find work as teachers or nurses, both highly desirable positions within the community. They are independent and educated enough to refuse being coerced into undergoing FGM upon their return. Notably, these high-school-educated Maasai girls also have a much higher value in the marriage market—again, regardless of whether they are cut.

Inspired by the success of the Simba Project, we took the insight on compensation and applied it to FGM. Our proposed incentive scheme is simple: we will pay for the girls' high school tuition, as long as they are not cut. Just before the beginning of the Maasai school year, we will have a health checkup for the eligible girls. If the checkup verifies that the girls are not cut, we will pay their high school tuition for the ensuing year. The plan is to repeat these health checkups annually until the girls graduate high school, at which point they will be independent and educated enough to resist FGM if it is attempted.

Under our incentive scheme, if a mother does not have her daughter cut, the team will pay for her daughter's high school tuition. The alternative to cutting now becomes much more attractive to the mothers—they have a strong incentive *not* to cut their daughters. The FGM Project ensures that if a mother chooses not to cut her daughter, the family will still be able to receive a high dowry, but her daughter will also remain healthy, obtain a high school education, and consequently have guaranteed career prospects (Outcome #3 in the game tree on the facing page). Her daughter will continue to be accepted by her peers as well, because having an education and career is highly respected within the community, overshadowing the fact that she is not cut.

Ending the lion-killing tradition was offset by the gains in tourism, while ending FGM will have no such immediate and tangible economic

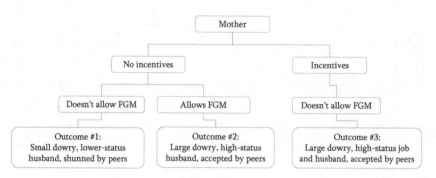

The FGM decision with proposed incentives

return at the community level. As is the case with smoking and exercising, a long-term commitment is required before the ultimate reward is reached. It will, however, promote well-being and health among the Maasai women for generations to come and, if successful, will lead to economic benefits in the future. As such, the advantage of our proposed incentive scheme goes far beyond simply preventing FGM: educating women empowers them, allows them to have their own source of income, and creates a ripple of positive effects throughout the community in the long run.

Methodology: What We Plan to Do

As always, we want to test the effectiveness of the incentive scheme. We plan to run a field experiment, also known as a *randomized control trial* (RCT), which will allow us to compare the outcomes of the girls who receive our incentives with the outcomes of the girls who do not (those in our control group). In so doing, we can quantify the effect of the incentives and compare their cost-effectiveness with the cost-effectiveness of other methods.

After we receive proper research permits, the first step will be to obtain the consent of the girls and their parents. All Maasai girls between the ages of eleven and fourteen at the start date will be eligible to participate in the study, because they are at the highest risk of being cut. After receiving consent, we plan to conduct health checkups in all twenty-two participating schools. As part of the health checkup, our team's nurses will record whether each girl is cut.

The second step will be to randomly assign eleven schools into the control group—in which the girls and their families will not receive incentives—and eleven schools into the treatment group with incentives. In the eleven treatment schools, we will tell the girls and their families about the incentive: every girl who is not circumcised will receive a scholarship for the coming year of high school. Our hope is that even for the younger girls, who are not yet ready to attend high school, the anticipation of the incentives will be enough to convince their families not to cut them. We plan on returning to the villages and repeating this annual checkup for six years.

Anticipating Problems

Just as with the Simba Project, we must foresee potential problems in order to avoid them. We identified three and have worked on solutions to the challenges we found most concerning in our proposed incentive scheme: (1) peer pressure, (2) the social norm, and (3) Maasai men.

Peer pressure. In the current environment, in which the majority of women are cut, being an uncut woman is hard. These ostracized women are considered to still be "girls," and their opinion is not taken seriously.[7] The other women call them "whores who are unfit to be married." Being the outcast is never easy, but it is especially hard within the Maasai, where being a part of the community is integral.

To stop this peer pressure that the uncut women in the community feel, the FGM Project purposefully targets a large fraction of girls in the community at the same time. Across the schools in which the program will be offered, we expect almost all twelve hundred girls between the ages of eleven and fourteen to take part. The goal is to stop the peer pressure that inflames FGM.

The social norm. What's to stop a mother from circumcising her daughter at the conclusion of the four years? Evidence shows that many high school graduates are not circumcised and are yet very successful in the marriage market in their village. In addition, in Kenyan boarding schools, FGM is publicly condemned, and the teachers there educate about the health consequences and risks associated with it. A girl who has spent four years in high school and knows her rights and the risks of FGM is much more likely to be able to successfully resist her parents if they try to have her cut around the age of eighteen. Once Maasai girls turn eighteen, they can no longer be coerced by their families. The FGM intervention aims to get them to that age, hopefully safe and unharmed.

We believe that the FGM Project will truly have a long-term impact and change the social norm in a positive direction by providing an alternate rite of passage in the form of a high school education, much like becoming a Simba Scout is now a Maasai boy's rite of passage. With a high school education in hand, these girls, in turn, will not circumcise their own daughters when the time comes, breaking a harmful cycle of tradition and establishing one that empowers women in its place.

Maasai men. Given how traditional the Maasai are, you may be wondering how the men fit into the FGM picture. Although the Maasai follow a patriarchal structure, the decision to perform FGM lies fully within the domain of the mothers. Maasai men prefer a circumcised wife mainly because they want her to be an accepted member of the community.

Would Maasai men be willing to marry an uncircumcised girl? When we asked them, the responses were a bit conflicting. On the one hand, they did want their wife to enjoy sex with them and avoid the health problems associated with FGM. On the other hand, they were also very concerned about the social status of their wife in the village. For this reason, the majority of Maasai men have grown to prefer marrying a woman who is cut, because she has a higher social status and is accepted by the community.

The FGM Project changes the men's incentives by resolving the dilemma and making the choice easier for them. An educated woman will have her own career and source of income and thus have a high social status regardless of whether she is cut. Under the FGM Project, Maasai men can have it all: if they marry an uncut woman with a high school education, she will enjoy sex, be healthy, and have a high social status within the community.

Two Alternative Futures

Our incentive scheme has been worked into the proposal just outlined, and we are now in the process of applying for grant money and research permits to conduct this experiment in the next few years. If its importance has not yet resonated with you, forget the game trees and the boxes and step into Kenya for a moment to meet Nangini. As the second youngest of five siblings, she lives her days trying to get away from the chaos. School is her

Nangini

one haven. Although she is young, she already has a clearly defined interest in helping others and wants to become a nurse. Envision her two futures: with and without our intervention.

The FGM Project is set to launch. Our partners in Kenya are hopeful and are working with us every step of the way. We hope to be able to change the lives of Nangini and thousands of young Maasai girls like her by using incentives.

TAKEAWAY: Design your incentives to get as many of the parties involved as possible on board.

PART SEVEN

Negotiate Your Signals

Putting Incentives to Work at the Negotiation Table

● ● ●

You just landed your dream job in San Diego. You're already walking along the gorgeous stretch of La Jolla beach mentally, but physically, you're still in Chicago and have a couple of logistics issues to sort out before you can move. The first big task is to sell your house, which you'd love to do as soon as possible. You own a nice greystone in Hyde Park that you bought back in 2012. Its value has since increased, but estimating an exact value for the house is difficult because it's one of the few rehabbed properties in the area. After doing a fair amount of research, you think you can reasonably expect to sell it for $750,000–$800,000.

You spend a couple of weeks cleaning out all the junk you've accumulated over the years, until finally, your place is ready to show. On the last Saturday of August, the day of your open house, you walk outside to a beautiful morning—you smile, feeling optimistic. A couple of people stop by during the first hour. They look around for a few minutes, politely ask a few questions, and then leave—clearly not serious buyers. During the second hour, a young woman walks through the door. She introduces herself as Jennifer, and you lead her to a table, where, after placing her bags down, she turns and enthusiastically tells you about the great farmers' market she stumbled across on the way to see the house. You smile. It's the same farmers' market on the corner you've visited every Saturday morning for the past twelve years, and it's one of the things you love most about your neighborhood. You cross your fingers and hope Jennifer will like the house as much as she liked the market.

She walks through the house, examining every nook and cranny. You sense her excitement—it's the same excitement you felt when you saw the view from the little beach condo you placed an offer on in San Diego. At the end of the tour, Jennifer informs you that she thinks your greystone is a good match for her and that she is very interested in it.

You are now ready to negotiate. You want to sell your house for the highest possible price, and Jennifer wants to purchase your house for the lowest possible price. How do you start such a negotiation? First, you should keep in mind the lowest you would be willing to sell the house for, or your "reservation price"—in your case, $750,000. Of course, you would prefer to sell it for much more. As in many negotiations, you do not know the most the other party, namely, Jennifer, is willing to pay.

This type of negotiation is termed a "zero-sum interaction," assuming an agreement is made. That is, the amount of profit to be made from the deal is fixed: your loss is the exact amount of Jennifer's gain. Naturally, you would like the bigger piece of the pie.

Before putting the house on the market, you had an important decision to make: How much should you ask for? You may think that the first offer is not that important. I'll try to convince you that it is and that your offer should be aggressive but reasonable. By doing so, you send a few very important signals to the buyer—signals that are likely to affect the buyer's subsequent behavior. In this part, we'll examine the four relevant behavioral principles that influence the signaling value of your first offer: *anchoring and insufficient adjustment, the contrast effect, price signals quality*, and *the norm of reciprocity*. I'll describe how these principles work and show them in action in the context of our example. By the last page in this part, you'll see that making the right first offer gives you the advantage in this type of negotiation. Even better, you'll be able to explain why.

25

Anchoring and Adjustment

The *anchoring effect* implies that the buyer's perception of the value of the object in question is not independent of the negotiation itself. In the case of your greystone, the maximum amount Jennifer would be willing to pay is positively correlated with your initial signal—your asking price.

Here's a great example of anchoring from Amos Tversky and Daniel Kahneman's classic 1974 experiment: They first asked participants to spin a "wheel of fortune." They then asked them whether they thought the percentage of African nations in the UN was higher or lower than the random number they obtained by the spin of the wheel. Their last question for participants was, "What is the percentage of African nations in the United Nations?"

Now, most people, including myself, do not know the answer to this question. What's interesting is what Tversky and Kahneman found: participants' guesses were significantly correlated with the number obtained from the spin of the wheel. Those who got a high anchor (a larger number from the wheel of fortune) guessed significantly higher percentages in response to the African-nations question than those who got a low anchor, even though none of the participants thought the result of the wheel of fortune had anything to do with the number of African nations in the UN. Put simply, the higher the spin result, the higher the guess. Tversky and Kahneman termed this phenomenon the "anchoring effect."[1]

I'm an Expert; I Wouldn't Fall for That!

An expert wouldn't be anchored by an initial offer, right? Looking to investigate this question, experimenters tested the effect of anchoring on experts.[2] In 1983, when the prime interest rate was around 11 percent, the experimenters asked a group of managers who worked in finance to estimate what the prime interest rate would be in six months. The average response was 10.9 percent. The experimenters asked another group of managers the same question but in a slightly different way. Managers were first asked whether they expected the prime interest rate to be above or below 8 percent in six months and then asked to estimate what the rate would be. The average response in this condition was 10.5 percent.

The experts in the second group gave lower estimates because they anchored on the very salient 8 percent they were given. The 8 percent value that was given to them served as a signal that the experimenter had expectations regarding the future interest rate. Expecting that the prime interest rate in six months would not be that much lower than the current 11 percent rate, the participants adjusted their estimates up but did so insufficiently, because their estimates were still biased downward toward the previously mentioned 8 percent. This phenomenon is known as *anchoring and insufficient adjustment*.

Similarly, despite being an expert, a real estate agent is likely to anchor their estimate of your reservation price on your asking price (referred to here as your first offer), just as Jennifer would. Because the number you give Jennifer is an initial offer, she will probably know that your asking price is a bit on the high side and will adjust the number down. However, she will use your asking price as a signal that you are expecting a higher price than she previously estimated, and her adjustment will probably be insufficient. The result? Her estimate of your reservation price will remain biased toward the original asking price.

Does This Phenomenon Happen in the Wild?

Real estate agents in Arizona were asked to assess the value of actual property for sale in Arizona on the basis of considerable written information, a physical tour of the property, and a listing price.[3] All agents received identical information, except for the listing price, which acted as an anchor. In post-experiment interviews, every real estate agent insisted that the listing price had no effect on their assessments. That is, the agents said that they did not use the asking price as a signal—but the results told a different story.

The participants who were given a lower listing price assessed the property as significantly lower in value than those who were given a higher listing price. Even in the face of all the other information available, the listing price served as a signal and had an effect. The signal value of anchoring works on nonexperts and experts alike: real estate agents estimate property values daily, yet they were still affected by the anchor.

Let's come back to our negotiations with Jennifer. On the basis of the results from the experiments just discussed, you expect Jennifer to be affected by anchoring. If your asking price essentially puts an anchor on the table that signals to Jennifer what your expectations are, she will try to estimate your reservation price, but her estimate will be biased toward this anchor. If you start with a high number, Jennifer's estimate will be biased toward that high number, thereby making her counteroffers higher.

But how high should the first offer be? Again, keep in mind that your offer should be high but not unreasonable. If you were to start with an asking price of $2 million, you'd signal that your expectations are not realistic or that you are not well informed. Jennifer would probably politely say thank you and then quickly make a beeline for the door. Your first offer should be optimistic: high enough that the buyer will be negatively surprised but reasonable enough that the buyer will come back with a counteroffer.

TAKEAWAY: Your first offer will affect the counteroffer. Make sure to signal that you expect a lot.

26

The Contrast Effect

A high but reasonable first offer not only anchors your counterpart but also provides benefits throughout the negotiation. It allows for something called the *contrast effect*. To elucidate the basic principle, I'll tell you a fable my parents told me when I was a young child.

Once there was a poor man who lived with his mother, wife, and six children in a little one-room hut. The poor man was thinking to himself about how loud, hectic, and cramped his hut was. He decided to ask his rabbi for advice.

The rabbi sat pensively stroking his beard and eventually advised the poor man to bring his chicken, roosters, and geese into the hut to live with the family. The poor man thought this advice was absurd, but he did as the rabbi suggested.

Shortly thereafter, the poor man realized that the situation had only gotten worse. Now, along with the crying and quarreling of his family, there was honking, crowing, and clucking. The birds were always getting in the way and leaving feathers everywhere. They only added to the mess and left less room for his family. So the poor man decided to go back to the rabbi. The rabbi continued giving seemingly absurd advice and told the man to add the goat to the hut. After a week of living under this horrid arrangement, the poor man visited the rabbi for the third and final time. This time the rabbi's advice came as music to the man's ears, for the rabbi recommended that the poor man remove all of the animals from the hut. The poor man gladly complied.

That night, the man and his family slept peacefully. There was no crowing, clucking, or honking. There was plenty of room. Now, when the poor man thought of his hut, with only his family, he thought of it as quiet, peaceful, and roomy.

A high-enough optimistic first offer, say, $875,000, serves not only as an anchor for Jennifer but also as a reference point for every consequent other offer and ultimately for the final selling price as well. It's the gift that keeps on giving. Everything that comes later in the negotiation will be compared and contrasted with your first offer. We refer to this automatic comparison as the *contrast effect*.

Basic experiments that demonstrate the contrast effect are so simple that you can try one for yourself—no need to pack your room with chickens and goats. Put your left hand into a bucket of ice water and your right hand into a bucket of warm water. Leave both hands in the buckets for about a minute. Then immerse both hands into a third bucket of lukewarm water. What's the temperature of the lukewarm water?

Your right hand probably will disagree with your left hand. Both hands are in the same bucket, but they feel quite different. The left hand, which was in cold water before, feels warm. The right hand, which was in warm water before, feels cool. The feeling is weird. Although you know the lukewarm water is a certain temperature, your brain receives different signals from each hand. The hands in the bucket feel the temperature difference relative to where they were before, and the signal they send to the brain is not "bucket temperature is 23° Celsius" but, rather, "it feels relatively hot (or cold)."

Judging things relatively instead of absolutely contradicts the rule that prescribes that the value of something is independent of its reference group.

It's the rule that economists often argue for—put differently, the value of a choice does not depend on irrelevant alternatives. In the bucket example, the water temperature does not depend on where our hand was before. We "understand" this when we think about it. Yet, our hands *feel* differently, as they are influenced by the contrast effect.

The contrast effect is not unique to psycho-physics experiments; it often arises in economic decisions, defying what economists would expect to see. Our knowledge about the brain can help make economic choices more or less attractive, by controlling the signals to the brain.

To demonstrate this effect in action, let's look at another example from the real estate world. Our friend—let's call her Julia—is an extremely successful realtor. When we hire new faculty members, we introduce them to Julia. She is honest, patient, and well connected and does not pressure buyers.

Usually, new faculty members set their parameters of interest in considering houses (area, size, price, etc.). Julia compiles a list of relevant houses on the market on the basis of these parameters and coordinates showings. The new faculty members come to visit the city for a few days, and on one of those days, Julia will take them to see potential houses. They spend the entire day on an extensive tour of houses that Julia coordinates in advance.

I got to see Julia in action when Martin joined our faculty. He is a friend of mine, so I accompanied him on the tour Julia arranged. On a nice spring morning, the three of us drove around looking at houses. One of Martin's prime considerations was location—with two young children, Martin was looking for a house in a suburb not too far from the university.

The first house on our tour was relatively old and not very well maintained. It had been rented out to students who had done a less-than-ideal job with upkeep. Additionally, the location of the house wasn't great—it was a bit far from the university and too close to the noisy freeway. To top it all off, the house was relatively expensive. When we left, Martin looked quietly dejected.

The second house we toured, however, was much better. It was in a quiet location, had a nice backyard, and was clearly well maintained. Julia told us the price, and Martin immediately beamed—it was even cheaper than the first house!

I looked at Martin's smile, feeling happy for him, and it was then that I had a sense of déjà vu. I realized I had a similar experience years ago with Julia. When my wife and I were looking to buy our first house in San Diego, Julia initially took us to see a bad house. I quietly turned the thought over in my head while we dropped Martin off at his hotel. Was it a coincidence?

It was not. As we drove back to La Jolla, Julia readily confirmed. It was not at all a coincidence. She said that she purposefully chooses to first tour a relatively bad property. Why? Because of the contrast effect. The bad house sets expectations: it sends a signal that maybe the housing market is expensive and not particularly nice. The following houses seem much better in comparison, and the buyer is more easily satisfied.

Julia knows to curate signals and leverage the contrast effect—she knows the buyers will compare the subsequent houses with the initial bad one. Relative to it, they're great. As the saying goes, the secret to happiness is low expectations.

You obviously can't control what house Jennifer views before yours, but you can still use the contrast effect. You already know you want to set an asking price (that is, a first offer) that will leverage the anchor effect and send a signal that you value your house highly, and your reservation price is probably high. The asking price will act as the contrast to all subsequent offers. Starting with a high first offer (which is bad in Jennifer's eyes) will artificially raise Jennifer's assessment of later offers. She is more likely to accept a subsequent lower offer if she is comparing it with an initial higher offer.

The contrast effect not only influences Jennifer's decisions but also directly affects her satisfaction. An experiment with undergraduate students demonstrates this part of the phenomenon. Participants in the experiment were presented with the following information:

Imagine you have just completed a graduate degree in communications and are considering one-year contracts at two different
magazines.

(A) Magazine A offers you a salary of $35,000. However, the
other workers, who have the same training and experience as you,
are making $38,000.

(B) Magazine B offers you a salary of $33,000. However, the
other workers, who have the same training and experience as you,
are making $30,000.

Half the students were asked, "Which job would you choose to take?"
Unsurprisingly, 84 percent opted for option A, with the higher salary. The
other half of the students were instead asked, "At which job would you be
happier?" The response is interesting. When confronted with this question,
62 percent of students chose option B: they thought they would be happier
in the job with the lower absolute salary but the higher relative salary as
compared to their peers.

Assuming that the students like to have more money, standard thinking would predict that they should receive greater happiness from the extra
$2,000 in salary that they would get from taking option A. The salary details
of colleagues shouldn't have mattered. This logic mispredicts the importance
of relative salary for satisfaction.

And it will matter in your negotiation with Jennifer as well. Imagine
two ways in which your negotiations with Jennifer could play out: In scenario A, you ask for $875,000, and after some negotiation, a deal is signed
for $825,000. In scenario B, you ask for $800,000, and after you adamantly
refuse to budge on the price, the house is sold for $800,000.

Which scenario would make Jennifer happier? Scenario A, in which
Jennifer was able to reduce the price by $50,000, or scenario B, in which she
dealt with a stubborn seller who was not willing to play the game? Jennifer

might be happier in scenario A because of the contrast effect: she will compare the $825,000 with the original price of $875,000, and that comparison will lead her to view the $825,000 more favorably.

TAKEAWAY: Our brain uses contrast to evaluate values. Make sure you create a high contrast with your first offer.

27

Price Signals Quality

Our high anchor sends the first signal, and the subsequent contrast effect sends the second. Peloton CEO John Foley discovered our third signal for himself through trial and error as he set the price for the now ubiquitous exercise bike. In a 2018 interview with Yahoo! Finance, he recalled, "It was interesting psychology that we teased out. In the very, very early days, we charged $1,200 for the Peloton bike for the first couple of months. And what turned out happening is we heard from customers that the bike must be poorly built if you're charging $1,200 for it. We charged $2,000 dollars for it, and sales increased, because people said, 'Oh, it must be a quality bike.'"[1]

This example demonstrates how consumers may use price as a signal of quality. We assume, like Peloton customers, that *price equals quality*. Research has shown that consumers often believe this and therefore judge higher-priced items to be of higher quality.[2]

Think of the following scenario: It's your birthday, and you want to bring home a nice bottle of wine to celebrate. Typically, you drink wine that costs about $20 a bottle, but given the special occasion, you decide to spring for the bottle with a $50 price tag. You don't have a specific wine in mind; you just assume that $50 wine tastes better than $20 wine.

In the spirit of this anecdote, Ayelet Gneezy, Dominique Lauga, and I ran a simple experiment in the summer of 2009 for Joe, a winery owner in Temecula, California.[3] Joe was trying to determine the best pricing strategy for his wines and asked us for advice. We jumped at the chance to help him. How often do you get to discuss pricing strategy while drinking quality wine?

At Joe's winery, visitors can taste different wines before choosing which to buy from the selection. Consumers typically go to the region specifically for wine tastings, making their way from one winery to another, sampling and buying wine. The wine with which we experimented was a 2005 cabernet sauvignon, "a prodigious wine, with complex notes of blueberry pie, black currant liqueur, acacia flowers, lead pencil shavings, and sweet foresty floor notes." (We could not figure out where the lead pencil shaving flavor came from, but some *poète manqué* must have discerned it.) Joe had it listed at $10, and it sold quite well.

To examine this price-equals-quality phenomenon, we manipulated the price of the cabernet to be $10, $20, or $40 on different days over the course of a few weeks. Each day, Joe greeted the visitors and told them about the tasting. The visitors then went to the counter, where they met the person who ran the tasting, and were handed a single printed page containing the names and prices of the nine included wines, ranging from $8 to $60. Visitors could try six of their choice. As in most wineries, the list was constructed "from light to heavy," starting with white wines, moving to red wines, and concluding with dessert wines. Visitors typically chose wines going down the list, and the cabernet sauvignon was always number 7. Tastings took between fifteen and thirty minutes, after which visitors would decide whether to buy any of the wines.

The results of the simple price change shocked Joe. Visitors were almost 50 percent more likely to buy the cabernet when he priced it at $20 than when he priced it at $10. That is, when we increased the price of the wine, it became more popular. By adjusting his prices accordingly, Joe increased the winery's total profits by 11 percent. Since then, Joe learned not to guess when setting prices, but rather to experiment.

You're already creating this association in your negotiation with Jennifer with a high asking price. As a first offer, this signals high quality. Imagine if you had instead started with a lower offer that was much closer to your reservation price, say $800,000. Instead of thinking, "Wow, what a great deal," Jennifer may interpret this low offer as a signal that the house has problems—the neighborhood runs wild at night, there's mold in the floorboards, your attic is home to a family of squirrels—her imagination will run wild. Regardless of the final selling price, a lower-than-expected asking price might cause the buyer to think she initially overvalued the house.

Price affects consumers' beliefs and expectations and can subsequently affect their subjective experiences, just as the contrast effect can affect satisfaction. During our experiment at Joe's winery, we also added a survey in which customers were asked how much they liked each wine they tried. It turns out that the higher we priced the cabernet, the higher they rated their enjoyment.

A similar result was found in an experiment with members of a fitness center.[4] Participants were given energy drinks to consume both before and during a workout session. One group of participants was told that the drink was purchased for the regular price of $2.89; another group was told that the regular price of the drink was $2.89 but that it was purchased at a discounted price of $0.89 as part of an institutional deal. After exercising, participants rated the intensity of their workout and how fatigued they felt. Participants in the reduced-price condition rated their workout intensity significantly lower than participants in the regular-price condition. Additionally, participants in the reduced-price condition indicated that they were more fatigued than did those in the regular-price condition.

How does this higher-price-equals-higher-quality-equals-higher-satisfaction effect relate to your negotiation with Jennifer? Making Jennifer view the product—your house—as more expensive can alter the perception of her own reservation price and may even give her more enjoyment from her new purchase.

TAKEAWAY: Price signals quality. Make sure to make the right impression.

28

The Norm of Reciprocity

Your high asking price anchors Jennifer, leverages the contrast effect, and signals high quality. The final psychological element that I want to discuss here is *reciprocity*, or the fact that humans are essentially hardwired to return favors. We feel obligated to act kindly in turn when someone has been kind to us.

In 1974, Phillip Kunz, a sociologist at Brigham Young University, ran a simple experiment: He sent Christmas cards to six hundred people randomly selected from the phone books of a few surrounding towns. A couple of weeks later, he had more than two hundred Christmas cards from complete strangers. Why? The *norm of reciprocity*.[1]

The norm of reciprocity is so deeply ingrained into our culture that we feel obligated to return favors even in situations with people we don't know or like or when we didn't even want the original kind gesture to begin with. In one well-known experiment showcasing this norm, participants thought their task was to rate paintings as part of an art-appreciation experiment. They were paired with a fellow participant, who was actually a researcher posing as a participant. In one condition, the researcher (let's call him Jim) left the room for a couple of minutes and came back with a free Coke for his fellow participant. In the other condition, Jim simply left the room and came back a couple of minutes later, no Coke involved. After Jim and the participant both finished rating the paintings, Jim asked his fellow participant to buy raffle tickets. The participants who received a free Coke bought in excess of two times as many raffle tickets as the participants who did not receive a Coke. The participants who had received a Coke felt indebted to Jim and reciprocated with higher purchase rates, even though they hadn't even asked for the drink.

Successful salespeople have long used the norm of reciprocity to produce higher sales. Robert Cialdini from Arizona State University argues convincingly in his classic book *Influence* that the norm of reciprocity elicits favors even when the initial kindness is not genuine but rather is synthetically created specifically to induce a return favor.[2] One of Cialdini's examples is Hare Krishna devotees, who give out flowers and ask for donations just a few seconds later.

Reciprocity is a powerful force. Remember this during your negotiation with Jennifer. If you start your negotiation with a high-enough first offer, you leave yourself plenty of room to be "nice" to Jennifer—by feigning a large concession. Say you start with $875,000. You don't really expect her to accept, but you've set the stage: you've anchored her, you've signaled that you consider your house to be of high quality, and you've ensured that all subsequent offers will be compared and contrasted with the $875,000. Jennifer counters your initial offer with a much-lower offer. Because of the high initial price, you can now come back with a large concession of, say, $30,000. You offer $845,000—still way above your reservation price but attractive relative to the initial offer. You signal to Jennifer your generosity in making that concession, and now it is her turn to reciprocate. The signal will probably also affect Jennifer's response. The $30,000 concession should have no influence on how she evaluates the second offer, but like all of us, she is influenced by social norms and will feel obligated to reciprocate this large "favor." She will be more likely to accept the second offer or respond with an offer more favorable to you. This give-and-take is considered "fair" in negotiations: I make a concession and then you make a concession. A higher first offer will allow you to play this give-and-take game, offering smaller and smaller concessions until Jennifer accepts. If you started low, at $800,000, instead, you wouldn't be able to leverage the first three signals, and you wouldn't be able to leverage the fourth: a large concession wouldn't be possible, and Jennifer wouldn't move from her even-lower counteroffer. You might both end up walking away from the table with a sour taste in your mouths—not a good outcome.

I've said that your offer should be "aggressive but reasonable," but what exactly makes an offer reasonable? As I said before, none of the signals will work if your asking price is so high that the buyer walks away. The price you are looking for is one that will surprise the buyer but not cause them to leave the table. As Margaret Neale (coauthor of *Negotiating Rationally*) puts it, your first offer should be "just this side of crazy."[3]

My favorite example of this negotiation tactic involves my then-nine-year-old son Ron (same guy from the Disney example in the introduction) and a lost tooth. Although my wife and I knew he no longer believed in the tooth fairy, we played the part, just as we had with our older daughters. I reminded him to put his tooth under his pillow before bed and asked how much he thought the tooth fairy was going to bring him. He shrugged his shoulders and went to put on his pajamas. A couple of hours later, my wife, aka the tooth fairy, went into his bedroom with $3. She reached under his pillow and found his tooth, along with the note shown here.

She brought the note out to show me, and after a good laugh, we decided that his creativity had earned him the $20 he requested. My son was

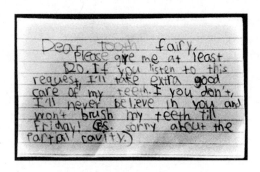

Incentivizing the tooth fairy

able to find the perfect asking price. If he had asked for more, we probably would have responded with "nice try" and left the original $3. Had he asked for $5, we wouldn't have hesitated and would have immediately pulled out an extra $2. By asking for $20, he surprised us but kept us at the table. It was high but not high enough to reject, and my son was able to pocket an extra $17 as a result.

Of course, what's considered "high but reasonable" can differ based on context and culture. If you are a seller negotiating in a bazaar in the Middle East, for example, you can probably get away with an opening of a few times more than your reservation price. This strategy would not work so well with your greystone, and you are probably better off listing the property at no more than 20 percent above the expected selling price or risk losing your credible signal otherwise. In some industries that have less room for negotiation, 1 percent might already be outrageous.

We've focused in this chapter on the "science" part of making the first offer. Calibrating it to the situation at hand is the "art" part of the negotiation. It requires preparation, data collection, experience, and intuition. But here's a good rule of thumb: if the other side gets back to you with a counteroffer (not a huff or a "Hand me the contract and I'll sign right now"), you weren't too aggressive in your original ask.

TAKEAWAY: Consider the signaling value of your first offer in negotiation. It can help you anchor the negotiation, create a contrast effect, increase the perceived value, and invite reciprocity.

From Mixed Signals to Clear Signals

I wrote most of this book during the COVID-19 pandemic in my garage-turned-office, reflecting on how the pandemic had turned the world into a real-life behavioral lab. People were debating in real time questions that are central to the themes in this book. Some questions were practical: Can we use incentives to increase vaccination rates? How can we control the signal these incentives send? Other questions were more on the ethical side: Even if we can use incentives and control their signals, should we?

Flash back to spring 2021: The vaccines were ready for use. There was a brief period of respite. The world was able to let out a collective sigh of relief, but it quickly became clear that celebration was premature—many people didn't want to get vaccinated. Organization after organization began to develop an interest in incentivizing people to get the vaccine.

The US government was front and center in this effort. On May 25, 2021, the Treasury Department released an update: states were allowed to use the billions of dollars in the coronavirus relief package on incentives, including lotteries, cash payments, and nonmonetary benefits, as long as these incentives were "reasonably expected" to increase vaccinations and the costs were "reasonably proportional" to the expected public health benefit. With both state and federal governments handing out hundreds of millions of dollars in incentives to encourage vaccination, many private companies followed suit and jumped at the opportunity to offer giveaways for vaccinated customers, in an effort to encourage vaccinations and boost business.

Regardless of one's stance on the COVID vaccine, it was an exciting time for both individuals and organizations interested in incentives.

The *New York Times* journalist Sarah Mervosh discussed one of the first lottery incentives used. She titled her story "Who Wants to Be a Millionaire? In Ohio, You Just Need Luck, and a Covid Vaccine." The article was about Ohio's "Vax-a-Million" plan, which offered residents who got at least one shot of the vaccine a ticket for a million-dollar lottery. Mervosh interviewed Jack Pepper, a health administrator in an Ohio county, who described the scene at his previously sleepy rural vaccination clinic: "For the first time in a while, there was a line at the door. Officials, who had been strategizing about how they might give away extra doses, were suddenly operating at full capacity. . . . Anywhere I go, people are joking with me, 'Hey, when am I going to win my million dollars?'"[1] And indeed, there was a lucky winner: the recipient of the first $1 million was Abbigail Bugenske of Silverton, Ohio, near Cincinnati. Good for her!

Ohio governor Mike DeWine was enthusiastic about the program's results, remarking, "I can't tell you how happy I am about it . . . it's been a marked change, a noticeable change." And indeed, it was a change that reached the ears of people in the federal government as well. White House COVID-19 advisor Andy Slavitt praised the governor: "Mike DeWine has unlocked a secret. . . . People care about COVID, but they also care about other things."[2] Other states, such as Maryland, New York, Colorado, and Oregon, adopted similar programs.

It's always nice to see someone "unlock the secret" of incentives. I love seeing incentives at work and appreciate it when people learn that incentives can be part of their toolbox. Of course—and you can sense the "but" coming—although the Vax-a-Million anecdote is a fun one, the real answer to whether the lottery incentive worked is much more complicated. DeWine noted the jump from fifteen thousand vaccinations per day before the lottery to twenty-six thousand per day during the lottery incentive and concluded, based on this information, that the lottery was a success. The problem with making such a conclusion is easy to identify: there was no control group in which people didn't receive incentives; therefore, the effect of the lottery incentive couldn't be isolated. The jump could have happened because of the implementation of better infrastructure at the time the lottery incentive was put into place or because the vaccine was approved for twelve-year-olds during the same period or for a myriad of other reasons. Without a control group, we can't disentangle the impact of the lottery from other events happening simultaneously. The real world is complicated.[3]

DeWine's conclusion was premature for another important reason: he observed the immediate aftermath of the lottery and failed to consider how incentives might backfire. You know this potential backfire effect well by now. Walk with me through this example. Imagine a scenario in which a medical school is testing a new vaccine and offers you $50 to participate in the clinical trial. The consent form you are asked to sign says that there are only mild known side effects and that the vaccine should be perfectly safe. Many people would consider helping for the greater good—in fact, this is essentially how medical research is currently being conducted. Now, imagine the same scenario, but instead of offering you $50, the medical school offers you $50,000 to participate. What might your reaction be? Mine would probably be something like, "Wait up, hold on, what am I getting into?" A large incentive in such a context signals that the researchers might be withholding information. I might choose to do it for the money, but I'll be concerned. The same might go for million-dollar lottery incentives. Such a payout inadvertently signals to some people, especially those who might already be suspicious of the vaccine and the government, that the vaccines are problematic; otherwise, why in the world would the state be paying so much for them to get it?

Even if everyone buys into the large payout and finds it reasonable given the gravity of the pandemic, the concern remains that the lottery incentive might backfire in the long run. If the lottery increases vaccination rates during the duration of the program, then great. But what happens to people's willingness to get vaccinated after the termination of the lottery incentive? Booster take-up, for example, might go way down. In that case, the state might have been better off not offering the lottery incentive in the first place.

The case of the COVID-19 vaccination effort perfectly demonstrates how the signals embedded in any incentive will work differently on different people. We can sort people into three general categories with respect to incentives. In the first category are those who don't need incentives to perform a given task. In the vaccine scenario, these people are the ones who follow the science and believe that the risk of not getting vaccinated is higher than the risks associated with getting it. In the second category are those who will not perform the task, no matter what the incentives are. Again in the vaccine scenario, these people are the ones who don't believe in the science or in the government and instead think that Bill Gates is using the vaccine to implant microchips into unsuspecting innocents. No incentive would get this group of people to get vaccinated—not even a million-dollar one. The third category includes those who are skeptical or confused and can be swayed either way. These people are the ones you want to target with incentives, and these are also the people who will look for every signal they can use to decide what to do. For them, a huge reward might be a bad signal, for the reasons just stated.

To be clear, the problem is not the use of lotteries as incentives. Consider an example of a lottery that, in my view, did a much better job than the million-dollar one. In May 2021, Phil Murphy, the governor of New Jersey, launched "Operation Jersey Summer." One of the prizes? Dinner with the governor and first lady. Residents who received at least one dose of the COVID-19 vaccination were eligible to enter the lottery. Even if you love Phil Murphy, the dollar value is clearly less than a million. But the incentive was better and smarter because it signaled that people getting vaccinated is important to the governor. It signaled that he takes vaccination seriously and is willing to donate his time to increase vaccination rates. Successful lotteries have also been offered by businesses. Los Angeles County ran a lottery in which the prize was a pair of Lakers season tickets, and the people eligible for it were those who came out the following weekend to get their vaccine. The tickets were donated by the Lakers, who received good PR. More importantly, the tickets signaled that the Lakers wanted to get the games up and running again, with an audience. To do this, they needed their audience to get vaccinated.

Although million-dollar lottery incentives make for great stories and clearly garner the attention of the public and the media, I prefer the less flashy Murphy-type incentives that some public and private organizations have offered—ones with a lower face value. New Jersey, for example, also offered free entrance to state parks for those who got vaccinated. What I like about this incentive is that it was associated with the right signal. As with the Lakers tickets, this incentive told residents that for the state to reopen, people needed to get vaccinated. The incentive—free state park admission—was directly associated with something that people can do safely only if they're vaccinated. To quote New Jersey Parks and Forestry Director John Cecil, "We look forward to welcoming everyone this summer and truly hope many people take advantage of this opportunity to save money while doing the right thing to help end the pandemic."[4] Similar incentives were offered all over the country; New Jersey's neighbor New York offered tickets to the New York City Aquarium, New York Botanical Garden, New York City Ferry, and so on.

My favorite COVID-19 vaccination incentives tie getting the vaccine with the success of local businesses. You probably felt the plea from your local businesses during the shelter-in-place orders. That's why I like the message, "Think of how much your local café/restaurant/bookstore suffered during the pandemic. To support them, you need to get vaccinated and visit them again." In this vein, public and private organizations tied cash-equivalent incentives with supporting local businesses to encourage vaccination. At the end of May 2020, Connecticut Governor Ned Lamont announced that residents who were fully vaccinated would receive a free drink at participating local restaurants.[5] The governor said, "We're doing everything we can to give you an incentive so that if you've been vaccinated, come on in." Scott Dolch, the executive director of the Connecticut Restaurant Association, noted, "It's kind of a 'thank you.' Like, we wouldn't have this date if it wasn't for everybody pitching in and helping our industry, but also going to get the vaccine because they know it's helping us protect the most vulnerable, and get us back to a sense of normalcy again this summer."[6] That's how you use your incentives to send the desired signal. Krispy Kreme implemented this message well, offering customers a free Original Glazed doughnut if they presented a vaccine card, and Shake Shack similarly had the "Get Vaxxed, Get Shack" campaign.[7] It's hard to think of a reason this type of incentive would backfire—they're smart incentives that send the right signal.

The vaccine incentives discussed so far were relatively easy for the public to accept, because the goal was to encourage people to get vaccinated, and the incentives for the most part accomplished that goal without harming those who chose not to get vaccinated. I say "for the most part" because framing the incentives in terms of "getting vaccinated protects you *and* others," as the businesses that encouraged people to get vaccinated did, comes with a cost. The flip side of this message is the implication that those who choose not to get vaccinated don't care about others. Personally, I trust the science and believe that people should get vaccinated, However, using incentives to impose beliefs could be a slippery slope.

The decision of whether such shaming is acceptable is not trivial. Vaccination was and is important enough to many public and private organizations that they have been willing to take a stance. However, others have pushed back. Some organizations have introduced regulations that are incentives in disguise. The most notable of these incentives is the "health pass" that was required in many places around the world to enter restaurants, shows, gyms, and so on. These health passes serve as a way of pushing reluctant individuals over the threshold by making their lives harder and harder.

Unvaccinated people were required either to test every few days or to stay out. Although these regulations stem from health concerns, they were also designed to be a negative incentive that would motivate reluctant individuals to get vaccinated.

Of course, at some point, incentives can turn into policy—in this case, vaccine mandates. The argument in favor of these mandates is clear: when people go to the hospital, they don't want to be treated by an unvaccinated health worker; when flying on an airline, they don't want to receive their pretzels from an unvaccinated flight attendant; when walking into my class, my students don't want to have to worry about an unvaccinated professor or unvaccinated peers. But as clear as the arguments in favor of these mandates are, so are the legal and moral objections.[8]

These are not new objections; similar ones were raised back when seatbelts were mandated. Daniel Ackerman made an interesting comparison in *Business Insider* between the objections to the seatbelts mandate back in the 1980s and the more recent objections to the COVID-19 vaccine mandate. Wearing seatbelts was strictly voluntary in the US until the 1980s. In 1956, a dismal 2 percent of Ford buyers took the $27 seatbelt option, and the death toll was rising. Evidence of the effectiveness of seatbelts in saving lives became clearer and clearer over the next couple of decades, and yet, in 1983, fewer than 15 percent of Americans said they used seatbelts consistently. In 1984, New York became the first state to pass a mandatory seatbelt law, with other states soon following. But, as Ackerman describes, the public was not happy. According to a Gallup poll conducted in July 1984, 65 percent of Americans opposed these mandatory seatbelt laws. As in the case of the vaccine, some objections, such as the claim that it was safer to be thrown clear from a wreckage than trapped inside one, were simply statistically wrong. Other objections cited by Ackerman were moral: "In this country, saving freedom is more important than trying to regulate lives through legislation," wrote an opponent in a 1987 *Chicago Tribune* editorial. Some protested by cutting the belts out of their cars; others challenged seatbelt laws in court. They took a hard stance on individual freedom, declaring, "You're not going to tie the American people up in seat belts."[9]

Just like the seatbelt case, the vaccine mandate sends a great signal precisely because of how strong the challenges against it are. When I think back to my childhood, I remember not even having seatbelts in the backseat. Can you imagine such cars today? The effort to make seatbelts part of our routine was successful. The data show that more than 90 percent of Americans today use seatbelts regularly. As Ackerman notes, this shift took time, public-service campaigns, legal enforcement, and even regular reminders from our cars themselves. All these efforts serve as signals of how important the behavior is to saving lives. Lawmakers don't easily mandate such laws. Similarly, car manufacturers don't add annoying noises to our cars because they think we'll like them. The fact that they chose to do so sends a clear, strong signal regarding the importance they place on the behavior. Whereas changing seatbelt behavior took decades (it took an entire century after invention for the mandate to happen), changing vaccine behavior will probably be faster.

It is in this spirit that we should read the July 2021 call to action from President Biden, urging states to offer $100 to the newly vaccinated, because "people are dying and will die who don't have to die." President Biden noted, "We all benefit if we can get more people vaccinated." He didn't just stop there—at the same time, he issued stricter safety policies for federal workers, requiring employees to show proof of vaccination or be subjected to mandatory testing and masking. He acknowledged the shortcomings of only using monetary incentives and bundled them with stricter measures to send a larger message on the importance of vaccination. As in the case of seatbelts, when the incentives and the extreme messages are aligned, the overall impact of mandates is stronger.[10]

The fact that mandates are such extreme measures signals just how strongly the administration believes that vaccines are important. We know from other examples that these strong signals work. Consider the following example on strong signals and taxes, adapted from Richard Thaler and Cass Sunstein's *Nudge*:

Sweden currently has the highest carbon price in the world, about $130 per metric ton. Since the tax was introduced in 1991 at about $28, and gradually increased to its current level, the country has seen an 83 percent increase in real GDP—comparable to that of other OECD member countries—and a 27 percent decrease in emissions. Though the tax increased gasoline prices, the response to the tax promoted significantly larger behavioral changes than would be expected under a gasoline-price increase alone. There is a general lesson here. If a tax is understood to be responding to a serious problem, people might respond even more than they would to the purely economic incentive. In this context, they might hear a signal that it's good to reduce greenhouse gas emissions—and they might be willing to do that even if it's not in their economic interest. Humans are like that.[11]

The carbon tax made the ultimate objective clear. The tax signaled the administration's priorities.

Another example of a strong signal is fees for disposable plastic shopping bags. The Israeli version of the law, which was introduced in 2017, stipulates that a large retailer must charge customers for the use of a disposable plastic bag and that this amount will be transferred to a fund dedicated to environmental protection. The motivation was stated as follows, "The purpose of this law is to reduce the use of carrier bags, the amount of waste generated as a result of their use, and the negative environmental effects of this waste, . . . including by imposing a surcharge on their sale, . . . to ensure a healthy environment, for the protection of biodiversity, for the prevention and reduction of environmental and health hazards, for the improvement of the quality of life and the environment, for the public and for future generations."[12]

The cost of three cents is very low, but the signal this surcharge sends is very strong. It sends the message that the environment is a high priority. As in the Swedish example, the effect was much larger than what you'd expect if you only looked at the monetary value of the incentive. The year the law was implemented, food-chain customers reduced the use of plastic bags by 80 percent. The data reveal that 378 million bags were sold in 2017, compared with 1.753 billion in 2016, before the law was passed. The total weight of the bags saved was 7,091 tons. Data from other countries show a similar change after passing such laws.

Why was the new Israeli law so successful? Because the message associated with it was clear, making the signaling value even stronger. The law successfully told people that using disposable bags is bad and that they shouldn't do it. There's even a small price associated with doing it, but please—we don't want your money; we want to protect the environment.

When you have a quantum mechanics problem, you consult a physicist. When you have a root canal, you visit a dentist. When your car engine decides to act out, you call a mechanic. In all these cases, you know to consult an expert. Some problems require less technical knowledge and fewer skills, and they're problems you might try solving yourself. My family can tell you all about the time I took it upon myself to build a deck for our house. After reading some articles and watching a couple of YouTube videos, I was hammering away. It took me way longer and cost me much more than if I'd hired a professional, and to top it all off, it resulted in a deck that was not actually stable. But I learned from that experience. A couple of years later, with a bit of consult from a guy who builds decks for a living, I built a second deck that was much more structurally sound, and I'm quite proud of that accomplishment.

The point is that very often, some level of expertise is needed when you're trying to solve a problem. The same is true for when you're designing incentives: when you face a problem that involves trying to get humans to change their behavior, you shouldn't consult only yourself. Doing some research and learning from experienced people can help. Designing incentives requires knowledge that needs to be acquired. It's not quite as difficult as, say, understanding string theory, but some knowledge and experience can help. One of my goals in writing this book was to provide you with that help.

Thank you for reading *Mixed Signals*. I hope you've enjoyed reading it as much as I enjoyed writing it. I'm lucky in that thinking about incentives and how they shape the world is both my hobby and my job, and I can't be any happier about that. It's how I've come to learn a lot about others and about myself. I hope I've inspired you to think about the meaning of incentives as well and how you can put them to work in your life, whether it's motivating your employees or getting one of your kids to potty train. If you are left with only one takeaway from this book, let it be this: incentives send a signal, and your objective is to make sure this signal is aligned with your goals.

Acknowledgments

Writing this book was a fun and rewarding journey. The book is based on many years of research with my coauthors and students—I was lucky to have the friendship and support of so many people along the way.

Early discussions with Katie Baca-Motes helped in forming the book. Sandy Campbell is the most critical reader I have ever had. We started working together just after she graduated college, yet she was never shy in telling me what to do. William Wang and Noam Gneezy read the book from cover to cover and made important contributions. Katie, Sandy, Will, and Noam—thank you!

My editor, Seth Ditchik, was crucial in shaping the message of the book and in making sure I stayed focused on it. A very special thanks to him and all the people at Yale University Press who trusted me. James Levine of the Levine Greenberg Rostan Literary Agency, provided the professional support and excellent guidance through the process. It was a pleasure working with Luigi Segre, who drew the cartoons in the book.

My friends say that Ayelet, my wife and coauthor, deserves a medal for sticking with me for so long; I agree. To her and our kids, Noam, Netta, and Ron, thank you for teaching me the limits of incentives—you are the best thing that has happened to me.

Notes

Introduction

1. Sally Black, "Do You Lie about Your Kids to Get Family Vacation Deals?," *Vacation-Kids*, September 16, 2013, https://www.vacationkids.com/Vacations-with-kids/bid/313333/Do-You-Lie-About-Your-Kids-To-Get-Family-Vacation-Deals.

2. See Emre Soyer and Robin Hogarth, *The Myth of Experience* (New York: Public Affairs, 2020), for more examples and discussion of the psychology literature.

3. Trif Alatzas, "Coke's Price Gouging," *Baltimore Sun*, October 12, 2018.

4. Paul Seabright, *The Company of Strangers: A Natural History of Economic Life* (Princeton, NJ: Princeton University Press, 2010), chap. 1.

5. See, for example, George A. Akerlof and Rachel E. Kranton, "Economics and Identity," *Quarterly Journal of Economics* 115, no. 3 (2000): 715–53; Roland Bénabou and Jean Tirole, "Incentives and Prosocial Behavior," *American Economic Review* 96, no. 5 (2006): 1652–78.

6. Daniel Pink, *Drive: The Surprising Truth about What Motivates Us* (New York: Riverhead, 2009), back cover.

Part One. How Signaling Wins Markets

1. Linda Ghent, Alan Grant, and George Lesica, "The Deal," *The Economics of Seinfeld*, 2010, http://yadayadayadaecon.com/.

Chapter 1. Credible Signals

1. Henry Farrell, "With Your Tattoos and Topknots, Who Do You Think You Are?," *Washington Post*, July 28, 2015, https://www.washingtonpost.com/news/monkey-cage/wp/2015/07/28/with-your-tattoos-and-topknots-who-do-you-think-you-are/.

2. Michael Spence, "Job Market Signaling," *Quarterly Journal of Economics* 87 (1973): 355–74.

Chapter 2. How Toyota Won the Hybrid Car Market

1. Alternative Fuels Data Center, "U.S. HEV Sales by Model," accessed December 2, 2020, https://www.afdc.energy.gov/data/10301.

2. Micheline Maynard, "Say 'Hybrid' and Many People Will Hear 'Prius,'" *New York Times*, July 4, 2007, https://www.nytimes.com/2007/07/04/business/04hybrid.html.

3. Robert J. Samuelson, "Prius Politics," *Washington Post*, July 25, 2007, https://www .washingtonpost.com/wp-dyn/content/article/2007/07/24/AR2007072401855.html.

Chapter 3. It's Just Who I Am

1. Ayelet Gneezy, Uri Gneezy, Gerhard Riener, and Leif D. Nelson, "Pay-What-You-Want, Identity, and Self-Signaling in Markets," *Proceedings of the National Academy of Sciences* 109, no. 19 (2012): 7236–40.

2. Eric Garland, "The 'In Rainbows' Experiment: Did It Work?," NPR, November 17, 2009, https://www.npr.org/sections/monitormix/2009/11/the_in_rainbows_experiment_did .html.

3. Brad VanAuken, "Toyota Prius—Vehicular Self-Expression," *Branding Strategy Insider*, July 10, 2007, https://www.brandingstrategyinsider.com/toyota-prius-ve/.

4. Robert Slonim, Carmen Wang, and Ellen Garbarino, "The Market for Blood," *Journal of Economic Perspectives* 28, no. 2 (2014): 177–96.

5. Dan Tracy, "Blood Is Big Business: Why Does It Cost So Much?," *Orlando Sentinel*, April 5, 2010.

6. Richard Titmuss, *The Gift Relationship: From Human Blood to Social Policy* (London: Allen and Unwin, 1970).

7. Timothy C. Bednall and Liliana L Bove, "Donating Blood: A Meta-Analytic Review of Self-Reported Motivators and Deterrents," *Transfusion Medicine Reviews* 25, no. 4 (2011): 317–34.

8. Robert Slonim, Carmen Wang, and Ellen Garbarino, "The Market for Blood," *Journal of Economic Perspectives* 28, no. 2 (2014): 177–96.

9. Nicola Lacetera and Mario Macis, "Social Image Concerns and Prosocial Behavior: Field Evidence from a Nonlinear Incentive Scheme," *Journal of Economic Behavior and Organization* 76, no. 2 (2010): 225–37.

10. Robert Slonim, Carmen Wang, Ellen Garbarino, and Danielle Merrett, "Opting-In: Participation Bias in Economic Experiments," *Journal of Economic Behavior & Organization* 90 (2013): 43–70.

11. Alois Stutzer, Lorenz Goette, and Michael Zehnder, "Active Decisions and Prosocial Behaviour: A Field Experiment on Blood Donation," *Economic Journal* 121 (2011): F476–F493.

Part Two. Avoid Mixed Signals

1. Bengt Holmstrom and Paul Milgrom, "Multitask Principal-Agent Analyses: Incentive Contracts, Asset Ownership, and Job Design," *Journal of Law, Economics, & Organization* 7 (1991): 24–52.

Chapter 4. When More Is Less

1. Linda Hall Library, "The Pacific Railway, A Brief History of the Pacific Railway," The Transcontinental Railroad, 2012, https://railroad.lindahall.org/essays/brief-history.html. If you want to learn more about Durant and his masterful methods of cheating with incentives, I strongly recommend AMC's Hell on Wheels TV series.

2. James D. Gwartney, *Common Sense Economics: What Everyone Should Know about Wealth and Prosperity* (New York: St. Martin's, 2016).

3. Austan Goolsbee, "Buses That Run on Time," *Slate*, March 16, 2006, https://slate.com/business/2006/03/buses-that-run-on-time.html.

4. Ryan M. Johnson, David H. Reiley, and Juan Carlos Muñoz, "'The War for the Fare': How Driver Compensation Affects Bus System Performance," *Economic Inquiry* 53, no. 3 (2015): 1401–19.

5. Nicole Tam, "A Millennial Investigates: Why Would Anyone Take a Taxi Instead of Uber or Lyft?," *Hawaii Business Magazine*, March 8, 2019, https://www.hawaiibusiness.com/a-millennial-investigates-why-would-anyone-take-a-taxi-instead-of-uber-or-lyft/.

6. Scott Wallsten, "Has Uber Forced Taxi Drivers to Step Up Their Game?," *Atlantic*, July 24, 2015, https://www.theatlantic.com/business/archive/2015/07/uber-taxi-drivers-complaints-chicago-newyork/397931/.

7. Alice Park, "Your Doctor Likely Orders More Tests than You Actually Need," *Time*, March 24, 2015, https://time.com/3754900/doctors-unnecessary-tests/.

8. Robert A. Berenson and Eugene C. Rich, "US Approaches to Physician Payment: The Deconstruction of Primary Care," *Journal of General Internal Medicine* 25, no. 6 (2010): 613–18.

9. Marshall Allen, "Unnecessary Medical Care: More Common than You Might Imagine," NPR, February 1, 2018, https://www.npr.org/sections/health shots/2018/02/01/582216198/unnecessary-medical-care-more-common-than-you-might-imagine.

10. Peter G. Peterson Foundation, "How Does the U.S. Healthcare System Compare to Other Countries?," July 14, 2020, https://www.pgpf.org/blog/2020/07/how-does-the-us-healthcare-system-compare-to-other-countries.

11. Lorie Konish, "This Is the Real Reason Most Americans File for Bankruptcy," CNBC, February 11, 2019, https://www.cnbc.com/2019/02/11/this-is-the-real-reason-most-americans-file-for-bankruptcy.html.

12. Kristen Fischer, "There Are Some Benefits to C-Sections, Researchers Say," *Healthline*, April 5, 2019, https://www.healthline.com/health-news/some-benefits-to-c-sections-researchers-say.

13. Emily Oster and W. Spencer McClelland, "Why the C-Section Rate Is So High," *Atlantic*, October 17, 2019, https://www.theatlantic.com/ideas/archive/2019/10/c-section-rate-high/600172/.

14. Shankar Vedantam, "Money May Be Motivating Doctors to Do More C-Sections," NPR, August 30, 2013, https://www.npr.org/sections/health-shots/2013/08/30/216479305/money-may-be-motivating-doctors-to-do-more-c-sections.

15. Jonathan Gruber and Maria Owings, "Physician Financial Incentives and Cesarean Section Delivery," *RAND Journal of Economics* 27, no. 1 (1996): 99–123.

16. Scott Hensley, "About a Third of Births, Even for First-Time Moms, Are Now by Cesarean," NPR, August 31, 2010, https://www.npr.org/sections/health-shots/2010/08/31/129552505/cesarean-sections-stay-popular/.

17. Erin M. Johnson and M. Marit Rehavi, "Physicians Treating Physicians: Information and Incentives in Childbirth," *American Economic Journal: Economic Policy* 8, no. 1 (2016): 115–41.

18. Joshua T. Cohen, Peter J. Neumann, and Milton C. Weinstein, "Does Preventive Care Save Money? Health Economics and the Presidential Candidates," *New England Journal of Medicine* 358, no. 7 (2008): 661–63.

19. Centers for Disease Control and Prevention, "Up to 40 Percent of Annual Deaths from Each of Five Leading US Causes Are Preventable," December 9, 2020, https://www.cdc.gov/media/releases/2014/p0501-preventable-deaths.html.

20. Shankar Vedantam, "Host, Hidden Brain," NPR, December 3, 2020, https://www.npr.org/people/137765146/shankar-vedantam. The book is Vivian Lee, *The Long Fix: Solving America's Health Care Crisis with Strategies That Work for Everyone* (New York: Norton, 2020).

21. Michael Hewak and Adam Kovacs-Litman, "Physician Compensation Structures and How They Incentivize Specific Patient Care Behaviour," *University of Western Ontario Medical Journal* 84, no. 1 (2015): 15–17.

22. NEJM Catalyst, "What Is Pay for Performance in Healthcare?," March 1, 2018, https://catalyst.nejm.org/doi/full/10.1056/CAT.18.0245.

23. Joshua Gans, "Episode 205: Allowance, Taxes and Potty Training," *Planet Money*, NPR, July 6, 2012, https://www.npr.org/sections/money/2012/07/06/156391538/episode-205-allowance-taxes-and-potty-training.

Chapter 5. Encouraging Innovation but Punishing Failure

1. Moral Stories, "Learning from Mistakes," October 8, 2019, https://www.moralstories.org/learning-from-mistakes/.

2. Franklin Institute, "Edison's Lightbulb," May 19, 2017, https://www.fi.edu/history-resources/edisons-lightbulb.

3. Dean Keith Simonton, *Origins of Genius* (Oxford: Oxford University Press, 1999).

4. Bob Sutton, "Why Rewarding People for Failure Makes Sense: Paying 'Kill Fees' for Bad Projects," *Bob Sutton Work Matters* (blog), October 4, 2007, https://bobsutton.typepad.com/my_weblog/2007/10/why-rewarding-p.html.

5. Arlene Weintraub, "Is Merck's Medicine Working?," *Bloomberg*, July 30, 2007, https://www.bloomberg.com/news/articles/2007-07-29/is-mercks-medicine-working.

6. Astro Teller, "The Unexpected Benefit of Celebrating Failure," TED, 2016, https://www.ted.com/talks/astro_teller_the_unexpected_benefit_of_celebrating_failure?language=en.

7. Rita Gunther McGrath, "Failure Is a Gold Mine for India's Tata," *Harvard Business Review*, April 11, 2011, https://hbr.org/2011/04/failure-is-a-gold-mine-for-ind.

8. Ben Unglesbee, "A Timeline of Blockbuster's Ride from Megahit to Flop," *Retail Dive*, October 7, 2019, https://www.retaildive.com/news/a-timeline-of-blockbusters-ride-from-megahit-to-flop/564305/.

9. Andy Ash, "The Rise and Fall of Blockbuster and How It's Surviving with Just One Store Left," *Business Insider*, August 12, 2020, https://www.businessinsider.com/the-rise-and-fall-of-blockbuster-video-streaming-2020-1.

10. Greg Satell, "A Look Back at Why Blockbuster Really Failed and Why It Didn't Have To," *Forbes*, September 21, 2014, https://www.forbes.com/sites/gregsatell/2014/09/05/a-look-back-at-why-blockbuster-really-failed-and-why-it-didnt-have-to/.

11. "Timeline of Netflix," Wikipedia, accessed April 23, 2022, https://en.wikipedia.org/wiki/Timeline_of_Netflix.

12. "Richard Branson," Wikipedia, accessed November 30, 2020, https://en.wikipedia.org/wiki/Richard_Branson.

13. Catherine Clifford, "What Richard Branson Learned When Coke Put Virgin Cola out of Business," CNBC, February 7, 2017, https://www.cnbc.com/2017/02/07/what-richard-branson-learned-when-coke-put-virgin-cola-out-of-business.html.

14. "14 Virgin Companies That Even Richard Branson Could Not Stop Going Bust," *Business Insider*, May 31, 2016, https://www.businessinsider.com/richard-branson-fails-virgin-companies-that-went-bust-2016-5.

Chapter 6. Encouraging Long-Term Goals but Rewarding Short-Term Results

1. Newman Ferrara LLP, "Corporate Governance Expert Tackles Acquisition Violation," December 22, 2014, https://www.nyrealestatelawblog.com/manhattan-litigation-blog/2014/december/professor-kicks-bazaarvoices-butt/.

2. Office of Public Affairs, US Department of Justice, "Justice Department Files Antitrust Lawsuit against Bazaarvoice Inc. Regarding the Company's Acquisition of PowerReviews Inc.," January 10, 2013, https://www.justice.gov/opa/pr/justice-department-files-antitrust-lawsuit-against-bazaarvoice-inc-regarding-company-s.

3. Tomislav Ladika and Zacharias Sautner, "Managerial Short-Termism and Investment: Evidence from Accelerated Option Vesting," Harvard Law School Forum on Corporate Governance, July 17, 2019, https://corpgov.law.harvard.edu/2019/07/17/managerial-short-termism-and-investment-evidence-from-accelerated-option-vesting/.

4. Alex Edmans, Vivian W. Fang, and Katharina A. Lewellen, "Equity Vesting and Investment," *Review of Financial Studies* 30, no. 7 (2017): 2229–71.

5. Lucian Bebchuk and Jesse Fried, *Pay without Performance: The Unfulfilled Promise of Executive Compensation* (Cambridge, MA: Harvard University Press, 2004); Lucian A. Bebchuk and Jesse M. Fried, "Paying for Long-Term Performance," *University of Pennsylvania Law Review* 158 (2010): 1915–59.

6. Caroline Banton, "Escrow," Investopedia, March 9, 2021, https://www.investopedia.com/terms/e/escrow.asp.

7. Glenn Davis and Ken Bertsch, "Policy Overhaul—Executive Compensation," Harvard Law School Forum on Corporate Governance, November 30, 2019, https://corpgov.law.harvard.edu/2019/11/30/policy-overhaul-executive-compensation/.

8. Ellen R. Delisio, "Pay for Performance: What Are the Issues?," *Education World*, accessed April 23, 2022, https://www.educationworld.com/a_issues/issues/issues374a.shtml.

9. Elaine McArdle, "Right on the Money," Harvard Graduate School of Education, 2010, https://www.gse.harvard.edu/news/ed/10/01/right-money.

10. Robin Chait and Raegen Miller, "Getting the Facts Straight on the Teacher Incentive Fund," Center for American Progress, June 13, 2009, https://www.americanprogress.org/issues/education-k-12/reports/2009/07/13/6390/getting-the-facts-straight-on-the-teacher-incentive-fund/.

11. US Department of Education, "Teacher Incentive Fund," September 27, 2016, https://www2.ed.gov/programs/teacherincentive/funding.html.

12. "No Child Left Behind Act," Wikipedia, accessed December 4, 2020, https://en.wikipedia.org/wiki/No_Child_Left_Behind_Act.

13. Rachel Tustin, "I'm a Teacher and Here's My Honest Opinion on Standardized Tests," Study.com, November 2017, https://study.com/blog/i-m-a-teacher-and-here-s-my-honest-opinion-on-standardized-tests.html.

14. Diane Stark Rentner, Nancy Kober, and Matthew Frizzell, "Listen to Us: Teacher Views and Voices," Center on Education Policy, May 5, 2016, https://www.cep-dc.org/displayDocument.cfm?DocumentID=1456.

15. PBS, "Finland: What's the Secret to Its Success?," *Where We Stand* (blog), September 5, 2008, https://www.pbs.org/wnet/wherewestand/blog/globalization-finland-whats-the-secret-to-its-success/206/.

16. Uri Gneezy and John List, *The Why Axis: Hidden Motives and the Undiscovered Economics of Everyday Life* (New York: Public Affairs, 2013).

Chapter 7. Encouraging Teamwork but Incentivizing Individual Success

1. Bill Taylor, "Great People Are Overrated," *Harvard Business Review*, June 20, 2011, https://hbr.org/2011/06/great-people-are-overrated.

2. "Tom Brady," Wikipedia, accessed April 23, 2022, https://en.wikipedia.org/wiki/Tom_Brady.

3. Greig Finlay, "Why Did Tom Brady Leave New England Patriots? Move to Tampa Bay Buccaneers Explained after Super Bowl 2021 Victory," *Scotsman*, February 8, 2021, https://www.scotsman.com/sport/other-sport/why-did-tom-brady-leave-new-england-patriots-move-tampa-bay-buccaneers-explained-after-super-bowl-2021-victory-3127497.

4. FC Barcelona, "Lionel Messi," accessed December 4, 2020, https://www.fcbarcelona.com/en/players/4974.

5. Marcel Desailly, "Messi's in a Mess and Doesn't Seem to Fit into the Argentina Collective," *Guardian*, June 28, 2018, https://www.theguardian.com/football/blog/2018/jun/28/lionel-messi-argentina-france-world-cup.

6. Rory Marsden, "Lionel Messi Has 'Different Attitude' with Argentina, Says Daniel Passarella," *Bleacher Report*, March 25, 2019, https://bleacherreport.com/articles/2827673?fb_comment_id=2244994605562520_2246297898765524.

7. Hayley Peterson, "A War Is Breaking Out between McDonald's, Burger King, and Wendy's—and That's Great News for Consumers," *Business Insider*, October 15, 2015, https://www.businessinsider.in/A-war-is-breaking-out-between-McDonalds-Burger-King-and-Wendys-and-thats-great-news-for-consumers/articleshow/49387367.cms.

8. Gary Bornstein and Uri Gneezy, "Price Competition between Teams," *Experimental Economics* 5 (2002): 29–38.

9. Reuben Pinder, "Paul Pogba and Alexis Sánchez's Goal Bonuses Have Caused Dressing Room Row at Manchester United," *JOE*, May 12, 2019, https://www.joe.co.uk/sport/paul-pogba-alexis-sanchez-goal-bonus-row-231299.

10. Joe Morphet, "Premier League Players' Jaw-Dropping Bonuses Revealed," *BeSoccer*, May 12, 2018, https://www.besoccer.com/new/premier-league-players-jaw-dropping-bonuses-revealed-426953.

11. Ken Lawrence, "Sanchez and Pogba at Heart of Man Utd Rift over Lucrative Goal Bonuses," *Sun*, May 11, 2019, https://www.thesun.co.uk/sport/football/9054278/sanchez-pogba-man-utd-goal-bonus-rift/.

12. Morphet, "Premier League Players' Jaw-Dropping Bonuses Revealed."

13. Joe Prince-Wright, "How Much? Zlatan's Goal Bonus Reportedly Leaked," *NBC Sports*, May 10, 2017, https://soccer.nbcsports.com/2017/05/10/how-much-zlatans-goal-bonus-reportedly-leaked/.

14. Michael Reis, "Next Time Firmino Scores He Receives £45000. From 11th Goal on £65000, from 16th £85000," Twitter, December 10, 2016, https://twitter.com/donreisino/status/807590847680233474?s=20.

15. Josh Lawless, "Roberto Firmino's Incredible Bonuses Have Been Revealed," *Sport Bible*, June 6, 2017, https://www.sportbible.com/football/news-roberto-firminos-incredible-bonuses-have-been-revealed-20170511.

16. Grant Wahl, "How Do MLS Financial Bonuses Work? A Look at One Player's Contract," *Sports Illustrated*, November 23, 2015, https://www.si.com/soccer/2015/11/23/mls-player-contract-bonuses.

17. Zach Links, "PFR Glossary: Contract Incentives," *Pro Football Rumors*, June 19, 2018, https://www.profootballrumors.com/2018/06/nfl-contract-incentives-football.

18. Mark Graban, "Individual NFL Player Incentives—Why Are They Necessary? Do They Distort the Game?," *Lean Blog*, January 2, 2011, https://www.leanblog.org/2011/01/individual-nfl-player-incentives-why-are-they-necessary-do-they-distort-the-game/.

19. "Terrell Suggs," Wikipedia, accessed December 4, 2020, https://en.wikipedia.org/wiki/Terrell_Suggs.

20. NFL, "2019 Performance-Based Pay Distributions Announced," 2019, https://nflcommunications.com/Pages/2019-PERFORMANCE-BASED-PAY-DISTRIBUTIONS-ANNOUNCED--.aspx.

Chapter 8. Stakes and Mistakes

1. Bethany McLean, "How Wells Fargo's Cutthroat Corporate Culture Allegedly Drove Bankers to Fraud," *Vanity Fair*, May 31, 2017, https://www.vanityfair.com/news/2017/05/wells-fargo-corporate-culture-fraud.

2. Jackie Wattles, Ben Geier, Matt Egan, and Danielle Wiener-Bronner, "Wells Fargo's 20-Month Nightmare," *CNN Money*, April 24, 2018, https://money.cnn.com/2018/04/24/news/companies/wells-fargo-timeline-shareholders/index.html.

3. Matt Egan, "Wells Fargo Admits to Signs of Worker Retaliation," *CNN Money*, January 23, 2017, https://money.cnn.com/2017/01/23/investing/wells-fargo-retaliation-ethics-line/index.html?iid=EL.

4. Uri Gneezy and Aldo Rustichini, "A Fine Is a Price," *Journal of Legal Studies* 29, no. 1 (2000): 1–17.

5. "Fining Parents 'Has No Effect on School Absence in Wales,'" *BBC News*, May 10, 2018, https://www.bbc.com/news/uk-wales-44054574.

6. Cecile Meier, "Mum Charged $55 for Being One Minute Late for Daycare Pickup." *Essential Baby*, August 2, 2018, http://www.essentialbaby.com.au/toddler/childcare/mum -charged-55-for-being-one-minute-late-for-daycare-pickup-20180801-h13ewo.

7. Sam Peltzman, "The Effects of Automobile Safety Regulation," *Journal of Political Economy* 83, no. 4 (1975): 677–725. Critical analysis found that Peltzman's model was wrong on many dimensions. A recent *Slate* article connects the concept to safety measures used during COVID-19. The bottom line: People do take more risks once safety measures are introduced, but this psychological impact is smaller than the technological improvement in safety. Tim Requarth, "Our Worst Idea about Safety.'" *Slate*, November 7, 2021.

8. Steven E. Landsburg, *The Armchair Economist* (New York: Macmillan, 1993).

9. Shay Maunz, "The Great Hanoi Rat Massacre of 1902 Did Not Go as Planned," *Atlas Obscura*, June 6, 2017, https://www.atlasobscura.com/articles/hanoi-rat-massacre-1902.

10. Michael Vann, "Of Rats, Rice, and Race: The Great Hanoi Rat Massacre, an Episode in French Colonial History," *French Colonial History* 4 (2003): 191–204. The Great Hanoi Rat Massacre, as it is now commonly referred to, is not unique in nature. Similar incidents have happened elsewhere. The British governor of Delhi in colonial India, for example, incentivized the killing of cobras, and local entrepreneurs reacted by creating cobra farms. See "The Cobra Effect," episode 96, *Freakonomics* (podcast), October 11, 2012, https://freakonomics .com/podcast/the-cobra-effect-2/.

11. "Puglia's Trulli," *The Thinking Traveller*, accessed December 4, 2020, https://www .thethinkingtraveller.com/italy/puglia/trulli.

12. Tony Traficante, "The Amazing 'Trulli,'" Italian Sons and Daughters of America, March 21, 2017, https://orderisda.org/culture/travel/the-amazing-trulli/.

13. Alex A., "Trulli: The Unique Stone Huts of Apulia," *Vintage News*, January 14, 2018, https://www.thevintagenews.com/2018/01/04/trulli-apulia/.

14. Italian Tourism, "The History of Alberobello's Trulli," accessed December 4, 2020, http://www.italia.it/en/discover-italy/apulia/poi/the-history-of-alberobellos-trulli.html.

15. UK Parliament, "Window Tax," accessed December 4, 2020, https://www.parliament .uk/about/living-heritage/transformingsociety/towncountry/towns/tyne-and-wear-case -study/about-the-group/housing/window-tax/; "Window Tax," Wikipedia.org.

16. "When Letting in Sunshine Could Cost You Money," *History House*, accessed December 4, 2020, https://historyhouse.co.uk/articles/window_tax.html.

17. Wallace E. Oates and Robert M. Schwab, "The Window Tax: A Case Study in Excess Burden," *Journal of Economic Perspectives* 29, no. 1 (2015): 163–80.

18. Tom Coggins, "A Brief History of Amsterdam's Narrow Canal Houses," *The Culture Trip*, December 7, 2016, Theculturetrip.com.

19. Karen Kingston, "Why Dutch Stairs Are So Steep," *Karen Kingston's Blog*, August 15, 2013, https://www.karenkingston.com/blog/why-dutch-stairs-are-so-steep/.

20. Nanlan Wu, "The Xiaogang Village Story," China.org.cn, March 6, 2008, http://www.china.org.cn/china/features/content_11778487.htm.

Chapter 9. Mental Accounting

1. Teke Wiggin, "Redfin CEO Glenn Kelman: Low Commission Fees Aren't 'Rational,'" Inman, June 30, 2015, https://www.inman.com/2015/06/30/redfin-ceo-glenn-kelman-low-commission-fees-arent-rational/.

2. Richard Thaler, "Transaction Utility Theory," *Advances in Consumer Research* 10 (1983): 229–32.

2. Richard Thaler, "Mental Accounting Matters," *Journal of Behavioral Decision Making* 12 (1999): 183–206.

3. Johannes Abeler and Felix Marklein, "Fungibility, Labels, and Consumption," *Journal of the European Economic Association* 15, no. 1 (2017): 99–127.

4. Uri Gneezy, Teck-Hua Ho, Marcel Bilger, and Eric A. Finkelstein, "Mental Accounting, Targeted Incentives, and the Non-fungibility of Incentives" (unpublished paper, 2019).

5. Roland Fryer, Steven D. Levitt, John List, and Sally Sadoff, "Enhancing the Efficacy of Teacher Incentives through Loss Aversion: A Field Experiment" (NBER Working Paper 18237, National Bureau of Economic Research, 2012).

6. The students were tested with the ThinkLink Predictive Assessment, a standardized diagnostic tool that is aligned with state achievement tests.

7. Daniel Kahneman and Amos Tversky, "Prospect Theory: An Analysis of Decision under Risk," *Econometrica* 47, no. 2 (1979): 263–91; Amos Tversky and Daniel Kahneman, "Loss Aversion in Riskless Choice: A Reference-Dependent Model," *Quarterly Journal of Economics* 106, no. 4 (1991): 1039–61.

8. Tanjim Hossain and John A. List, "The Behavioralist Visits the Factory: Increasing Productivity Using Simple Framing Manipulations," *Management Science* 58 (2012): 2151–67.

Chapter 10. Regret as Incentives

1. S. Lock, "Sales of State Lotteries in the U.S. 2009–2019," Statista, March 31, 2020, https://www.statista.com/statistics/215265/sales-of-us-state-and-provincial-lotteries/.

2. Daniel Kahneman and Amos Tversky, "Prospect Theory: An Analysis of Decision Making under Risk," *Econometrica* 47 (1979): 263–91.

3. Marcel Zeelenberg and Rik Pieters, "Consequences of Regret Aversion in Real Life: The Case of the Dutch Postcode Lottery," *Organizational Behavior and Human Decision Processes* 93, no. 2 (2004): 155–68.

4. Zeelenberg and Pieters.

5. Eric Van Dijk and Marcel Zeelenberg, "On the Psychology of 'If Only': Regret and the Comparison between Factual and Counterfactual Outcomes," *Organizational Behavior and Human Decision Processes* 97, no. 2 (2005): 152–60.

6. Linda L. Golden, Thomas W. Anderson, and Louis K. Sharpe, "The Effects of Salutation, Monetary Incentive, and Degree of Urbanization on Mail Questionnaire Response Rate, Speed, and Quality," in *Advances in Consumer Research*, vol. 8, ed. Kent S. Monroe (Ann Arbor, MI: Association for Consumer Research, 1980), 292–98; James R. Rudd and E. Scott Geller, "A University-based Incentive Program to Increase Safety Belt Use: Toward Cost-Effective Institutionalization," *Journal of Applied Behavior Analysis* 18, no. 3 (1985): 215–26.

7. Kevin G. Volpp, George Loewenstein, Andrea B. Troxel, Jalpa Doshi, Maureen Price, Mitchell Laskin, and Stephen E Kimmel, "A Test of Financial Incentives to Improve Warfarin Adherence," *BMC Health Services Research* 8 (2008): 272.

Chapter 11. Prosocial Incentives

1. Uri Gneezy and Aldo Rustichini, "Pay Enough or Don't Pay at All," *Quarterly Journal of Economics* 115, no. 3 (2000): 791–810.

2. Ron Roy, "Volunteer Firefighters: Why We Do What We Do," *Fire Engineering*, January 23, 2020, https://www.fireengineering.com/2020/01/23/483462/volunteer-firefighters -why-we-do-what-we-do/.

3. Ben Evarts and Gary P. Stein, "NFPA's 'U.S. Fire Department Profile,'" NFPA, February 2020, https://www.nfpa.org/News-and-Research/Data-research-and-tools/Emergency -Responders/US-fire-department-profile.

4. "Volunteer Fire Department," Wikipedia, accessed December 8, 2020, https://en .wikipedia.org/wiki/Volunteer_fire_department.

5. Alex Imas, "Working for the 'Warm Glow': On the Benefits and Limits of Prosocial Incentives," *Journal of Public Economics* 114 (2014): 14–18.

6. Stephanie Clifford, "Would You Like a Smile with That?," *New York Times*, August 6, 2011, https://www.nytimes.com/2011/08/07/business/pret-a-manger-with-new-fast -food-ideas-gains-a-foothold-in-united-states.html?pagewanted=all.

Chapter 12. Awards as Signals

1. Eulalie McDowell, "Medal of Honor Winner Says Feat Was Miracle," *Knoxville News-Sentinel*, October 12, 1945, accessed at https://www.newspapers.com/clip/40200051/the -knoxville-news-sentinel/.

2. Erin Kelly, "The True Story of WWII Medic Desmond Doss Was Too Heroic Even for 'Hacksaw Ridge,'" *All That's Interesting*, September 20, 2017, https://allthatsinteresting.com/desmond-doss.

3. Kelly.

4. Uri Gneezy, Sandy Campbell, and Jana Gallus, "Tangibility, Self-Signaling and Signaling to Others" (unpublished paper, 2022).

5. Matt Straz, "4 Ways Innovative Companies Are Celebrating Their Employees," *Entrepreneur*, August 17, 2015, https://www.entrepreneur.com/article/249460.

6. "Navy Cross," Wikipedia, accessed December 5, 2020, https://en.wikipedia.org/wiki/Navy_Cross.

7. Tom Vanden Brook, "Almost 20% of Top Medals Awarded Secretly since 9/11," *USA Today*, February 29, 2016, https://www.usatoday.com/story/news/nation/2016/02/29/almost-20-top-medals-awarded-secretly-since-911/81119316/.

8. Lin Edwards, "Report Claims Wikipedia Losing Editors in Droves." Phys.org, November 30, 2009, https://phys.org/news/2009-11-wikipedia-editors-droves.html.

9. "Wikipedia: Awards," Wikipedia, accessed December 9, 2020, https://en.wikipedia.org/wiki/Wikipedia:Awards.

10. Jana Gallus, "Fostering Public Good Contributions with Symbolic Awards: A Large-Scale Natural Field Experiment at Wikipedia," *Management Science* 63, no. 12 (2017): 3999–4015.

11. "Top Five Most Difficult Sports Trophies to Win," CBS Miami, July 1, 2014, https://miami.cbslocal.com/2014/07/01/top-five-most-difficult-sports-trophies-to-win/.

12. Carly D. Robinson, Jana Gallus, and Todd Rogers, "The Demotivating Effect (and Unintended Message) of Awards," *Organizational Behavior and Human Decision Processes*, May 29, 2019.

13. Melia Robinson, "The Unbelievable Story of Why Marlon Brando Rejected His 1973 Oscar for 'The Godfather,'" *Business Insider*, February 24, 2017, https://www.businessinsider.com/marlon-brando-rejected-godfather-oscar-2017-2.

14. Oscars, "Marlon Brando's Oscar Win for 'The Godfather,'" YouTube, October 2, 2008, https://www.youtube.com/watch?v=2QUacUoI4yU&ab_channel=Oscars.

15. "Sacheen Littlefeather," Wikipedia, accessed December 5, 2020, https://en.wikipedia.org/wiki/Sacheen_Littlefeather.

16. Becky Little, "Academy Award Winners Who Rejected Their Oscars," History, February 26, 2018, https://www.history.com/news/brando-oscar-protest-sacheen-littlefeather-academy-award-refusal.

17. Gallus, "Fostering Public Good Contributions."

18. Golden Globes, "The Cecil B. DeMille Award," accessed December 5, 2020, https://www.goldenglobes.com/cecil-b-demille-award-0.

19. Zainab Akande, "Denzel Washington So Earned the DeMille Award," *Bustle*, December 10, 2015, https://www.bustle.com/articles/128808-who-is-the-2016-cecil-b-demille-award-winner-this-years-winner-completely-deserves-the-honor.

20. Meena Jang, "Golden Globes: Denzel Washington Accepts Cecil B. DeMille Award," *Hollywood Reporter*, January 10, 2016, https://www.hollywoodreporter.com/news/golden-globes-2016-denzel-washington-853375.

21. Tom Shone, "The Golden Globes Are More Fun than the Oscars—and They Pick Better Winners, Too," *Slate*, January 13, 2012, https://slate.com/culture/2012/01/golden-globes-better-than-the-oscars.html.

Part Four. Use Incentives to Identify the Problem

1. Jessica Firger, "12 Million Americans Misdiagnosed Each Year," CBS News, April 17, 2014, https://www.cbsnews.com/news/12-million-americans-misdiagnosed-each-year-study-says/.

Chapter 13. Are US Students Really So Bad?

1. "Effort, Not Ability, May Explain the Gap between American and Chinese Pupils," *Economist*, August 17, 2017, https://www.economist.com/news/united-states/21726745-when-greenbacks-are-offer-american-schoolchildren-seem-try-harder-effort-not.

2. National Center for Education Statistics, "Program for International Student Assessment (PISA)—Overview," accessed December 5, 2020, https://nces.ed.gov/surveys/pisa/index.asp.

3. Organisation for Economic Co-operation and Development, "PISA 2015 Results in Focus," 2018, https://www.oecd.org/pisa/pisa-2015-results-in-focus.pdf.

4. Sotiria Grek, "Governing by Numbers: The PISA 'Effect' in Europe," *Journal of Education Policy* 24 (2009): 23–37.

5. Organisation for Economic Co-operation and Development, "PISA 2012 Results: What Students Know and Can Do, Student Performance in Mathematics, Reading and Science, Volume I," 2014, https://www.oecd.org/pisa/keyfindings/pisa-2012-results-volume-I.pdf.

6. Sam Dillon, "Top Test Scores from Shanghai Stun Educators," *New York Times*, December 7, 2010, https://www.nytimes.com/2010/12/07/education/07education.html.

7. Martin Carnoy and Richard Rothstein, "What Do International Tests Really Show about U.S. Student Performance?," Economic Policy Institute, January 28, 2013, https://www.epi.org/publication/us-student-performance-testing/; Harold W. Stevenson and James W.

Stigler, *The Learning Gap: Why Our Schools Are Failing and What We Can Learn from Japanese and Chinese Education* (New York: Summit Books, 1992); Eric A. Hanushek and Ludger Woessmann, "How Much Do Educational Outcomes Matter in OECD Countries?," *Economic Policy* 26, no. 67 (2011): 427–91.

8. Uri Gneezy, John A. List, Jeffrey A. Livingston, Xiangdong Qin, Sally Sadoff, and Yang Xu, "Measuring Success in Education: The Role of Effort on the Test Itself," *American Economic Review: Insights* 1, no. 3 (2019): 291–308.

9. Ben Leubsdorf, "Maybe American Students Are Bad at Standardized Tests Because They Don't Try Very Hard," *Wall Street Journal*, November 27, 2017, https://blogs.wsj.com/economics/2017/11/27/maybe-american-students-are-bad-at-standardized-tests-because-they-dont-try-very-hard/.

Chapter 14. Overhead Aversion

1. National Philanthropic Trust, "Charitable Giving Statistics," accessed December 5, 2020, https://www.nptrust.org/philanthropic-resources/charitable-giving-statistics/.

2. Dan Pallotta, "The Way We Think about Charity Is Dead Wrong," TED, March 2013, https://www.ted.com/talks/dan_pallotta_the_way_we_think_about_charity_is_dead_wrong.

3. Jonathan Baron and Ewa Szymanska, "Heuristics and Biases in Charity," in *The Science of Giving: Experimental Approaches to the Study of Charity*, ed. Daniel M. Oppenheimer and Christopher Y. Olivola (New York: Psychology Press, 2011), 215–36; Lucius Caviola, Nadira Faulmüller, Jim A. C. Everett, Julian Savulescu, and Guy Kahane, "The Evaluability Bias in Charitable Giving: Saving Administration Costs or Saving Lives," *Judgment and Decision Making* 9 (2014): 303–16.

4. Uri Gneezy, Elizabeth A. Keenan, and Ayelet Gneezy, "Avoiding Overhead Aversion in Charity," *Science* 346, no. 6209 (2014): 632–35.

5. Lise Vesterlund, "Why Do People Give?," in *The Nonprofit Sector: A Research Handbook*, 2nd ed., ed. Walter W. Powell and Richard Steinberg (New Haven, CT: Yale University Press, 2006), 568–88.

6. Aleron, "Why Charities Should Look at New Ways of Measuring Impact," 2013, https://aleronpartners.com/why-charities-should-look-at-new-ways-of-measuring-impact/.

7. charity:water, "The 100% Model: Charity: Water," accessed December 9, 2020, https://www.charitywater.org/our-approach/100-percent-model.

Chapter 15. "Pay to Quit" Strategy

1. Jim Edwards, "This Company Pays Employees $25,000 to Quit—No Strings Attached—Even If They Were Just Hired," *Business Insider*, June 20, 2014, https://www.businessinsider.com/riot-games-pays-employees-25000-to-quit-2014-6.

2. Jim Edwards, "Amazon Pays Employees Up to $5,000 to Quit," *Slate*, April 10, 2014, https://slate.com/business/2014/04/amazon-jeff-bezos-shareholder-letter-the-company-pays-workers-up-to-5000-to-quit.html.

3. Ian Ayres and Giuseppe Dari-Mattiacci, "Reactive Incentives: Harnessing the Impact of Sunk Opportunity Costs" (Columbia Law and Economics Working Paper 612, 2019).

4. Bill Taylor, "Why Zappos Pays New Employees to Quit—And You Should Too," *Harvard Business Review*, March 19, 2008, https://hbr.org/2008/05/why-zappos-pays-new-employees.

5. Christopher G. Harris, "The Effects of Pay-to-Quit Incentives on Crowdworker Task Quality," in *Proceedings of the 18th ACM Conference on Computer Supported Cooperative Work & Social Computing* (New York: Association for Computing Machinery, 2015), 1801–12.

6. Harris.

Chapter 16. Bribing the Self

1. Institute of Medicine, Committee on the Learning Health Care System in America, Mark Smith, Robert Saunders, Leigh Stuckhardt, and J. Michael McGinnis, eds., *Best Care at Lower Cost: The Path to Continuously Learning Health Care in America* (Washington, DC: National Academies Press, 2013).

2. John N. Mafi, Ellen P. McCarthy, Roger B. Davis, and Bruce E. Landon, "Worsening Trends in the Management and Treatment of Back Pain," *JAMA Internal Medicine* 173, no. 17 (2013): 1573–81.

3. Colette DeJong, Thomas Aguilar, Chien-Wen Tseng, Grace A. Lin, W. John Boscardin, and R. Adam Dudley, "Pharmaceutical Industry-Sponsored Meals and Physician Prescribing Patterns for Medicare Beneficiaries," *JAMA Internal Medicine* 176, no. 8 (2016): 1114–22.

4. Rickie Houston, "Your Financial Advisor's Conflicts of Interest," *SmartAsset*, January 16, 2020, https://smartasset.com/financial-advisor/financial-advisor-conflicts-of-interest.

5. Uri Gneezy, Silvia Saccardo, Marta Serra-Garcia, and Roel van Veldhuizen, "Bribing the Self," *Games and Economic Behavior* 120 (2020): 311–24.

6. Charles Ornstein, Mike Tigas, and Ryann Grochowski Jones, "Now There's Proof: Docs Who Get Company Cash Tend to Prescribe More Brand-Name Meds," ProPublica, March 17, 2016, https://www.propublica.org/article/doctors-who-take-company-cash-tend-to-prescribe-more-brand-name-drugs.

Part Five. How Incentives Lead to Behavior Change

1. Olivia B. Waxman, "Trying to Get in Shape in 2020? Here's the History behind the Common New Year's Resolution," *Time*, January 8, 2020, https://time.com/5753774/new-years-resolutions-exercise/.

2. Nadra Nittle, "How Gyms Convince New Members to Stay Past January," *Vox*, January 9, 2019, https://www.vox.com/the-goods/2019/1/9/18175978/planet-fitness-crunch-gyms-memberships-new-years-resolutions.

3. Stefano DellaVigna and Ulrike Malmendier, "Paying Not to Go to the Gym," *American Economic Review* 96, no. 3 (2006): 694–719.

4. See https://www.vizerapp.com/.

5. Uri Gneezy, Agne Kajackaite, and Stephan Meier, "Incentive-Based interventions," in *The Handbook of Behavior Change*, ed. Martin S. Hagger, Linda D. Cameron, Kyra Hamilton, Nelli Hankonen, and Taru Lintunen (Cambridge: Cambridge University Press, 2020), 523–36. (This article includes a more detailed discussion of the relevant literature. See also Alain Samson, ed., *The Behavioral Economics Guide 2019*, introd. Uri Gneezy (Behavioral Science Solutions, 2019), https://www.behavioraleconomics.com/the-be-guide/the-behavioral-economics-guide-2019/.

Chapter 17. Creating Habits

1. Gary Charness and Uri Gneezy, "Incentives to Exercise," *Econometrica* 77 (2009): 909–31.

2. Dan Acland and Matthew Levy, "Naiveté, Projection Bias, and Habit Formation in Gym Attendance," *Management Science* 61, no. 1 (2015): 146–60.

3. "Commitment Device," Wikipedia, accessed December 8, 2020, https://en.wikipedia.org/wiki/Commitment_device.

4. Heather Royer, Mark Stehr, and Justin Sydnor, "Incentives, Commitments, and Habit Formation in Exercise: Evidence from a Field Experiment with Workers at a Fortune-500 Company," *American Economic Journal: Applied Economics* 7, no. 3 (2015): 51–84.

5. Philip S. Babcock and John L. Hartman, "Networks and Workouts: Treatment Size and Status Specific Peer Effects in a Randomized Field Experiment" (NBER Working Paper 16581, National Bureau of Economic Research, 2010).

6. Simon Condliffe, Ebru Işgın, and Brynne Fitzgerald, "Get Thee to the Gym! A Field Experiment on Improving Exercise Habits," *Journal of Behavioral and Experimental Economics* 70 (2017): 23–32.

7. Wendy Wood and Dennis Rünger, "Psychology of Habit," *Annual Review of Psychology* 67 (2016): 289–314.

8. John Beshears, Hae Nim Lee, Katherine L. Milkman, Robert Mislavsky, and Jessica Wisdom, "Creating Exercise Habits Using Incentives: The Trade-Off between Flexibility and Routinization," *Management Science* 67, no. 7 (2021): 3985–4642.

Chapter 18. Breaking Habits

1. Centers for Disease Control and Prevention, "Tobacco-Related Mortality," accessed December 8, 2020, https://www.cdc.gov/tobacco/data_statistics/fact_sheets/health_effects/tobacco_related_mortality/index.htm.

2. Centers for Disease Control and Prevention, "Cigarette Smoking among Adults—United States, 2000," *MMWR: Morbidity and Mortality Weekly Report* 51, no. 29 (2002): 642–45; Centers for Disease Control and Prevention, "Annual Smoking-Attributable Mortality, Years of Potential Life Lost, and Productivity Losses—United States, 1997–2001," *MMWR: Morbidity and Mortality Weekly Rep*ort 54, no. 25 (2005): 625–28.

3. Kevin G. Volpp et al., "A Randomized, Controlled Trial of Financial Incentives for Smoking Cessation," *New England Journal of Medicine* 360 (2009): 699–709.

4. John R. Hughes, Josue Keely, and Shelly Naud, "Shape of the Relapse Curve and Long-Term Abstinence among Untreated Smokers," *Addiction* 99 (2004): 29–38.

5. SRNT Subcommittee on Biochemical Verification, "Biochemical Verification of Tobacco Use and Cessation," *Nicotine & Tobacco Research* 4 (2002): 149–59.

6. Richard J. Bonnie, Kathleen R. Stratton, and Robert B. Wallace, *Ending the Tobacco Problem: A Blueprint for the Nation* (Washington DC: National Academies Press, 2007); Centers for Disease Control and Prevention, "Smoking during Pregnancy," accessed December 8, 2020, https://www.cdc.gov/tobacco/basic_information/health_effects/pregnancy/index.htm.

7. Daniel Ershoff, Trinita H. Ashford, and Robert Goldenberg, "Helping Pregnant Women Quit Smoking: An Overview," *Nicotine and Tobacco Research* 6 (2004): S101—S105; C. L. Melvin and C. A. Gaffney, "Treating Nicotine Use and Dependence of Pregnant and Parenting Smokers: An Update," *Nicotine and Tobacco Research* 6 (2004): S107—S124.

8. Carolyn Davis Cockey, "Amanda's Story," Healthy Mom & Baby, accessed December 8, 2020, https://www.health4mom.org/amandas-story/.

9. Stephen T. Higgins, Yukiko Washio, Sarah H. Heil, Laura J. Solomon, Diann E. Gaalema, Tara M. Higgins, and Ira M. Bernstein, "Financial Incentives for Smoking Cessation among Pregnant and Newly Postpartum Women," *Preventive Medicine* 55 (2012): S33–S40.

10. Xavier Giné, Dean Karlan, and Jonathan Zinman, "Put Your Money Where Your Butt Is: A Commitment Contract for Smoking Cessation," *American Economic Journal: Applied Economics* 2 (2010): 213–35.

11. Nava Ashraf, Dean Karlan, and Wesley Yin, "Tying Odysseus to the Mast: Evidence from a Commitment Savings Product in the Philippines," *Quarterly Journal of Economics* 121, no. 2 (2006): 635–72.

12. Scott D. Halpern, Benjamin French, Dylan S. Small, Kathryn Saulsgiver, Michael Harhay, Janet Audrain-McGovern, George Loewenstein, Troyen Brennan, David Asch, and Kevin Volpp, "Randomized Trial of Four Financial-Incentive Programs for Smoking Cessation," *New England Journal of Medicine* 372, no. 22 (2015): 2108–17.

13. "Why Are 72% of Smokers from Lower-Income Communities?," Truth Initiative, January 24, 2018, https://truthinitiative.org/research-resources/targeted-communities/why -are-72-smokers-lower-income-communities.

14. Jean-François Etter and Felicia Schmid, "Effects of Large Financial Incentives for Long-Term Smoking Cessation: A Randomized Trial," *Journal of the American College of Cardiology* 68, no. 8 (2016): 777–85.

Chapter 19. I Want It Now!

1. Katherine Milkman, Julia A. Minson, and Kevin G. M. Vlopp, "Holding the Hunger Games Hostage at the Gym: An Evaluation of Temptation Bundling," *Management Science* 60, no. 2 (2014): 283–99.

2. Daniel Read and Barbara van Leeuwen, "Predicting Hunger: The Effects of Appetite and Delay on Choice," *Organizational Behavior and Human Decision Processes* 76, no. 2 (1998): 189–205.

3. Stephan Meier and Charles Sprenger, "Present-Biased Preferences and Credit Card Borrowing," *American Economic Journal: Applied Economics* 2, no. 1 (2010): 193–210.

Chapter 20. Removing Barriers

1. Centers for Disease Control and Prevention, "Benefits of Physical Activity," accessed December 8, 2020, https://www.cdc.gov/physicalactivity/basics/pa-health/index.htm.

2. Editorial Board, "Exercise and Academic Performance," *New York Times*, May 24, 2013, https://www.nytimes.com/2013/05/25/opinion/exercise-and-academic-performance.html.

3. Alexander W. Cappelen, Gary Charness, Mathias Ekström, Uri Gneezy, and Bertil Tungodden, "Exercise Improves Academic Performance" (NHH Department of Economics Discussion Paper 08, 2017).

4. Donna De La Cruz, "Why Kids Shouldn't Sit Still in Class," *New York Times*, March 21, 2017, https://www.nytimes.com/2017/03/21/well/family/why-kids-shouldnt-sit-still-in-class .html.

5. Tatiana Homonoff, Barton Willage, and Alexander Willén, "Rebates as Incentives: The Effects of a Gym Membership Reimbursement Program," *Journal of Health Economics* 70 (2020): 102285.

6. Hunt Allcott and Todd Rogers, "The Short-Run and Long-Run Effects of Behavioral Interventions: Experimental Evidence from Energy Conservation," *American Economic Review* 104, no. 10 (2014): 3003–37.

7. Alec Brandon, Paul J. Ferraro, John A. List, Robert D. Metcalfe, Michael K. Price, and Florian Rundhammer, "Do the Effects of Social Nudges Persist? Theory and Evidence from 38 Natural Field Experiments" (NBER Working Paper 23277, National Bureau of Economic Research, 2017).

8. Thomas A. Burnham, Judy K. Frels, and Vijay Mahajan, "Consumer Switching Costs: A Typology, Antecedents, and Consequences," *Journal of the Academy of Marketing Science* 31, no. 2 (2003): 109–26.

9. T-Mobile, "How to Switch to T-Mobile," accessed December 8, 2020, https://www.t -mobile.com/resources/how-to-join-us.

10. Minjung Park, "The Economic Impact of Wireless Number Portability," *Journal of Industrial Economics* 59, no. 4 (2011): 714–45.

Chapter 21. From Lion Killers to Lion Savers

1. "Maasai People," Wikipedia, accessed December 8, 2020, https://en.wikipedia.org/ wiki/Maasai_people.

2. "Kenya: Country in Africa," Datacommons.org, accessed February 15, 2022, https:// datacommons.org/place/country/KEN?utm_medium=explore&mprop=count&popt= Person&hl=en.

3. Rachel David, "Lion Populations to Halve in Most of Africa in Next 20 Years," *New Scientist*, October 26, 2015, https://www.newscientist.com/article/dn28390-lion-populations -to-halve-in-most-of-africa-in-next-20-years/.

4. Safaritalk, "Wildlife Environment Communities," accessed December 12, 2019, http:// safaritalk.net/topic/257-luca-belpietro-the-maasai-wilderness-conservation-trust/.

5. Maasai Wilderness Conservation Trust, "Kenya Wildlife Conservation," accessed December 8, 2020, http://maasaiwilderness.org/.

6. Seamus D. Maclennan, Rosemary J. Groom, David W. Macdonald, and Laurence G. Frank, "Evaluation of a Compensation Scheme to Bring About Pastoralist Tolerance of Lions," *Biological Conservation* 142 (2009): 2419–27; Laurence Frank, Seamus Maclennan, Leela Hazzah, Richard Bonham, and Tom Hill, "Lion Killing in the Amboseli-Tsavo Ecosystem, 2001–2006, and Its Implications for Kenya's Lion Population" (unpublished paper, 2006), http:// livingwithlions.org/AnnualReports/2006-Lion-killing-in-Amboseli-Tsavo-ecosystem.pdf.

Chapter 22. Insurance Fraud and Moral Hazard

1. "'The Sopranos': Whoever Did This," aired November 10, 2002, IMDb, accessed April 24, 2022, https://www.imdb.com/title/tt0705295/.

2. Maasai Wilderness Conservation Trust, "Predator Protection—Creating Harmony between Wildlife and Community," accessed December 8, 2020, http://maasaiwilderness.org/ programs/predator-protection/.

Chapter 24. Changing the Economics of Female Genital Mutilation

1. Kenya National Bureau of Statistics, "Kenya Demographic and Health Survey 2014," Demographic and Health Surveys Program, December 2015, https://dhsprogram.com/pubs/pdf/FR308/FR308.pdf.

2. Sarah Boseley, "FGM: Kenya Acts against Unkindest Cut," *Guardian*, September 8, 2011, https://www.theguardian.com/society/sarah-boseley-global-health/2011/sep/08/women-africa; World Health Organization, "Female Genital Mutilation," February 3, 2020, https://www.who.int/en/news-room/fact-sheets/detail/female-genital-mutilation.

3. World Health Organization, Department of Reproductive Health and Research, and UNAIDS, *Male Circumcision: Global Trends and Determinants of Prevalence, Safety and Acceptability* (Geneva: World Health Organization, 2007).

4. R. Elise B. Johansen, Nafissatou J. Diop, Glenn Laverack, and Els Leye, "What Works and What Does Not: A Discussion of Popular Approaches for the Abandonment of Female Genital Mutilation," *Obstetrics and Gynecology International* 2013 (2013): 348248.

5. Damaris Seleina Parsitau, "How Girls' Education Intersects with Maasai Culture in Kenya," Brookings, July 25, 2017, https://www.brookings.edu/blog/education-plus-development/2017/07/25/how-girls-education-intersects-with-maasai-culture-in-kenya/.

6. Netta Ahituv, "Can Economists Stop Kenya's Maasai from Mutilating Their Girls?," *Haaretz*, March 14, 2016, https://www.haaretz.com/world-news/.premium.MAGAZINE-can-economists-stop-the-maasai-from-mutilating-their-girls-1.5415945.

7. UNICEF, *Changing a Harmful Social Convention: Female Genital Mutilation/Cutting*, technical report (Florence, Italy: UNICEF Innocenti Research Centre, 2005).

Chapter 25. Anchoring and Adjustment

1. Amos Tversky and Daniel Kahneman, "Judgment under Uncertainty: Heuristics and Biases," *Science* 185, no. 4157 (1974): 1124–31.

2. J. Edward Russo and Paul J. H. Schoemaker, *Winning Decisions: Getting It Right the First Time* (New York: Currency, 2001).

3. Gregory B. Northcraft and Margaret A. Neale, "Experts, Amateurs, and Real Estate: An Anchoring-and-Adjustment Perspective on Property Pricing Decisions," *Organizational Behavior and Human Decision Process* 39 (1987): 84–97.

Chapter 27. Price Signals Quality

1. J. P. Mangalindan, "Peloton CEO: Sales Increased after We Raised Prices to $2,245 per Bike," Yahoo! Finance, June 5, 2019, https://finance.yahoo.com/news/peloton-ceo-says-sales-increased-raised-prices-2245-exercise-bike-132256225.html.

2. See, for example, Eitan Gerstner, "Do Higher Prices Signal Higher Quality?," *Journal of Marketing Research* 22 (1985): 209–15; Joel Huber and John McCann, "The Impact of Inferential Beliefs on Product Evaluations," *Journal of Marketing Research* 19 (1982): 324–33; Akashay R. Rao and Kent B. Monroe, "The Effect of Price, Brand Name, and Store Name on Buyers' Perceptions of Product Quality: An Integrative Review," *Journal of Marketing Research* 36 (1989): 351–57.

3. Ayelet Gneezy, Uri Gneezy, and Dominique Lauga, "Reference-Dependent Model of the Price-Quality Heuristic," *Journal of Marketing Research* 51, no. 2 (2014): 153–64.

4. Baba Shiv, Ziv Carmon, and Dan Ariely, "Placebo Effects of Marketing Actions: Consumers May Get What They Pay For," *Journal of Marketing Research* 42 (2005): 383–93.

Chapter 28. The Norm of Reciprocity

1. Phillip R. Kunz and Michael Woolcott, "Season's Greetings: From My Status to Yours," *Social Science Research* 5 (1976): 269–78.

2. Robert B. Cialdini, *Influence: Science and Practice*, 3rd ed. (New York: HarperCollins, 1993).

3. Stanford GSB Staff, "Margaret Neale: Why You Should Make the First Move in a Negotiation," Stanford Graduate School of Business, September 1, 2007, https://www.gsb.stanford.edu/insights/margaret-neale-why-you-should-make-first-move-negotiation.

Conclusion

1. Sarah Mervosh, "Who Wants to Be a Millionaire? In Ohio, You Just Need Luck, and a Covid Vaccine," *New York Times*, May 26, 2021.

2. Justin Boggs, "White House on Vax-a-Million Drawing: DeWine Has Unlocked a Secret," *Spectrum News 1*, May 25, 2021.

3. A controlled experiment in Sweden found encouraging evidence: a $24 incentive to get vaccinated increased vaccination rates by 4.2 percentage points, from a baseline rate of 71.6 percent. See Pol Campos-Mercade, Armando N. Meier, Florian H. Schneider, Stephan Meier, Devin Pope, and Erik Wengström, "Monetary Incentives Increase COVID-19 Vaccinations," *Science* 374 (2021): 879–82.

4. State of New Jersey, "Governor Murphy Announces New Incentives to Encourage COVID-19 Vaccinations, Including Free Entrance to State Parks and Free Wine at Participating Wineries," press release, May 19, 2021.

5. "Vaccinated Individuals Will Be Able to Get a Free Drink at Certain Restaurants," NBC CT, April 26, 2021, https://www.nbcconnecticut.com/news/coronavirus/vaccinated-individuals-will-be-able-to-get-a-free-drink-at-certain-restaurants/2474928/.

6. Rich Coppola and Samaia Hernandez, "'Drinks on Us': Participating CT Restaurants, Bars Offering Free Drinks with Proof of Vaccination Starting This Week," WTNH, April 26, 2021, https://www.wtnh.com/news/business/participating-ct-restaurants-and-bars-offering -free-drinks-with-proof-of-vaccination/.

7. John Cheang, "Krispy Kreme Offers Free Glazed Donut to Those Who Show Covid Vaccine Card," NBC News, March 22, 2021, https://www.nbcnews.com/news/us-news/ krispy-kreme-offers-free-glazed-donut-those-who-show-covid-n1261768.

8. Nicholas Tampio, "A Weakness in the Argument for Vaccine Mandates," *Boston Globe*, August 25, 2021.

9. Daniel Ackerman, "Before Face Masks, Americans Went to War against Seat Belts," *Business Insider*, May 26, 2020, https://www.businessinsider.in/Before-face-masks-Americans -went-to-war-against-seat-belts/articleshow/76010870.cms.

10. "Covid-19: Biden Tells States to Offer $100 Vaccine Incentive as Cases Rise," BBC News, July 30, 2021, https://www.bbc.com/news/world-us-canada-58020090.

11. Richard H. Thaler and Cass R. Sunstein, *Nudge: The Final Edition* (New Haven, CT: Yale University Press, 2021).

12. "Plastic Shopping Bag," Wikipedia (in Hebrew), https://he.wikipedia.org/wiki/%D7 %A9%D7%A7%D7%99%D7%AA_%D7%A7%D7%A0%D7%99%D7%95%D7%AA_%D7 %9E%D7%A4%D7%9C%D7%A1%D7%98%D7%99%D7%A7.

Index

Figures are indicated by "f" following the page number.